CONTESTED AMERICANS

LATINA/O SOCIOLOGY SERIES

General Editors: Pierrette Hondagneu-Sotelo and Victor M. Rios

Family Secrets: Stories of Incest and Sexual Violence in Mexico
Gloria González-López

Deported: Immigrant Policing, Disposable Labor, and Global Capitalism
Tanya Maria Golash-Boza

From Deportation to Prison: The Politics of Immigration Enforcement in Post–Civil Rights America
Patrisia Macías-Rojas

Latina Teachers: Creating Careers and Guarding Culture
Glenda M. Flores

Citizens but Not Americans: Race and Belonging among Latino Millennials
Nilda Flores-González

Immigrants under Threat: Risk and Resistance in Deportation Nation
Greg Prieto

Kids at Work: Latinx Families Selling Food on the Streets of Los Angeles
Emir Estrada

Organizing While Undocumented: Immigrant Youth's Political Activism under the Law
Kevin Escudero

Front of the House, Back of the House: Race and Inequality in the Lives of Restaurant Workers
Eli Revelle Yano Wilson

Building a Better Chicago: Race and Community Resistance to Urban Redevelopment
Teresa Irene Gonzales

South Central Dreams: Finding Home and Building Community in South L.A.
Pierrette Hondagneu-Sotelo and Manuel Pastor

Latinas in the Criminal Justice System: Victims, Targets, and Offenders
Edited by Vera Lopez and Lisa Pasko

Uninsured in Chicago: How the Social Safety Net Leaves Latinos Behind
Robert Vargas

Medical Legal Violence: Health Care and Immigration Enforcement
Meredith Van Natta

Contested Americans: Mixed-Status Families in Anti-Immigrant Times
Cassaundra Rodriguez

Contested Americans

Mixed-Status Families in Anti-Immigrant Times

Cassaundra Rodriguez

NEW YORK UNIVERSITY PRESS
New York

NEW YORK UNIVERSITY PRESS
New York
www.nyupress.org

© 2023 by New York University
All rights reserved

Please contact the Library of Congress for Cataloging-in-Publication data.
ISBN: 9781479800537 (hardback)
ISBN: 9781479800544 (paperback)
ISBN: 9781479800605 (library ebook)
ISBN: 9781479800599 (consumer ebook)

New York University Press books are printed on acid-free paper, and their binding materials
are chosen for strength and durability. We strive to use environmentally responsible suppli-
ers and materials to the greatest extent possible in publishing our books.

Manufactured in the United States of America

10 9 8 7 6 5 4 3 2 1

Also available as an ebook

CONTENTS

Introduction

Mixed-Status Families

Sometimes when Natalia speaks with her hands, I think about the fluttering of birds and her talent for telling stories about her life in a mixed-status family.[1] Twenty-something Natalia was born in the United States and therefore has US citizenship, but this is not the case for everyone in her family. Her parents, undocumented at the time of her birth, remain so. Still, the United States is their home. Natalia sits back in her chair to assert, "My parents have been here so long, so it's not sensible to think that you should go back to your country when you've made a home for yourself in another." It is in the United States—Los Angeles specifically—where Natalia's Mexican immigrant parents have set roots and raised their children.

Natalia is a college graduate, speaks fluent English, has a professional career, and tells me she is doing all that she can to access upward mobility for her family. She also worries about the well-being of her undocumented family members and the possibility of a loved one's deportation. "We don't want to imagine the worst," Natalia explains as she describes the ways her family copes with deportation fears. This, too, is hard when proposed policy changes and news reports rattle her family's sense of security. The country is reckoning with particularly anti-immigrant times. She elaborates, "There is a sense or idea that all the undocumented and their offspring are out to get us in America. That has an impact on everybody who is an immigrant or a child from immigrant parents. You can't escape it. . . . Oh, man! There are a lot of bigots in this country!"

Natalia complicates the assumption that citizenship equates belonging, saying, "I think it has to do with how society accepts you. If society doesn't accept you, then you feel like you are not American because they think you are not American." She recognizes that citizenship is more than just legal rights. For one to experience full citizenship, membership

1

must be acknowledged by other society members. Natalia has a legal claim to belong in the country, but her social experience of this membership is conditional, negotiated, and challenged. Her undocumented family members' ties to American membership are even more tenuous despite their extended time living in the country.

Natalia's thoughts get to the crux of a current dilemma in American politics: the place of undocumented immigrants and their (citizen) children in American society. For some elected officials, bureaucrats, and political pundits, the rightful place of Americans born to undocumented parents is anywhere but the United States. There has been a sustained attempt among conservative elected officials to amend or eliminate birthright citizenship to make the children of undocumented immigrant parents ineligible. In these debates, Mexican undocumented mothers are castigated for having children or "anchor babies" for the purpose of helping them access legal residency. Several hate groups and elected officials have gone as far as to suggest that mixed-status families reproduce like rats and rabbits.[2] Donald Trump joined the conservative chorus to argue that the American children of undocumented parents are legal loopholes and otherwise illegitimate American citizens.[3] The citizenship of these Americans is, therefore, contested. This rhetoric often goes hand in hand with the denigration of Mexican undocumented immigrants—a group Trump publicly referred to as criminals, rapists, and thieves.[4]

The Obama-era program known as Deferred Action for Parents of Americans and Legal Residents (DAPA) would have provided an estimated 4.4 million eligible undocumented parents temporary protection from deportation. However, DAPA was never implemented. Along with this blocked program, undocumented youth have faced a constant battle to access the Deferred Action for Childhood Arrivals (DACA) program, which provides protection from deportation and other tangible benefits.[5] Researchers have well captured undocumented young adults' challenges and resilience in activism, school, work, and family and dating contexts.[6] Yet, researchers know little about the lives of their citizen counterparts who have undocumented family members. It remains a question if and how members of mixed-status families experience belonging in the United States, and how adult citizen children may manage part of the undocumented experience in their own lives.

If we are to believe conservative rhetoric about mixed-status families, Natalia should be able to legalize her parents without any problem, thereby serving her role as an anchor baby. Because she is an adult and no longer legally dependent on her family, we could also imagine that Natalia can escape her connection to the undocumented experience. Instead, Natalia's age, citizenship, or efforts to become upwardly mobile do not prevent the possibility of her parents' deportation, mitigate the family responsibilities she holds as a citizen, or erase her racialized experiences as a Latina or Mexican American woman. For an American like Natalia, her own and her undocumented family members' membership in the United States is a socially contested issue and question. *Contested Americans* tackles this dilemma.

How, then, do adult-age citizen children in mixed-status families experience and articulate US belonging? How do both US citizens and undocumented immigrants in Mexican mixed-status families make sense of their US membership? Importantly, how do families like Natalia's manage differences in legal status and map out plans and responsibilities? This book answers precisely these difficult, but critically important questions about these contested Americans.

I find that citizenship is a negotiated ideal for Mexicans and Mexican Americans who are intimately connected to undocumented status. Undocumented status or illegality is created by governments, but it is also continuously reproduced and shaped sociopolitically.[7] What I call "family illegality" describes how family members negotiate illegality in their lives. They must contend with family illegality because immigration status is meaningful, and because the nation-state perpetrates what sociologists Cecilia Menjívar and Leisy Abrego call "legal violence" against immigrant communities.[8] Policies and programs that separate families, cause fear of separation, and otherwise prevent immigrant families from living secure, healthy lives are all state-sanctioned forms of violence. As we will see for the adult-age children of undocumented parents, their relationship to family illegality can change over time as they become adults and face new freedoms, as well as new responsibilities.

Each person in a mixed-status family tries to mitigate family illegality by making choices or claims to help their loved ones. For undocumented parents, negotiating family illegality is an effort to eliminate the spillover of illegality to their children. In practice, this often means if parents are deported, they are willing to endure the emotional struggle of physical separation to keep children in the United States. Parents do this to protect what they see as their children's citizenship right to remain in the United States in order to continue their US-based academic and professional futures. These are difficult decisions born out of love and a sense of how sacrifices may yield the best results for children down the road.

For adult-age, primarily educated citizen children in mixed-status families (eighteen to twenty-eight years old), citizenship is experienced as a responsibility to help their families manage the challenges of illegality. In their lives, sometimes family illegality is made less salient because of their age and independence, while simultaneously these same two factors entail new pressures and family obligations. Members of mixed-status families also discursively challenge popular anti-immigrant sentiments about immigrants and immigrant families. At a symbolic level, family illegality is also managed when undocumented immigrants claim their belonging by emphasizing their economic contributions and their clean criminal records. Citizen youth also deconstruct the derogatory term "anchor baby" and dispute harmful narratives about their families. Although US citizenship is the goal for many undocumented immigrants, this book also points to the limits of legal citizenship as citizen participants experience various forms of racialized nonbelonging when they spatially navigate segregated Los Angeles.

Research(er) Background

I conducted this project as a feminist scholar and as both an insider and an outsider in the communities I researched.[9] I was an insider in terms of my Mexican/Latino identity and immigrant family and working-class upbringing. My outsider status depended on who I was interviewing or what kind of data I was collecting. Sometimes I shared the immigration status and age range of the participants, and other times I did not. With young adults, our shared age range and similar family and educational backgrounds were often points of connection. With older undocumented adults, we had a shared ethnicity and the Spanish language in common, but our immigration statuses were certainly different, and often so were our educational backgrounds. I suspect, however, that undocumented parents' willingness to participate in the study had something to do with supporting a young, aspiring Latina professional—a professional status they hoped their own children would eventually achieve.

Like the participants, I also have roots in Los Angeles. I was a young child living in a heavily Mexican and immigrant community in the San Fernando Valley when California was undergoing a state budget crisis in the early 1990s. Immigrant women and their children were increasingly blamed for these budget woes and were depicted as part of a larger problem of waves, tsunamis, and hordes of immigrants coming from the southern border.[10] At the time, Governor Pete Wilson ran a reelection campaign that centered on saving the state from what was framed as the perils of undocumented immigration. His 1994 campaign ads included grainy black-and-white security footage of anonymous (assumed brown) bodies running past a US-Mexico border checkpoint and across Golden State freeways. The ad depicts undocumented immigration as an invasion, until Wilson comes on the screen promising to fight against undocumented immigration and deny state services to "illegal immigrants." In doing this, he promises to protect law-abiding, taxpaying Americans. "Enough is enough," Wilson concludes at the end of his ad. As young as I was at the time, I was privy to how such rhetoric implicated my Mexican immigrant family, even if I could not articulate my discomfort. But my nuclear family was also *legally* protected. Like many of my particular ethnic background and age/immigrant generation, I personally understood the meaningful benefits that the last broad amnesty program in 1986 offered not just to immigrants but also to their families.

Later, I would make sense of these matters more thoroughly in college, where I learned the importance of critical scholarship and broad activist movements. When I left Southern California to attend graduate school in Massachusetts in the summer of 2011, I left behind a vibrant student and local community invested in fighting for student, immigrant, and workers' rights, as well as racial and feminist justice. At the time, these important social issues felt all the more salient given the economic uncertainty and devastation that was occurring following the Great Recession. In graduate school, I became more intensely aware of the record-breaking deportation rates of immigrants under the Obama administration. Increasingly, I noticed documentaries and other media on the strife of immigrant and mixed-status families. As sympathetic as some of these narratives were, there were still many anti-immigrant discourses about immigrant lawbreakers and immigrant mothers irresponsibly bearing "illegal" or anchor baby US citizen children. Children, however, do eventually grow up, and in Los Angeles, these so-called anchor babies included many of my peers—adult-age children whose parents migrated in the 1980s and 1990s and were part of my community. I could not look away from the cruelties of immigration policy. I left New England to make the cross-country move back to Los Angeles.

There is an urgency in this work. Perhaps I approached this research as a story that I could facilitate for people whose lives are often told in a constraining dichotomy: immigrants and their families are undesirable threats (lawbreakers, job stealers, economic drains) or else they are family-oriented victims working hard at backbreaking jobs. Real life, however, is more complicated. Yet, at the same time, it was and is certainly true that mixed-status families face a range of challenges tied to illegality—from the mundane to the terror of family separation. In thinking about my motivation for this research, I found some relevance in Chicana writer Sandra Cisneros's explanation for why people of color write: "We do this because the world we live in is a house on fire and the people we love are burning."[11] I could not look away from the flames. In these politically incendiary times, I seek to present a nuanced account of how members of mixed-status families make sense of their family ties and membership in the United States.

Making an Undocumented and Mixed-Status Population

The fact that mixed-status families call the United States home is by no means accidental. Instead, the presence of these families has largely been facilitated by US policies that have incentivized immigrants' permanent settlement. Part of this background is explained by policies that militarized the border and, in turn, effectively cut off much of the seasonal or circular migration that immigrants would undertake between the United States and Mexico. These enforcement policies were a political move on behalf of opportunistic elected officials and political pundits who helped construct undocumented immigration as a moral panic. The militarization of the border and the decrease in circular migration began with the Immigration and Reform and Control Act (IRCA) of 1986, followed by the Illegal Immigration Reform and Immigrant Responsibility Act (IIRIRA) in 1996. IRCA represented a three-pronged approach to curbing undocumented migration by granting amnesty to an eligible 2.3 million undocumented immigrants while also increasing border enforcement and providing employer sanctions for employing unauthorized workers.[12] Funding for border enforcement programs was funneled into Operation Gatekeeper in California and Operation Hold the Line in Texas. As a result of pressures to address what was considered the racialized problem of "illegal" immigration, the budget for Operation Gatekeeper doubled, resulting in a significant increase in the number of border patrol agents and the incorporation of new technologies of surveillance.[13] While IRCA and subsequent border policing programs made the border more durable, they did not curb unauthorized migration as intended. Instead, they made border crossing more dangerous and permanent settlement more likely.[14] These policies, coupled with border-enforcing programs following September 11, 2001, made clandestine border crossing more dangerous. As the border became less porous, this transformed a pattern of circular migration to a population of undocumented immigrants deciding to remain in the country and make the United States their permanent home.

Although immigration statuses are not fixed, the absence of immigration reform has also solidified—for many—an undocumented status that has been unchanged for decades. Now well over thirty-five years since the last broad legalization offered under IRCA in 1986, more than half of the undocumented population has been in the United States for at least ten years.[15] The demand for feminized service work also meant that since the 1980s, women began migrating much more than in previous periods.[16] Moreover, immigration status differences among parents and children are made possible by birthright citizenship that grants citizenship to children born on US soil. Not surprisingly, the majority of undocumented parents in the country have citizen children. About 85 percent of undocumented immigrants have US citizen family members, and 62 percent of undocumented immigrants have at least one US citizen child.[17] American children in mixed-status families are also no small population; about 5.8 million American-born children live with an unauthorized family member in their household.[18]

Not only do undocumented immigrants remain stuck as undocumented and their families as mixed-status, but undocumented status has also become increasingly criminalized. This has been possible through a coordinated governmental apparatus that oversees immigration enforcement. Following the events of September 11, 2001, the newly established Department of Homeland Security (DHS) and Immigration Control and Enforcement (ICE) began to oversee immigration enforcement programs and processes. Thanks to both IIRIRA and the Anti-Terrorism and Effective Death Penalty Act, undocumented immigrants are subject to an increased risk for deportation for a wide variety of offenses, and they face fewer options to successfully contest an order of deportation. Immigrants are under greater surveillance when federal programs, such as those established under 287(g) agreements, partner immigration authorities with local law enforcement to identify and detain undocumented immigrants. Other programs, such as the widely scrutinized Secure Communities (S-Comm) program worked to notify ICE when immigrants are arrested and fingerprinted as part of their processing in local jails. The result of these policies and programs is the increase in the detention and deportation rates of immigrants. Further, in many cases, individuals have been caught in the immigration enforcement dragnet because of minor infractions, such as traffic violations.[19] The detention and removal of immigrants who have committed minor violations suggests enforcement programs are not about removing violent criminals but about criminalizing noncitizens under the state.[20]

The state's surveilling of undocumented immigrants serves as a mechanism to control families with the threat of deportation. This threat feels all the more real when among the major outcomes of increased policing are considerably higher rates of immigrants detained and deported. In the years leading up to this study, the United States deported a record-breaking number of people in 2012 and 2013 (approximately 419,000 and 438,000, respectively), while hundreds of thousands also voluntarily left the country from 2011 to 2013.[21] In 2014, the removals had dropped somewhat but still were over 400,000.[22] These numbers leave behind impacted families that must manage difficult decisions. When children leave with deported parents, they also experience a form of deportation and can face poverty, reduced educational opportunities, and violence in their ancestral homeland—life circumstances that their parents hoped to leave behind by migrating to the United States in the first place. Children who leave with deported parents become "exiles," and children who remain in the United States may become "orphans" without the presence of their parents.[23] Family members who remain in the United States may also have to deal with dramatically altered caregiving and financial supports when parents and primary breadwinners are suddenly detained and deported.[24] As a result of immigration policies, in effect, mixed-status families contend with complex realities.

Record-breaking deportation rates did not go unnoticed and were met with anti-deportation resistance. By November 2014, President Obama suspended the controversial S-Comm program. Citing harsh criticism, cities being unwilling to participate, and a general misunderstanding of the program, DHS replaced S-Comm with the Priority Enforcement Program (PEP) in 2015.[25] The newer program worked similarly to S-Comm because immigrants who are arrested still have their information and fingerprints transferred to ICE databases, which can then flag ICE about an immigrant being in police custody. The difference is that PEP was meant to prioritize criminals or those considered threats to public safety. Once an immigrant is flagged in the system, ICE can request a hold on the detainee to pick them up. According to advisory materials developed by the Immigrant Legal Resource Center, "SComm = PEP. S-Comm was dismantled in name, but in fact it continued in practice as 'PEP.'"[26] I also observed that activists at various community events were quick to point out the similarities between PEP and S-Comm. The new program did not necessarily represent a victory for immigrants, and of course, it did nothing to help families already impacted by deportation. For them, the damage was done. This was the federal immigration policy context when I collected data, although the following years would bring forth more restrictive immigration proposals and policies from the Trump administration, including discontinuing PEP and reviving the S-Comm program in 2017.

The Question of Belonging

Eschewing sociological questions of assimilation, *Contested Americans* centers on members of mixed-status families' meaning-making concerning citizenship and belonging.[27] While there is substantial literature on immigrant families and the undocumented immigrant experience, there is comparatively very little research on how citizenship is experienced within mixed-status families. This gap is especially glaring considering how citizen children are sometimes used for conflicting political purposes. Some antideportation activists have centered their campaigns on the family by claiming parents of US citizens deserve to remain in the United States, while at the same time citizen children in mixed-status families are constructed as a problem in anti-immigrant debates.[28] Centering on citizenship provides a meaningful investigation into how everyday belonging is articulated and experienced when much of the policy and discursive context constructs citizens and noncitizens in these families as undesirable and even harmful to the United States.

In this book, we see how members of mixed-status families engage with family illegality, which underscores both the real limitations and the possibilities of citizenship for those who possess legal status, and for those who do not. Scholars have theorized citizenship as "a form of membership in a political and geographical community . . . [that includes] legal status, rights, political and other forms of participation in society, and a sense of belonging."[29] Traditional sociological approaches to citizenship have included sociologist T. H. Marshall's formulation of citizenship as entailing legal status, rights, participation, and belonging.[30] The legal status that citizenship provides is prized in mixed-status families because it does allow some access to areas of social life that are deeply consequential—such as a right to remain in the United States without the fear of deportation and legal access to wage labor. Yet, for undocumented family members and those who love them, they know that legal status—even with its limitations—is not something to take for granted.

However, many of the legal status advantages that exist for citizen children in mixed-status families may be accessible into adulthood or when there is less dependency on parents. Theories of citizenship have paid less attention to the role of families. In the lives of my participants, though, family matters a great deal when it comes to their relationships with immigration status and citizenship. When scholars examine how citizens' rights are challenged in mixed-status families, they do so by examining how Americans may feel betrayed by their country as they experience the challenges of immigration laws and enforcement alongside their undocumented romantic partners.[31] In families with young children, researchers study how children are collateral damage in immigration enforcement actions.[32] Somewhat relatedly, scholars also study how minor children are prevented from accessing resources they are entitled to, such as educational, social, and medical programs.[33] In this way, the state's very treatment of immigrants prevents US citizen children from realizing the full promise of their legal status. In effect, children are penalized because of the intimate and dependent relationship they have with undocumented immigrant parents. However, the existing scholarship has not fully accounted for how family relationships may alter both access and the promises of US citizenship when children of undocumented parents are adults.

Adult children and their family members have a somewhat different relationship to the political and administrative realities of immigration status. The rewards of citizenship are in some ways better realized for *adult* children compared with their dependent years as minors. In other ways, these privileges result in new family responsibilities and concerns. Concurrently, some of the punishments of immigration policies continue to harm the undocumented and citizen members in families. Even as members of mixed-status families attempt to access the broad privileges attached to legal status, there remains the larger question of how family members access belonging—a key component to citizenship.

Aside from differences in legal status, members of Mexican mixed-status families contend with racialized experiences that further complicate their sense of belonging. Since members of Mexican or Latino mixed-status families may be racialized as non-White, even the citizens among them may find themselves feeling like they occupy a second-class status in the United States. Scholars have pointed out how Marshall's theoretical foundations of citizenship are arguably less relevant to individuals marginalized by class, gender, and/or race.[34] Shaped by these social locations, marginalized Americans may have formal citizenship but cannot fully exercise substantive citizenship or experience belonging in their country.

A focus on belonging can capture discrepancies between legal recognition of membership and how groups are accepted in practice. For instance, if we consider the case of Black Americans, they were granted recognition of US citizenship in 1868 by the Fourteenth Amendment.

Still, Jim Crow policies and contemporary mass incarceration and discrimination have long excluded members of this group from the promises of citizenship.[35] Certainly, then, legal status matters, but the intersection with race and other social locations can impact how one is excluded from full citizenship. Legal status is not the only prerequisite for feeling a sense of membership either. Immigrants without legal claims to a country might experience inclusion in the national polity when they have access to education, labor protections, and other privileges.[36] Noncitizens may also feel a sense of territorial belonging after living in a country for an extended number of years.[37] Looking at belonging allows a deeper examination of the lives of both citizens and immigrants in mixed-status families. It can reveal what formal citizenship *offers* and *still denies* racialized members of the United States.

One indicator of this nonbelonging for American-born Latinos has been their reluctance to identify as American. In this study, citizens do not usually identify themselves as American in their everyday lives.[38] These Americans reject this label because of their marginalization and their inability to be marked as White or English monolingual and because of how they see their immigrant families are treated in US society.[39] In other research, Mexican American and Asian American youth view citizenship as racialized White and may not identify as Americans because of how they are often treated as racialized outsiders.[40] In other words, these young adults could claim American identity if they felt that they were truly accepted as part of the nation and that their claim to this identity would not be challenged. However, for members of Mexican mixed-status families, both their racialized experiences and their immigrant status or ties may shape their sense of inclusion in the United States. In everyday language, these racialized connotations of citizenship are sometimes reinforced by citizen and undocumented members of mixed-status families when they, for example, would use the term *los americanos*, or Americans, as a synonym for Whites.

Sociologist Evelyn Nakano Glenn has argued that citizenship is first and foremost a category that denotes membership, and one that is enforced by the state *and* laypersons.[41] In this book, I share and build on this argument espoused by Glenn in that citizenship implicates questions of belonging by community members. As she has noted:

Citizenship is not just a matter of formal legal status; it is a matter of belonging, including recognition by other members of the community. Formal law and legal rulings create a structure that legitimates the granting or denial of recognition. However, the maintenance of boundaries relies on "enforcement" not only by designated officials but also by so-called members of the public.[42]

For citizens and non-citizens in mixed-status families, any legal claim to belong can be contested. Popular support among state and non-state actors to amend birthright citizenship for the children born of undocumented immigrants exemplifies how even citizen members in mixed-status families are deemed unworthy of inclusion. Citizenship, then, is based on an experience of belonging that is also shaped by whether other members of a community acknowledge your membership.

Looking at citizenship through the lens of belonging is particularly pertinent given the politics surrounding birthright citizenship and mixed-status families. If citizenship is imagined as a consensual admittance between members, immigration restrictionists loudly and adamantly reject the children of undocumented immigrants who gain access to citizenship via birthright.[43] Restrictionists see these American children as nothing more than legal loopholes. It is in this way that immigration restrictionists do not consent to or accept the children of undocumented immigrants as part of the American "imagined community."[44] While the fervor against citizen children born to undocumented immigrants may be imagined as stemming from a small extremist segment of the population, national polls suggest otherwise. According to a recent poll, as many as 49 percent of respondents oppose granting birthright citizenship to children born to undocumented immigrants.[45] These challenges to citizenship, therefore, necessitate an understanding of how members of mixed-status families, deemed nonconsensually admitted to the polity, experience and articulate their own sense of belonging.

Questions concerning citizenship and belonging have interested researchers in and across fields. In this book, I look closely at how members of mixed-status families articulate their own sense of belonging in the United States, and how they make efforts to fight for the right to physically belong in the country. I find that members of mixed-status families explain how the United States *is* their home despite their immigration status, their connection to illegality, or their racialized identity. In addition, scholars have examined how undocumented immigrants and their loved ones may assert their right to belong in the country by analyzing political mobilization and/or participation in cultural or ethnoreligious festivals.[46] Here, I find value in exploring how people advocate for themselves and their families in less public ways.

Racialization and Mexican Mixed-Status Families

Given the share of Mexican immigrants in the overall undocumented population, it is perhaps unsurprising that many mixed-status families are of Mexican origin. As a result, current immigration laws that impact mixed-status and undocumented families also significantly affect Mexican and Mexican American communities. Partly because of this demographic reality and the ongoing social, legal, political, and cultural association of illegality with Mexicans,[47] family illegality is not just a legal or familial negotiation but also one shaped by the racialization of immigration.

Mexican-origin groups occupy a unique space in the American racial landscape. As any sociologist will tell you, Mexicans are not a race but an ethnic group. While race is a social construction based on meanings typically assigned to physical characteristics, ethnicity is based on a broad array of religious, cultural, and ancestral origins. As a result, race—even while a social construction—is theorized as more fixed, whereas ethnicity can be optional or symbolic.[48] However, I find that Mexicans and Mexican Americans did not talk about their ethnicity as optional in the way many descendants of European immigrants do. Instead, Mexican Americans are often treated and made to identify themselves as a distinct racial group.[49]

Based on the experiences of participants, and the way they engage in family illegality—especially at the discursive level—I argue that Mexicans and Mexican Americans are a racialized group, similar to how scholars have described them as a "racialized ethnic group" or a "racialized ethnicity."[50] Groups can become racialized, since race itself has always been a category of shifting meanings and contestation.[51] Further,

Mexicans are not simply racialized as non-White; instead, they are often explicitly racialized as foreigners and "illegals."[52] Immigrant replenishment or the long-standing presence of Mexican immigrants in the United States means Mexican Americans are sometimes mistaken for foreigners based on their skin color, physical features, and/or surname.[53]

The racialization of Mexican Americans has never been straightforward. Groups can be considered bureaucratically White but treated and racialized as non-White in practice. This discrepancy is certainly true for Mexican Americans. Following the Mexican-American War, the Treaty of Guadalupe Hidalgo in 1848 granted Mexicans on newly annexed US land the option to become American citizens. At the time, only Whites were eligible for US citizenship. Therefore, this expansion of citizenship essentially marked Mexican Americans as legally White. However, they were ostensibly treated as non-White in their everyday life.[54] Despite Mexican Americans being legally White, nineteenth-century public officials considered them a distinct and *racially inferior racial* group.[55] Later, Mexican Americans would at one point have their own racial category in the 1930 US Census.

Despite the obvious racial implications of studying immigration, immigration research as a whole can be improved by better accounting for how immigrants are racialized. Immigration enforcement programs are also not race-neutral in practice or in outcome. Current punitive immigration enforcement policies violate the human rights of immigrants and the civil rights of citizens of color.[56] For example, immigrant policing programs have led to the racial profiling of Latino people.[57] Latinos of all legal statuses can experience racial profiling when raids and immigration sweeps occur in their Latino mixed-status communities. In these circumstances, law enforcement or immigration agents use apparent markers of Mexican identity to racially profile people as undocumented immigrants.[58] Consequently, Mexican and Mexican American families can be subject to the immigration enforcement regime regardless of their legal status.

The racial underpinnings of immigration enforcement are hard to deny when the majority of detained and deported migrants are from Mexico.[59] Yet, while many Mexican immigrants are deported or deportable, there remain limited opportunities for undocumented immigrants to change their status. This predicament is why one immigration scholar refers to deportation as "racial expulsion."[60] Deportation has long been a racialized project, particularly for the Mexican American community. In the 1930s the US government initiated "Mexican repatriation" that deported both Mexican immigrants and Americans of Mexican origin. As agents relied on race/ethnicity to target potential deportees, they made little distinction among those with and without legal status. As a result, during the 1930s, an estimated 60 percent of deportees were actual US citizens.[61] The racialized foundation of punitive immigration enforcement is clear.

More recently, these racialized patterns of removal have continued. The representation of Latino men in deportation rates and the sites of workplace raids where Latino migrant men are overrepresented mark these men as the targets of punitive immigration enforcement.[62] This was particularly the case during the 2008 economic recession when Latino migrant labor became disposable.[63] These raced and gendered logics of disposability make Latino immigrant men deportable while ongoing depictions of Mexican bodies as criminal may have more easily advanced the immigration policy shifts toward "crimmigration."[64] The discourse on national security was effective in criminalizing Latino immigrants precisely because this group has been constructed as archetypal criminals.[65] Indeed, national discourses have long criminalized Mexican Americans and Mexican migrants as *bandidos* (bandits) or criminals and gang members who are prone to violence and lawlessness.[66] Certainly, the latest incarnation of this depiction was reintroduced in Donald Trump's final 2016 presidential debate when he referred to undocumented immigrants as "bad *hombres*," or bad men.[67] The criminalization of Mexican migrants has consequences that severely impact immigrant and mixed-status families.

While I draw from sociological perspectives on citizenship and racialization, this discussion has parallels to critical race theory (CRT) perspectives. Pulling from the tradition of CRT, and specifically Latino/a critical theory (LatCrit), the fact that Mexican immigrants and Mexican-origin US citizens are racialized as "other" is not coincidental. Such othering processes can be reflective of what LatCrit scholars refer to as "racist nativism."[68] Acknowledging how racism and nativism often go hand in hand in the Latino experience, Pérez Huber and colleagues conceptualize racist nativism as the assigning of values to real or imagined differences, in order to justify the superiority of the native, who is perceived to be white, over that of the non-native, who is perceived to be People and Immigrants of Color, and thereby defend the right of whites, or the natives, to dominance.[69]

In other words, how Latinos and immigrants are subjugated works to protect White supremacy. In this case, Mexicans and Mexican Americans in mixed-status families have to shoulder double burdens, one of which is that they must often manage *family illegality* in their lives. To be clear, it wouldn't have to be this way if it were not for immigration policies making undocumented status so consequential. In addition, Mexicans, regardless of their legal status, also have to manage their discursive marking as non-American others—a burden not usually experienced by Whites, who are presumed to be prototypical Americans.[70]

Researching Mixed-Status Families

Studying members of mixed-status families is important not only because they form part of a large population of sixteen million but also because debates about immigration would be sorely ill-informed without acknowledging these families and their experiences. As Heide Castañeda notes, mixed-status families are a "primary and enduring feature of the immigrant experience in the United States today."[71] Researching mixed-status families also represents an opportunity to better understand the impacts of illegality, as legal status differences within the family may reveal power and penalty in managing this social and legal status. Some immigration scholars are increasingly noting how current immigration laws cement undocumented status as a *social* identity that may be similar to some of the social consequences of race and gender.[72] Thus, immigration policies can make the lives of mixed-status families difficult, while the citizenship of some family members may mitigate some of the challenges of illegality. When it comes to being an adult child in a mixed-status family, adult citizens do not face the same challenges as minor citizen children, nor do many of these citizens have the privilege of eschewing responsibilities that would not be expected of adults with legal status parents. Citizens can also face distinct responsibilities that are not necessarily expected of their undocumented peers.[73]

Focusing on the lives of adult citizen children also provides an opportunity to look at the lives we may have ignored. Too often it is easy to forget that Americans are part of immigrant families, or, when we do think of them, we are perhaps reminded of the popular image of *young children* struggling to make sense of family separation. Yet, without widespread amnesty, the United States' inevitable future includes citizen children in mixed-status families who will age into adulthood. This is especially true in California, where US citizen children are estimated to have the highest number of undocumented parents—approximately two million US citizen children live with an undocumented family member.[74] Learning about the experiences of young adults can be helpful in understanding challenges current and new young citizens in mixed-status families will face in the years to come. Understanding these challenges provides essential information for these young adults, individuals who serve this population, and academics who have long been interested in understanding the immigrant second generation.

This book draws on in-depth interviews conducted during the years 2015 and 2016 with sixty-seven individuals who are part of mixed-status families. Most of the families were living in working-class neighborhoods in Los Angeles County. Interviewees were part of Mexican mixed-status families, but they also reflect the diversity of Los Angeles and bi-ethnic/biracial identities and partnerships that are found there. For example, while participants shared ethnic, familial, or intimate ties with Mexicans, six participants also identified with Salvadoran, Guatemalan, or Armenian origins.[75] Interviewees were part of families that included at least one US citizen and one undocumented immigrant family member. Interviews were conducted with 41 adult-age children, 20 parents, and 6 individuals connected to mixed-status families through partner or grandparental ties. In terms of immigration status, I interviewed 42 US citizens, 7 DACA recipients/DACAmented immigrants, and 18 undocumented immigrants who were part of mixed-status families. The terms "undocumented" and "unauthorized" are used to describe immigrants without government authorization to reside in the United States. This includes individuals who entered without authorization, as well as those who initially had authorization but then overstayed their visas. DACAmented immigrants include young adults who gained access to the DACA program.

Participants in this study were largely part of families headed by undocumented parents with citizen children or a combination of undocumented, citizen, or DACAmented children. However, aware of the critiques on how antideportation mobilizing, immigration law, and immigration research often have privileged heteronormative families, I chose not to explicitly define family for participants when making recruitment efforts.[76] While no queer families participated, leaving this family definition open meant that I didn't disqualify participants whose household and family extended beyond the traditional nuclear family. Doing this is particularly important for working-class families of color, many of which have historically relied on or lived with extended family and "fictive kin."[77]

Interviews were conducted in English or Spanish depending on the preference of the interviewee. Sometimes participants also responded in a combination of English and Spanish words. The interviews took place in locations chosen by the participant, typically in homes, cafés, and restaurants and on college campuses. Interview themes centered on questions pertaining to experiences of citizenship, belonging, discrimination, familial responsibilities, and details of their familial relationships. Additionally, I asked respondents about media representations of mixed-status families and immigration policies, and I asked parents about parenting, migration, and plans for their children. Aside from these questions, participants often volunteered rich, detailed information about themselves and their lives. Interviews ranged from about 1 hour to 3.5 hours in length, averaging about 1.5 hours for an interview.

I was able to access participants through several means, including tapping into established personal networks that I had developed during some of my college years between 2008 and 2011. Participants were also directly sampled from Latina/o student or community groups. When possible, I also accessed participants from family members I had already interviewed; this snowball sampling strategy was most effective in accessing siblings or partners. After realizing I could not access enough parents through youth/young adult networks, I also sought to recruit parents while serving as a volunteer English as a second language (ESL) instructor at a local nonprofit. After several months, I invited my students and students from other ESL classes to participate in the research study by making classroom announcements and distributing flyers. Ultimately, this strategy was not effective. Some of my students, I assume, already had legal status, while others may not have been interested in investing additional time away from work or family when the class was already a significant time commitment. Yet my participation as a volunteer teacher gave me insights into the broader Latino immigrant experience and provided me with a sense of camaraderie and joy during this time. Thankfully, my volunteer partnership with the nonprofit eventually allowed me to recruit potential participants from another department where I was able to approach mothers waiting for their children who were taking part in after-school services.

In trying to recruit young adults, I made direct contact with potential participants by making announcements during student group or community-based general body meetings, posting on their social media pages, and meeting with members at their group events. Through these channels, college students in the social sciences and humanities also learned about my study from university staff who shared the study flyer or a recruitment email with them. Recruiting adult children from educational institutions means the young adult sample comprises mostly educated young people. Doing this was intentional, although I tapped into personal networks and community organizations to help diversify the sample. Yet, we can learn a lot by looking at a privileged group that may meet all the proverbial checklist measures for how social scientists think about integration for immigrants and their children—English language fluency, educational attainment, and professional occupational status, to name a few. Yet, despite efforts for upward mobility and US integration, these young adults may be marked as American outsiders. Knowing the challenges of educated young adults in mixed-status families also allows educators in particular to learn of their experiences and perhaps, with this awareness, to develop strategies of support. Understanding the limitations of my sample, the goal here is not generalizability. Instead, I seek to provide an in-depth account of actual lives that we may know so little about—and voices the public may so often ignore or refuse to include.

Alongside the interviews, over the course of a year from 2015 to 2016, I was a participant observer in private homes and immigrant-friendly spaces. In doing this research, I often found myself in immigrant- and Latino-centered spaces, including know-your-rights workshops, public demonstrations, and group meetings and events hosted by organizations that were invested in immigrant rights and/or Latino/a empowerment. I was able to interact with immigrants in a number of community programs and with broad groups of people that included immigrants, the children of immigrants, community service providers, and allies. Most of all, I observed families during their mundane routines at home, as well as during celebratory moments, such as birthday parties and baptisms. I observed and spent the most time with the Garcia-Mendez mixed-status family in the evenings when family members enjoyed each other's company following school and work obligations.[78] I draw from little of the participant observation data explicitly, although these observations did inform this study.

Understandably, undocumented immigrants and their family members were sometimes reluctant to participate in this research, particularly in the "magnified moment" in which I conducted interviews. Sociologist Arlie Hochschild describes magnified moments as "episodes of heightened importance, either epiphanies, moments of intense glee or unusual insight, or moments in which things go intensely but meaningfully wrong."[79] As I conducted interviews and fieldwork, I saw firsthand how mixed-status families experienced both the 2016 presidential race and the possibility of DAPA and their heightened feelings of relief, confusion, and/or disappointment. Importantly, I also saw the discrepancies in hope and optimism—for some families, DAPA was never a possibility.[80]

Los Angeles County Context

Los Angeles County—homeland to the indigenous communities of the Chumash, Tataviam, and Tongva—represents eighty-eight cities, several regions, and a sprawl of neighborhoods with distinct cultural and political histories. As a county, Los Angeles is the most populated in the United States, comprising approximately ten million people, with 33.7 percent of the population being foreign born.[81] Los Angeles remains today a racially diverse metropolis and immigrant gateway. Participants were mainly from or living in Central Los Angeles, East and Southeast Los Angeles, and the San Fernando Valley. These regions include communities that have long-established Mexican neighborhoods as well as those that have experienced an increased Mexican and Latino population since the 1980s.

Doing this research in Los Angeles was ideal for locating mixed-status families, as well as older immigrant families that would include adult-age children. The county is also home to a large settled undocumented population, meaning that about 68 percent of the undocumented Angeleno population has resided in the United States for over ten years.[82] California is home to the largest concentration of Latinos in the United States, at 39 percent of the population; in Los Angeles County, this population is nearly 50 percent.[83] Out of the Latino population in California, 84 percent are of Mexican origin.[84] A sizable number of those Mexican-origin Californians call Los Angeles home. As Roberto Gonzales notes, Los Angeles is "distinctly Mexican . . . [and] Angelenos of Mexican descent make up the municipality's single largest ethnic group."[85] With over 6.5 million Mexicans and Mexican Americans living in Los Angeles, the location is ideal for studying questions that relate to Mexican American incorporation.[86] Additionally, since one out of every five Los Angeles County residents is undocumented or shares a household with an undocumented immigrant, this demographic reality makes the case for why studying mixed-status families in Los Angeles County is imperative.[87]

Although this book joins a long list of immigration studies out of California and Los Angeles, the City of Angels continues to be a puzzle for the curious mind interested in questions of belonging. The integration experiences of immigrants and their children are shaped by the "context of reception," which includes a host society's laws and racial/ethnic makeup.[88] Immigrant residents of Los Angeles have access to accommodating immigrant policies, large immigrant and co-ethnic communities, and a robust infrastructure of immigrant-serving community and civic organizations. Los Angeles is also approximately 135 miles north of the US-Mexico border. Therefore, undocumented immigrants and their loved ones can avoid the constant surveilling and presence of border patrol agents that characterize life in border towns.[89] For these reasons, we can consider my findings are shaped by the context of Los Angeles as a relatively hospitable place for undocumented immigrants and their families. On the other hand, we should not be too quick to laud Los Angeles as a Mexican/Latino, immigrant, or multiracial utopia. As racially and ethnically diverse as Los Angeles is, the area is an epicenter of residential hypersegregation and is one of the most segregated US cities for Latinos.[90] Further, while having co-ethnic networks can be helpful for new immigrants, the saturation of Latino immigrants in Los Angeles also means immigrants face more competition for work and housing. Historically in the not-too-distant past, California was also the site of virulent anti-immigrant policies and discourse. Further, while California and Los Angeles can represent the vanguard in pro-immigrant policies, not all undocumented immigrants may be eligible for or choose to access such protections.[91] Nor does living in Los Angeles mean undocumented immigrants and their families are immune from federal policies or national rhetoric.[92] One cannot underestimate the role of immigration policies that are national in scope, or the fact that on the ground, hate crimes and unauthorized policing tactics can make immigrants vulnerable even in accommodating immigration contexts.

Nevertheless, undocumented immigrants in Los Angeles live in a context of reception that is more immigrant-friendly than not, and these data were collected before the years of the Trump administration. This distinction is important as readers make sense of my findings. Understandably, the experiences described here may differ from those in mixed-status families that live in more hostile immigrant contexts where the fear of deportation may be more pronounced and subsequently may impact undocumented immigrant spatial mobility, presentation of self, and other routines and family responsibilities.[93] In Los Angeles, Special Order 40 has mandated that police officers refrain from interacting with a member of the public for the sole purpose of determining their immigration status.[94] Furthermore, former California governor Jerry Brown signed the Trust Act in 2013, which prevents California counties from putting a hold on a jailed detainee so that ICE can take them into immigration custody, although there are some exceptions. Later, in May 2015, the County Board of Supervisors ended the 287(g) agreement between the federal government and the Los Angeles County Sheriff's Department.[95] These policies established the local context for the immigrant families in this book.

Organization of the Book

In chapter 1, I outline how undocumented parents conceptualize the citizenship status of their American children. Although their own status is insecure, undocumented parents value the US educational opportunities available to their children and perceive it as their children's right to continue accessing this resource. As a result, most parents are willing to fragment their families if they or their partners are deported. Parents use the phrasing *no quiero cortarles las alas* (I do not want to cut their wings) to emphasize their roles in protecting their children's educational opportunities. Parents' plans regarding their possible deportation involve protecting their citizen children's rights, while for their undocumented children, parents rely on moral logics and extended time in the United States to encourage their children's continued residence in the United States. Although parents do experience some ambivalence about their plans, this language highlights the importance of education in undocumented parents' hopes and dreams for their children.

In chapter 2, I track how young adults manage family illegality. Citizen children who have undocumented parents manage family illegality in new ways when they become adults. Adult-age children come to learn that their legal status affords them newfound mobility as well as partial relief regarding parental deportability. The transition to adulthood also represents a new relationship to illegality as young adults are able to develop new ways to cope with and understand parental deportability. Young adults also shift their relationship to illegality when they transition to college, negotiate sponsoring their parents for residency, and participate in family breadwinning. First, my analysis reveals that the pathway to college is made more difficult for citizen college-goers when financial aid processes ask for parents' Social Security numbers and other US authorization information. I also find that the responsibility to sponsor parents for legalization is not a family-friendly option for families who do not want to separate and wait out an extended bar outside the United States. These harsh realities stand in stark contrast to any public discourse about so-called anchor babies and the opportunistic use of citizen children's privileges. Moreover, my findings complicate how we understand gendered family breadwinning, since citizen daughters are expected to financially help their families even if they have adult undocumented brothers.

Chapter 3 chronicles how young Americans "talk back" to public rhetoric about anchor babies and birthright citizenship. Mexican Americans share counterstories that challenge the mainstream anchor baby myth by using several claims that speak to their lived experience and knowledge. Young Americans position anchor baby discourse as illogical, hypocritical, and racist. They argue for the dignity they seek for their families and themselves as a way to counter how elected officials warn of the so-called dangers of birthright citizenship for children born in mixed-status families. While I focus on young adult narratives, I also outline how this rhetoric impacts the lives of mothers and young children. Ultimately, members of mixed-status families resist how they are depicted in public debates and consider this another example of how their membership in the United States is unfairly tenuous.

Chapter 4 examines how undocumented immigrants express their belonging in the United States. Undocumented immigrants construct their worthiness of being in the United States by articulating how their labor provides economic contributions to the country. From these narratives we also get a glimpse of immigrants' visions for immigration reform and their longing for formal recognition from the state. In these narratives, however, not all undocumented immigrants are constructed as worthy. In their attempts to mitigate their own stigma, undocumented immigrants also create moral hierarchies of worth based on clean criminal records and labor history. They do so partly because they place blame on the actions of a few immigrants for creating or maintaining stereotypes of undocumented immigrants as rapists, murderers, and drug dealers. These narratives and hierarchies surrounding criminal activity also reveal how belonging can be stratified for undocumented immigrants.

Chapter 5 focuses on how citizens in mixed-status families experience belonging at the local level. In multiethnic segregated Los Angeles, participants generally feel belonging in their local hometown neighborhoods but experience racism and racial microaggressions in predominantly White communities. It is in White communities where Mexican Americans are told to go back to Mexico, are racially profiled, and experience a range of indignities that mark them as "illegals," undesirable, and/or inferior. These racialized experiences also shape how Mexican Americans exercise agency in responding to or preparing for microaggressions. These Americans primarily use language, self-presentation, and family strategies to mitigate racism.

In the conclusion, I summarize the main findings and unpack some of the contradictions in this work. Despite the challenges youth may face in the event of a parental deportation or in navigating higher education, parents have an optimistic view of their children's futures. Parents feel a responsibility to protect what they see as their children's citizenship or moral right to get an education—but this perception is also based on a dual frame of reference, where parents value and better appreciate US education opportunities over those they believe are available in their home countries. For this reason, if a parent is deported, forced separation is deemed preferable. On the other hand, going through a legalization process in which a parent voluntarily exits the country and waits through a several-year ban is not considered an appropriate plan when families want to stay together. In the conclusion, I also raise pertinent questions about what living in a Trump era of politics meant for mixed-status families and what the future can hold for families if immigration reform and other immigration policies are accomplished. Finally, I provide policy recommendations and challenge readers to consider what change would look like beyond the confines of respectability politics. Ultimately, belonging for members of mixed-status families is a complicated and negotiated ideal. This book centers on the unique subjectivities of these contested Americans who grapple with the realities of illegality and their own racialized belonging.

1

Parents Mitigating Family Illegality in Deportation Plans

Walking to Luz's home, I am struck by the contradiction of overarching roaring freeways and the sweet aroma of what I think is a guava tree. I try to locate this tree but can only imagine it from its delectable scent. It is a weekday, midday—too early for most children to be out of school. It is well into autumn, but the heat would make you think otherwise. As I turn the corner and near Luz's home, there is little noise except for the occasional barking dog and the rumble of a distant garbage truck. "Call me when you get to the house, so I can let you into the back," Luz had told me when we first met. With some mild confusion as to where I am going, I walk through this working-class neighborhood—the kind that reminds me so much of home—to meet Luz once again.

We first met when I received an invitation to attend a birthday cel-ebration for Luz's daughter. When I arrived at the party, I was greeted with the smell of delicious, fragrant food and the splash of the yellows and blues of the themed party. Images of colorful characters were dis-played throughout. These playful characters would surface time after time in the backdrop as I collected data—appearing at other family gath-erings, displayed on TVs and electronic devices, and as stuffed plushies held by toddlers and teens alike. At the party, small, carefree children ran, tumbling themselves into the bounce castle as adults settled into seats lining the rectangular party tables. Luz and her husband, Alfredo, would come by to the table moments later with decorated treats inge-niously made from snack cakes and bouquets of clown lollipops that playfully grin back at you. The food, the decor, all of it caught my eye, but it was Luz and Alfredo's care for each other that was most obvious; their occasional embraces and gleaming eyes made me think they could not be prouder of their small family.

A few weeks later, on this sweltering hot day, I find myself walking alongside a chain link fence that might be enclosing Luz's home. In the hot sun, nothing looks familiar. I pull out my phone to call Luz and let her know I am in front of her house. I make my way to her front door as I let her know where I am. As I walk farther onto the property, I see Luz slowly opening the squeaky screen door while holding back Esme, her young daughter.

Like many immigrants, Luz didn't necessarily plan on migrating to the United States. While growing up in a small town in a coastal state of southern Mexico, she thought she would continue to live in the country, go to school, and later have a family. Her memories of Mexico are fond, often reflecting on the tranquility of her town and the familiar sounds and comforts of children playing freely outside. It wasn't until after she married Alfredo and had their first child that her partner first proposed the possibility of migrating to the United States for work. By then, at the young age of 20 and with a two-year-old, they had already left their hometown and moved to an urban center in Mexico. The idea of migrating seemed like a suitable option to Alfredo, who was hoping to earn money to send back home to Luz, but she had her doubts. *¿Para que? ¿Para que enfrentar el riesgo?* For what? Why risk it? *¿Porque nos quieres dejar? Why do you want to leave us?* she had asked him. By Luz's account, they were not in extreme poverty, but her husband was lured by the prospect of earning higher wages to support their family. The idea of him migrating on his own, she expressed, was also an especially anxiety-producing thought. "Sometimes you hear a lot about how the men go to the United States and they find a new partner and they don't return to their families," Luz said. In the end, he left to work in El Norte, the United States. A few months later, he sent for Luz and their son to come join him in Los Angeles.

Now, at the kitchen table of her small home, she shares her experience as an immigrant mother with twelve years in the United States. It has also been twelve years since seeing her parents, siblings, and extended family, and a little over twelve years since that fateful moment when her husband first raised the prospect of migrating. Her son, an adolescent, is in high school and has deferred action, or DACA. On her lap, sometimes restless, sits Esme, the only US citizen in the family. Esme is a chubby-cheeked toddler with short dark hair. Her large brown eyes convey curiosity as she looks inquisitively at me. She alternates between sitting on her mother's lap and sitting on the tile floor at her mother's feet with a classic toy. Esme pulls down the lever of her bright yellow "farmer says" toy; the colorful arrow spins and lands on a farm animal and its appropriate sound. *Mooooo*, I hear.

When Luz talks about her children, she speaks of opportunity. She hopes her son will find a professional career in the United States and that her young citizen daughter will do well in school. As she discusses her children's education at length, that is what eventually brings her to the subject of deportation. Her deportation, if it were to happen, is something that stands in stark contrast to the plans she has for her family. To Luz, having her children return to Mexico would mean that she would be foreclosing the opportunities available to them in the United States, especially opportunities that relate to schooling and economic advancement. Referring to a family return to Mexico, she said, "Sería como cortarles las alas a mis hijos" (It would be like cutting my children's wings). This was the first time I would hear this specific phrase in the context of this research, but it was certainly not the last. It is in this way we see how parents think about family sacrifice and separation and how much they value protecting their children's futures.

Sometimes, to my surprise, participants often discussed the topic of education at length without any prompting. When I began the interviews, I asked participants to tell me about themselves. It was then that participants sometimes would discuss their educational goals and experiences. Education is often articulated as a matter that is particularly salient for both parents and children in mixed-status families. Regardless of their actual educational attainment, narratives about their or other family members' educational journeys are significant to many of the participants. No matter how concerned or unconcerned they are about the possibility of deportation, parents disclose how they would facilitate family fragmentation if it meant their children could remain in the United States. The few who express their plan to leave as a family unit possibly do so only after carefully considering their children's futures while balancing caregiving and mental health concerns. Moreover, for a select few of my participants, the actual experience of a parental deportation means a complete restructuring of family plans to accommodate caregiving and educational priorities.

In this chapter I focus on one type of narrative that centers on how participants think about their family members' educational futures in the event of a deportation. In these narratives we see how families—

and parents in particular—strategize and conceptualize their children's citizenship when considering the possibility of a family return to their country of origin or, more commonly, family fragmentation. In these narratives, I find that parents conceptualize the US-based belonging of their children as tied to their ability to matriculate through US schools and colleges. Thus, for many parents, possible deportation means that they will do whatever they can to avoid cutting their children's wings, allowing them to grow and fly into professional futures and financial security in the United States. This figurative language is telling, for it emphasizes the parents' role in a child's ability to strive for a success-ful, well-rounded life. However, to be clear, whatever plans parents may have, their choices are made in the context of legal violence.[1] This is to say, if anyone or any system is cutting the wings and dreams of immi-grant families, it is immigration enforcement policies that are usually to blame. As parents in my study build family lives and plans within this context, about 60 percent of those who reported their plans expressed a preference for family fragmentation if a deportation should occur. Other parents expressed a preference for return migration as a family or expressed ambivalence about what they would do in the event of a deportation.[2] For parents who report ambivalence or a definite plan of leaving the United States as a family, their narratives still center on their children's educational opportunities. Still, the decision to return migrate often implicates a lack of available caregiver options for their children if they remain in the United States. These plans, even when ambivalent, are often based on valuing and supporting children's education, although this does not mean children have an easy road ahead either.

These plans are based on parents' conceptualization of their children's citizenship rights, but they are also expressed as a pragmatic approach to class-based realities and educational aspirations. While citizen and un-documented children can access educational opportunities in the United States, parents believe that quality schooling and higher education in their country of origin are affordable only for solidly middle-class and wealthy families. As parents do what they can to mitigate illegality, their plans are in fact just that—plans. In real terms, this means that families may ultimately prefer family reunification, or that in the aftermath of a detention and deportation, there may be little choice or time to carry out even carefully made plans. In the next chapter, I show how even when deportation does not occur, or family arrangements go according to plan, children grow up to face educational barriers and challenges shaped by illegality.

While parents try to manage their illegality in relation to their children and exercise considerable agency in doing so, what I call family illegality is present in the parents' narratives about deportation. While "illegality" is constructed as akin to "deportability," managing and mitigating illegality is a familial practice for mixed-status families.[3] Citizens theoretically should not fear deportation, but as part of mixed-status families, the deportation of a parent might mean leaving the US to live a life in a country that is likely unfamiliar. These family deliberations complicate family plans, and specifically trouble family arrangements surrounding children's educational futures. For example, children who remain in the United States after a parent's deportation can exhibit mental and physical symptoms that make their school learning difficult.[4] On the other hand, children who return with their deported parents face institutional barriers in a new context where they may be ineligible for educational resources because they are not Mexican nationals.[5] In the transition, students might experience difficulty enrolling in school and may be placed a grade back because credits do not transfer or because children first need to reach grade-level standards.[6] Bureaucratic obstacles aside, children can face significant challenges in adjusting to a different linguistic, cultural, instructional, and academic environment.[7] These are difficult considerations that are part of the work of managing family illegality. Before discussing deportation in more depth, I turn now to the matter of education—a matter held dear by parents.

Latinos and Education

Many scholars have critiqued the deficit model approach to understanding Latino or Mexican American educational achievement in the United States. This model assumes that when students of color have lower educational achievement they are to blame because "they and their families have internal defects, or deficits, that thwart the learning process."[8] This model largely casts parents as unwilling to help their children succeed while ignoring structural and institutional barriers that might impede

Latino educational success.[9] One structural issue is that Latino students are concentrated in schools with few resources and little information about attending college.[10] When Latino immigrant parents get involved in advocating for their children's access to good schools and educational resources, school staff and experts can disregard or discount parental suggestions or knowledge.[11] Schools may exclude Latino parents through bureaucratic requirements and culturally insensitive practices.[12] School staff sometimes also perpetuate a Latino achievement gap by tracking Latino students into remedial or non–college preparatory classes and use racialized logics to discipline their bodies.[13] Indeed, schools can be viewed as racial sites where teachers, administrators, and staff rely on racialized stereotypes about Mexican American students.[14] As Mexican American youth find themselves in underfunded schools and tracked into vocational courses in lieu of college preparatory classes, educational attainment for this group can decline, which inhibits their mobility and their incorporation into the mainstream.[15]

There is a long history of tracking students of color away from college preparatory classes and into classes that train students for vocational and service careers. In their study of four West Coast high schools, researchers found that Latino students were believed to be the most appropriate pupils for vocational courses, more so than any other racial or ethnic student group population.[16] High school principals, school security guards, and teachers also criminalize young boys of color by excessively surveilling them and assuming these students are headed to prison.[17]

Another structural issue faced by Mexican undocumented parents is the fear that their immigration status might make them vulnerable to deportation if they seek educational programs or resources for their children.[18] Indeed, parental immigration status shapes how children and families navigate schooling and developmental programs.[19] Parental undocumented status also has other indirect effects on children's educational success. For example, a parent's precarious immigration status often contributes to poverty and the need to move frequently, impacting children's educational stability and performance.[20] Undocumented students have access to US K-12 education through the decision made in *Plyer v. Doe*. However, once undocumented students come of age and attempt to transition to higher education, they face a lack of institutional support and extremely limited financial aid options.[21] Therefore, there are many structural barriers and immigration-related obstacles that can contribute to Latino educational attainment.

The structural barrier of undocumented status can profoundly influence Latino educational advancement. For example, the long-term consequences of Mexican parental undocumented status impact children's educational attainment. Scholars of immigration argue that undocumented immigrants and their children experience "membership exclusion," which is alleviated for the second generation once parents do become legalized.[22] This research suggests that while undocumented status is durable and can impact generations, legalization would do much to relieve the structural exclusion faced by many Mexican Americans.

Despite the deficit assumptions that Latinos and Mexicans do not value education, my research participants, regardless of age, gender, family relationship, or citizenship status, often discussed the importance of education. Across the board, participants of all levels of educational attainment discussed the value of education for their own or their children's lives. This valuing of education is supported by recent data. In a Pew Research Center survey, for example, over 77 percent of young Latinos reported their parents believe that college is the most important next step after high school.[23] Research with Mexican families confirms that parents believe education to be the key to the American Dream.[24] Mexican undocumented parents also do not differ from other ethnic groups or legalized immigrants in terms of engaging their young children in educational or cognitively stimulating activities in the home.[25]

Many of the parents in this study are also involved in their children's educational development. Parents of younger children report going to parent-teacher conferences and occasional school events or programs. Parents also sought out information about educational opportunities for their children where they could—with either kin, friends, community nonprofits, or sometimes, with me. I also saw firsthand how parents carefully structured time for homework and other academic activities. During my observations with the Garcia-Mendez family, I saw how their daily routines centered on twelve-year-old Lana's homework. When Lana asked about playing a DVD or visiting her aunt, her parents would ask, "Is your homework done?" Indeed, this was one of the most common questions asked during my time with the family, and my image of

Lana is of her sitting at the kitchen table, head bent over a textbook as we try to figure out how to solve a math equation.

During my time observing families, I did not find parents to be culturally averse to the idea of working toward a good education or earning a college degree. Instead, they were resourceful and took opportunities to ask me questions about how to help their children navigate K-12 schooling, college, or possible professional careers. Despite the challenges that exist for Latino students and their families, parents in this study assess American educational systems with a dual frame of reference by comparing US educational opportunities to those available in their home countries.[26] Parents perceive US educational opportunities to be better and more accessible than those in Mexico, and they worry that their children may experience structural, educational, social, and/or linguistic challenges if they were to suddenly transition to Mexican schooling.[27] For mixed-status families, the question of education is inextricably linked with the question of deportation. For all the barriers undocumented parents face, their articulations surrounding their children's citizenship and education highlight how family illegality is managed.

Deporting Dreams

Los Angeles County and the state of California arguably represent the gold standard in implementing immigrant-friendly policy solutions. Nevertheless, parents in this study were also aware that the nature of their legal status made their position in the country precarious. In the backdrop of their daily lives, undocumented parents were aware of anti-immigrant national discourses that permeate their TV screens, radios, and everyday conversations. Collecting interviews during 2015–2016 meant the presidential election was in full swing and Donald Trump's particularly virulent rhetoric about deporting Mexicans was on their minds and raging in their hearts. This national rhetoric sometimes inspired a sense of uncertainty for parents.

Deportation, parents knew, may not have always been a direct concern given the relatively accommodating immigrant policy context of Los Angeles. Still, many of the participants had known someone who had been deported. Eleven participants (16 percent) volunteered in their interview that they personally knew someone who had been deported. Out of these participants, nine (13 percent) had a family member deported at some point in time.[28] Knowing someone who has been deported is certainly not uncommon in Latino communities. National data suggest that at least one in four Latinos know an immigrant who has been detained or deported.[29] While about a quarter of Latinos know what it is like to experience the deportation of a friend or family member, over half of Latinos worry about their own or their loved one's deportation.[30] These deportations disproportionately impact Mexican communities.[31]

For some participants, deportation is also visual; they knew deportation could happen because they had seen immigration enforcement vehicles in their communities. In some cases, participants had seen family members or neighbors being taken away by immigration agents, often in the early mornings. However, immigrants had access to resources and information about their rights thanks to a broad patchwork of committed community organizations, nonprofits, and activists. Youth activists, for example, made communities aware of how ICE does in fact apprehend people across LA. Their efforts also manifested in workshops and events across various communities in Los Angeles County to inform immigrants on how to legally deal with an ICE encounter. The labor of the Immigrant Youth Coalition (IYC) and members of the ICE out of LA Coalition also resisted deportations by publicizing petitions for detained immigrants.

In January 2016, deportation could not escape the imagination of immigrant communities. Just a few days after the New Year, DHS confirmed that President Barack Obama had given them the green light to conduct raids to detain Central American families that had migrated illegally after 2014.[32] While the raids were targeting specific families outside of California, the announcement and reporting of these enforcement tactics sent a resounding message to immigrant communities across Los Angeles. Ultimately, the days and weeks surrounding the announcement reminded immigrant communities that they may not be safe.

Even if not the direct target of an ICE raid or apprehension, Latino activists and research participants were critical of what they considered the racial profiling and targeting of Latino communities. These concerns are well documented by sociologists and legal scholars who find that immigration authorities (or those acting as immigration enforcement surrogates) use "Mexicanness" or apparent Latino identity as a reason to suspect a person is in the United States unlawfully and to enforce immigration policing in Latino communities.[33] These punitive immigration enforcement programs therefore impact Latinos and Mexicans in particular, regardless of immigration status.

Once apprehended, immigrants can contest their case, but these efforts are difficult. Parents can claim that their deportation would be damaging to their families, but current policies can make this claim an uphill battle. The Illegal Immigration Reform and Immigrant Responsibility Act of 1996 fundamentally changed the options for undocumented immigrants attempting to contest their deportation. First, IIRIRA made it harder for detained migrants to demonstrate that their removal from the United States would be an "extreme hardship" for their children.[34] Courts have also ruled that US citizen children cannot claim that a parent's removal infringes upon the child's constitutional rights because citizen children can remain in the United States and exit and reenter the country at any time.[35] With few options to contest deportation, an encounter with ICE is an even more frightening prospect. It is a form of legal violence that families contend with when they face the threat or the experience of separation.[36]

"It Would Be an Injustice": Parental Plans and Sacrifices

For Luz, clipping the wings of her children meant cutting off their opportunities. Parents, Luz included, frame the cutting of their citizen children's wings as an act against their children's US citizenship, while doing this to undocumented or DACAmented children is framed as an injustice on moral grounds. For parents like Luz, forcing an undocumented child to return to their country of birth is wrong because they have been socialized and educated in the United States. In our interview, Luz shares the following:

> It's an injustice and very bad luck if immigration caught me and sent me back. We have heard that it is extremely difficult to come back. It would also be an injustice to ask my husband to come back to Mexico just because I am no longer in the US or to ask that of my son. How could I cut off all his dreams that could actually be possible in the US? He could

realize his dreams here as a professional, so it would be unjust to tell him to return to Mexico to be with me. It's a lot to think about. It's something that we know can happen when we live in this country, but it would be an injustice to have them all return if something happened to me.

Parental considerations about what to do in the event of a deportation mean wrestling with the reality that return migration to the United States after a deportation—whether lawful or unauthorized—would be unlikely or challenging. In this sense, parents are keenly aware of the somewhat permanent nature of separation, at least until children may be able to freely visit parents in Mexico. In Luz's words, her own deportation would mean an injustice for all of the family if she asked them to come back to Mexico with her. Moreover, since her son is in high school and close to the time of possible college enrollment, Luz worries that returning to Mexico might signal an end to his professional future.

Luz shares that she and her family have had conversations about what would happen to the children if one or both parents are deported. Fortunately, for Luz, careful considerations about what would be done are possible because she can count on trusted family friends to temporarily house and care for her children. She tells me, "We have talked about it. If something should happen, we have good [family friends], and I think they would help." Luz has discussed these plans with her son and knows that these arrangements will temporarily suffice, at least until her son is independent or adult age. As families think about what might happen after a parental deportation, the possibility of family fragmentation suggests that someone must remain in the United States to care for minor children. In Luz's case, while she has no immediate family in the United States, she trusts some family friends to possibly partake in caregiving if the need arises. Luz's plans for such an arrangement, I hope, will not be necessary. But, it should be noted, Luz's clean criminal record and her knowledge of no active deportation order in her name may suggest that she is not particularly at risk for being detained and deported. Even so, while Luz lives in the comfort of her Mexican community with a relatively accommodating policy context for immigrants, the national discourse surrounding immigration does not escape her. The heated debates revolving around the 2016 presidential election (occurring at the time of the interview) worry her:

What I can tell you is that I am worried. I've heard [Donald Trump] wants to take away my son's DACA too, so it worries me. More than anything, I want my children to stay in the US and to be upwardly mobile and become important people. With all the comments and hate language that some people use, you get to thinking: what kind of future will there be for my children? For my children to return to Mexico it would be so complicated.

Luz was already very familiar with Trump's call to deport undocumented immigrants, build a wall between Mexico and the United States, and eliminate DACA. Luz was concerned about what a new presidential administration would mean for the future of her son, an adolescent who had grown up in the United States. For her citizen daughter, remaining in the United States to matriculate in American schools would be ideal, but also incredibly complicated given her young age. Luz's thoughts point to how she is exercising agency in a circumstance of significant external constraints. Ostensibly, she doesn't want to cut her children's wings and prevent them from flying. However, Luz profoundly articulates the other side of this dilemma: the United States can be a hostile place for children like hers. So, as parents work to secure the American Dream for their children, there is perhaps still an understanding that children can face racism along the way that may chip away at this hope.

When I meet Berta, we are at a nonprofit waiting room filled with mothers and young children. With some trepidation, I have been walking around the room, prepared with my three-ring binder and flyers to talk to mothers about my project.[37] Almost like a shield, I let my binder rest against my body as I look around the buzzing room. It's not that I am scared, but I worry about being intrusive. I squeeze through tight spaces between chairs and toddlers to ask each mother if I could have a couple of minutes of her time. Berta is the last person I spot after making my way around the room.

Berta is jovial and very friendly when I approach her. She has been talking to two women who are about to leave. I sit with her and tell her about my research project. A few moments later, her son skips over to her with outstretched arms that precariously hold his books and an open backpack that spills out a flow of white school paper. It's an image that makes me think of a tree in autumn with falling leaves. Berta greets him,

gets up from her chair, and then turns to me to say, "I will come participate, but right now, I have to leave. I will be back tomorrow if you want
to interview me." I understand immediately that this is likely the polite
way she is declining to participate. To my pleasant surprise, however,
Berta's words are sincere. I return in a few days to interview her.

In the privacy of a brightly lit room, we sit and carry out the interview. Berta prefaces the interview by sharing how difficult her migration
journey was. Like many immigrants, she crossed the border with the
help of a *coyota*, or woman human smuggler. The journey was particularly long, requiring days of travel by train, bus, and long-distance walking through La Rumorosa.[38] While Berta calmly tells me her story, she
emphasizes how she and others on the trek contended with conditions
she describes as fit only for animals. At one point, she leans in slightly
as she tells me, "It was very, very bad." When she senses the implication
of what she said, Berta leans closer and waves her hands to dismiss my
possible interpretation: "No, no, no, it's not like other women, you know,
they are assaulted and raped. Nothing like that."

Berta's migration journey was difficult at many points. While she had
started out with two male family members, the *coyota* in charge separated migrants into groups, leaving Berta with a set of strangers. Aside
from contentious encounters with Mexican police even before reaching
the US border, Berta was at one point separated from her group and
lost in the desert—hungry, thirsty, and exhausted—with two men and a
woman. After recalling this arduous journey, Berta reaches out with her
hands and says she will never voluntarily go back to her country. It cost
her so much to get here.

Berta and I talk about how she and her husband decided on settling
in Los Angeles and what her family's plan is now that they have been in
the United States for ten years. Like many immigrants, Berta and her
husband did not think they would settle in the United States. The initial
plan had been to work in the country for five years and save enough
money to return home. After having children in the United States, however, their plans changed. Berta says now the only way she would go
back is if she was deported, but this thought was not a topic of conversation she liked to discuss with her husband and children. To her, a return
to her country would mean a blow to the educational plans she has for
her children, and as she notes, she wouldn't want to rob them of that.

Berta takes an active role in her children's schooling and shares, "I tell them they have to advance themselves." For that reason, she wouldn't want to rob them of their rights as American citizens to live and study in the United States.

In considering the possibility of her deportation, Berta expresses her agency to think through how she can help keep her children rooted in the United States when being undocumented entails constrained choices. For parents like Berta, migrating to the United States is a temporary plan that only becomes permanent once children are part of the family. Unlike any anchor baby or otherwise elaborate plan of reproducing for the purposes of legalizing in the United States, parents tend to prioritize the needs of their minor children. If anything, parents want to remain in the United States to continue to raise and guide their children so that they can achieve their goals. In the event of an emergency and subsequent family fragmentation, parents certainly believe in anchoring their children to the United States, but this is not the same anchor evoked in popular media narratives of mothers bearing anchor babies to legalize themselves in the United States.

While institutional forces create the barriers that restrain Berta's choices, parents exercise their agency to mitigate family illegality. The decision to separate the family is difficult for several reasons. Berta shares that if deportation is going to happen, it would be best when her children are older. She sighs, "They can stay here. I think that a child who is fifteen or over can stay here." Certainly, these choices are made by balancing educational goals, caregiving, and the realities of family fragmentation. The age of her children would be a significant factor because Berta reiterates that given her crossing experience, she would never do it again. Before leaving the interview, she smiles broadly. With kids and backpacks in tow, I watch Berta leave the nonprofit for the day. For weeks, I will see her smiling and cracking jokes with the other mothers.

On the day I introduced myself to Berta, I chatted briefly with another woman, who I came to know later as Angélica. I am immediately drawn to Angélica because she looks like the youngest mother in the waiting room and probably the closest in age to me. I sit next to her and ask politely about her children. They are little and sort of stumbling about by the tables and toys in the lobby. But my timing is off because, just as soon as we start talking, her son joins us and lets us know he is ready to leave. Then, weeks later, I see her again.

It turns out that Angélica and I are the same age, but our lives are quite different. As a child-free and at the time unmarried citizen, I do not have the same experience she does as an undocumented wife and mother of three small children. But within a short time, Angélica is very open to me about her status. When I talk about my research on mixed-status families, she asks, "Would that include a family like mine? Where the parents are undocumented? Because that is my situation." Angélica's three children range in age from two to eleven, and all but one was born in the United States. Her oldest, a son, was brought to the states when he was just five months old.

After a brief stint in Chicago, Angélica and her husband made it to California. When I ask if she will stay in Los Angeles, Angélica responds, "Well, yes, while they don't kick us out." She laughs as she asks me, "How do you call him? The guy who wants to be president?" And in that moment, I know she is probably thinking about Trump's anti-immigrant rhetoric and his proposed plan for mass deportations. Unless she experiences deportation, Angélica plans to stay in the United States permanently. When I ask her how she had adapted to the United States, Angélica admits the following:

> Yes, it is very different. It's hard to be far from family. One thing is that if I go to Mexico, my children won't be able to study their own language because they were born here. It would be like I am cutting their wings when they want to fly. Yes, because over there they can learn Spanish and choose whatever career they'd like, but over there, education doesn't count. So, as a parent, you put up with what you can here.

For Angélica, like most parents in my study, the metaphor of not wanting to cut children's wings remains a powerful articulation of parental sacrifice. Angélica also recognizes the linguistic challenges her children may face in Mexico. There are Mexican educational policies meant to promote English-Spanish bilingualism, but few students in Mexican schools have access to a qualified bilingual teacher, and most of the teachers who can offer competent English instruction are in private schools.[39] The other side to this challenge is that American or US-raised children may confront challenges in acclimating to schooling in Mexico, where they will need to speak, write, and read in Spanish. These challenges mean American children in Mexico may fall behind academically.[40]

While undocumented parents who have both undocumented and citizen children discuss not wanting to cut their children's wings, parents make claims around citizen children having the right to fly since they are citizens born on US soil. In this sense, parents articulate and create meaning around their children's citizenship. Angélica's comment also reveals practical concerns about what a collective family return to Mexico would mean. While children can return to their parents' country of birth, go to school, and still earn a college degree, Angélica fears that a Mexican degree would "not count" or transfer in the country of her citizen children.[41] Therefore, the metaphor of not wanting to cut off children's wings reflects parents' understanding of their children's citizenship and attempts to manage their own illegality while balancing practical concerns about their children's professional work possibilities.

Not all families can plan to have children remain in the United States in the event of a deportation. For a mother like Paloma, family fragmentation would not be possible because she is a single parent with limited social networks. Paloma would probably have no choice but to arrange to have her children accompany her if she was deported to Mexico. Her husband has been out of the picture for over a year now—a family arrangement that pains Paloma to tell me as we sit together. In addition to this, her other loved ones are in Mexico. She explains, "I don't have family here. It's just me. Out of my five siblings, I am the only one here." As a result, Paloma has no family or close friends in the area who could be entrusted to take on any caregiving. This is unfortunate because her young son has been receiving extensive speech therapy since he was a young toddler. Paloma is concerned that her children will lose access to important US programs that have helped them develop socially, cognitively, and academically if they were to move outside the country.[42] Although her children are young, she hopes they will continue to meet developmental milestones and eventually go to college and pursue a fulfilling career. She tells me, "More than anything, I want my children to surpass me academically. I made it to high school but I want them to complete a degree and access a professional career." Since all her children are US citizens, she believes their status will serve as an advantage to them as they work toward completing their educations. As she explains, "They have the privilege to really advance themselves. I have an obstacle that really keeps me stuck, but they don't. They can really go far. They don't have a barrier." A deportation would drastically impact Paloma's hopes. Single parents do not want to cut their children's wings, but they also have few options for arranging for their children's care in the United States if they do not have family or social networks to access suitable guardians.

Mothers are not the only ones to share narratives about not wanting to cut their children's wings. Fathers, too, think about their precarious status and the possibilities their children can have if they remain and are educated in the United States. Hernán, a father of three, migrated in the 1980s and was particularly outspoken about the educational opportunities available in the United States. In an apartment in the San Fernando Valley, Hernán tells me about his hopes for his children, especially given his own experiences with hardship. When we meet, it is late evening, and his family is getting ready to eat dinner while a Spanish-language news program plays in the background. The backdrop of our interview features the usual sounds of family dinnertime and the interruptions of the family's two exuberant dogs.

Hernán grew up in the Mexican state of Guadalajara with his parents and eight siblings. He recounts his childhood as being a simpler time, but one marked by poverty, and sometimes with very little to eat. Despite this, Hernán was able to complete a few college classes and had not grown up with any intentions of migrating. When he was a bachelor, it was a work trip that sent him to the US South for a brief time before returning to Mexico. Years later, a rock concert inspired his return to the United States. At this point, he was married with a young child. When he made it back to the United States in the early 1990s, this time to Los Angeles, he had his wife and child in tow. Now, having been in the United States for over twenty-five years, Hernán feels comfortable in the country and no longer necessarily worries much about the possibility of an ICE encounter. He is mainly focused on the educational future of his children. More than anything, Hernán makes the distinction that in Mexico you can earn a higher education if you have money, whereas in the United States, he argues, class status matters less. For this reason, his deportation would not mean a family return to Mexico, as this would alter the dreams he has for his children. He tells me, "What I want is for my children to get a good education, and luckily my oldest daughter has her career." If Hernán was compelled to return to Mexico, he would try to find work and send money to his family in the United States. He elaborates, "[My children] would need to stay because they have the right to get a good education, and in my country, you know, you have to have a lot of financial resources to keep studying." For Hernán, family fragmentation would make practical sense. He perceives a family return to Mexico in the wake of his deportation as leading to a significant reduction in his children's educational opportunities. He tells me his son, a high school student, is thinking about colleges. Hernán communicates some of the advice he gives his son, which is to bring home good grades. Since Hernán's son has matriculated through US schools all his life and has an idea of what kind of profession he wants to pursue, they both already have specific US universities in mind—one in California and another farther east.

Although many parents discuss their children's educational opportunities, fathers also discuss their economic contributions if they were deported. Hernán makes clear that if he were deported, he would still send money to his family. Mothers who think about their possible deportation do not discuss plans to send money to the United States. Indeed, deportations take on different meanings for mothers and fathers, even though their reasons for leaving their children in the United States are the same. Such differences make sense considering how undocumented fathers can feel their sense of worth is tied to their ability to financially support their families.[43] While Hernán does not definitively say he would return to the United States, deported fathers often express motivation to return to better fulfill their roles as breadwinners for their families.[44]

Although both mothers and fathers talk about what they would do if they are caught in the immigration enforcement dragnet, it is disproportionately Latino working-class men who are detained and deported.[45] In the more common circumstance in which male partners are deported and leave a family behind, women become solo family caregivers and providers.[46] The parents I interviewed recognize the investment in education for their children, but they also understand family disruption is emotionally and financially taxing, particularly when the deportee is the main breadwinner.

Importantly, financial constraints can be an issue even when parents return migrate as a family. Even as Hernán is particularly invested in his children's careers, he also noted that if he was deported and his family joined him, they would all be in dire straits in Mexico. In effect, not only would he be concerned about constrained educational advancement, but also more general quality of life issues. He expressed:

> It's just not the same quality of life to support your children. How are you going to support them over there? The communities are different. The children would not be used to it. Another thing is the language. For the children, it's not the same. They won't understand. We already have a life made here. Honestly, we already have twenty-five years here. That is already half my life. I was twenty-six, twenty-seven, something like that when I got here. Now my kids, all their lives have been here. Not half their lives, their whole lives. They were raised here. They would not be able to speak [the language] over there. They will not be comfortable at all. It will not be the same. There are a lot of circumstances where there will not be enough money.

Already being accustomed to US customs, norms, and English language ubiquity all seem to suggest life in Mexico would be difficult for Hernán's family. This compounded with relatively depressed wages in Mexico would make it hard to support a family. Hernán later sums up some of his thoughts with a new word that I've never heard before: *carencias*. This word, Hernán explains to me, means scarcity. In other words, if his family were in Mexico, "There [would] not be enough money." These are some of the important considerations that parents, but especially fathers, think about.

Miguel, a father of three, has a similar stance on what would happen to his family in an immigration-related emergency. Miguel, like Hernán, is not worried that he will come into contact with ICE but recognizes that it is a possibility. I made initial contact with him through his wife, Ximena, a US citizen. When we talk on the phone about the possibility of doing an interview, I speak in Spanish. Ximena responds to me in English and asks me about the research. Ximena admits she has tried to find research that reflects the realities of her family and found only a few studies about families like hers. We agree to meet for an interview.

Miguel and Ximena meet with me on a Sunday after attending church. They are exceptionally warm and greet me with smiles and hugs as they make their way into the home. We sit together for a while talking about the research project. Then Ximena asks if we could pray, so together we join hands, and Ximena asks God to protect us and grant help to mixed-status families across the country. With this wish and eager for Miguel's interview to begin, Ximena agrees to stay with the children in the other room.

Miguel sits on a couch, and I roll over in an office chair to sit across from him. With a tray table between us and the dimming light of the sun setting against the windows, we begin the interview. Miguel has been in the United States for about twenty-five years, which is now over half his life. Like Hernán, Luz, and Berta, Miguel, did not grow up thinking he would eventually migrate to the United States. Things changed when a brother living in Los Angeles convinced him to migrate, and as a single man, he thought he would take his chances. Miguel later met Ximena. Now, they are married and have children together. When I ask Miguel what he appreciates most about the United States, he shares:

> Well, I see it from the academic perspective. You can reach your goals if you are willing. There are ways to reach your academic goals, and that is something that in my country I did not have or it's just much harder. To access an education is not possible in my country if you are not economically privileged, whereas in the US the government gives you more help to grow in that sense.

For Miguel, the United States represents a country of educational opportunity. He clarifies that a quality education, including a university degree, is possible in Mexico, but only if one has sufficient financial resources.[47] Miguel argues that US after-school programs and government financial aid for college-bound high school students prove that educational opportunity is feasible in the United States. These comparisons make sense for immigrant parents who have a dual frame of reference between their home countries and the United States.[48] With this frame,

US educational opportunities seem more plentiful, far superior, and more economically accessible than educational pathways in Mexico.

Miguel tells me that he wants his children to love God and get a good education so that they can help people. As citizens, he believes, this goal is possible. For this reason, when we talk about what would happen in a situation with ICE, Miguel states:

> We have discussed it, and I tell them that if I had to leave, I would still try to help financially. I feel that for them, the opportunities are here to educate themselves. They would stay for this reason because there are more opportunities here than in my country. Like I was saying, in my country you can study if you have money. In the US, however, there are more opportunities to realize your dreams and study.

Miguel is quite explicit in recognizing that family fragmentation is a preferable option, since it means his children would be able to continue their education in US schools. Miguel and Ximena both work, but Miguel emphasizes he would also continue to serve as a breadwinner by sending remittances to the United States from Mexico, a reversal of the more common trend of sending financial resources to Mexico from the United States. His rationalizing about keeping his children's wings uncut is also made within a larger context of class-based constraints. Parents know that their working-class children may be able to secure college financial aid and possibly enroll in high-performing or career-specific public schools. This US educational context—in parents' eyes—stands in stark contrast to Mexican educational contexts where parents believe class status serves as an even greater sorting mechanism for educational access and opportunity.

Even as parents believe family fragmentation might be the best choice for their children's educational futures, thinking about mitigating family illegality involves considerations about family caregiving and mental health. Keeping children rooted in the United States requires someone to care for them. Many of the participants could rely on a partner, older child, family member, or close friend to take on this important responsibility. These narratives are also fraught with ambivalence as parents try to balance a strong desire to protect their children's futures and the family's emotional needs. For some families, however, the question of what would be done in the event of a deportation hits close to home. Unlike Miguel and Ximena, another pair of parents—Ruben and Carmela— face a much more pressing reality. Thinking about deportation is made more real when a loved one has been detained and awaits their hearing to know the outcome of their immigration case. This was the situation Ruben and Carmela were facing. For this couple, the reported deportation plan was ambivalent as they sought to balance family emotional needs with the US-based educational opportunities of their children.

Ruben had been detained about a month prior to our interview. A local activist group had been working to get media attention on his case, circulating a petition to get Ruben out of detention. When we have a chance to meet in person, Ruben is out on bond, but he and Carmela express the dire uncertainty about what lies ahead. At the time of the interview, they are working with local activists to figure out how to move forward with the now urgent matter of financial resources: they must repay a loan for the bond and also pay their lawyer. Ruben and Carmela don't know what will be next for Ruben. His fate—and whether he will be deported to Mexico—is still to be determined.

On a spring afternoon, I set out to meet Ruben and Carmela at their church. The church is somewhat nondescript, and its exterior reminds me of many public-schools in the area. It is located on a busy street nestled in a dense neighborhood of primarily apartment buildings and the occasional food vendor. I agreed to meet them after church, so when I made it there, I worried about calling Carmela's phone during what might be the respectful silence of a congregation listening to a sermon. I wait in front of the church for a while before making my way to the side entrance where parishioners start to trickle out. I later find myself in a room with parishioners gathering in the church's recreation hall to eat a potluck dinner. The church congregation is mostly Latino, but there are also Black and White parishioners who have gathered for a feast of tostadas and *pupusas*.

I recognize Ruben from the petition photo posted online by local immigrant youth activists. I smile as I approach to shake his hand. I also meet Carmela, Ruben's sister, and little Tiffany, who is nine years old and noticeably timid. As we eat, several churchgoers approach Ruben, and it becomes obvious to me that the church is involved in the fight against his deportation. A moment later, a parishioner sits near the family to catch up with Carmela. *Es una desgracia*, a disgrace, I overhear. I think they are talking about Ruben's case. The woman continues, "They were chasing after the wrong guy, but he must have been scared because he ran. They caught up with him on the corner and shot the poor kid. Just right here. He was in high school." She was not talking about Ruben. The women at the table shake their heads in disapproval. These are the realities of life here in this working-class Latino community.

Ruben, Carmela, and I eventually make our way outside to talk privately. The interview is unique in that much of what they have to share is on the urgent matter of Ruben's possible deportation. Ruben migrated to the United States in 2000 and was joined by Carmela and their son three years later. After fifteen years in the country and with a US-born daughter in elementary school, Ruben and Carmela are actively thinking about what returning to Mexico would mean for their family. But they acknowledge that Ruben's deportation would not necessarily be a return home. Instead, Ruben describes his country of birth as a place that is no longer what it once was: "We are used to the lifestyle here and supposedly our country has become a harder place to live. There are assassinations, kidnappings, and lots of insecurity." For Ruben, returning to Mexico would not be a return to the home he remembers; his sister in Mexico sometimes calls to share with him the rumors of violence and threats there that make his fear of violence all the more understandable.

More than anything, Carmela wants her children to grow up to be good, professional people. She has ambitious hopes for both children, but she concedes that she can't force her son to study and that his lack of legal authorization makes it difficult for him to continue his education and find work. She sighs, "He will have to make more of an effort to study." She brings her hands together as if praying as she tells me about her daughter, Tiffany. Her little girl wants to become a veterinarian. Carmela says, "We hope that they can be something, someone especially in this country where we think it's possible."

As we sit outdoors, the day melts into the night. Occasional sirens interrupt the stillness of this clear spring evening. Ruben tells me about his experience with how immigration agents managed to enter his house and later returned to handcuff him on his way to taking his daughter to school. They talk freely and openly about the ambivalence ahead and the possible deportation; the plan is tenuous but has been discussed. For the moment, Carmela says she focuses on her routine and hearing her daughter share about her days at school. She is pleased with Tiffany's school because she sees how they are focused on inspiring students to go to college by including field trips to UCLA and other local universities:

> I think her school motivates her so much. In that respect, it would cost her a lot if she had to go to Mexico. In our country, schooling is not the same. It would be similar if we enrolled her in a private school in Mexico, but we wouldn't have the money for a private school, right. If she stays with me and my husband goes, for her it would be so difficult because she is very attached to her father. He is the one that takes her and picks her up from school. . . . While he was in detention, she was distracted in school. I noticed she was worried about him. When they would talk on the phone, I would see how sad she gets. She would start crying. . . . But while we can continue being a family, I want my daughter to grow up that way and my son.

Carmela's words underscore how parents considering these choices find themselves between a rock and a hard place. On the one hand, the quality education she desires for her daughter would likely be out of reach financially in Mexico. On the other hand, remaining in the United States could result in Tiffany struggling in school as she manages the emotional trauma of being separated from her father.

During the interview, I catch a glimpse of Ruben and Carmela's family dynamic with Tiffany. From time to time, parishioners briefly stop by our table to say goodbye to Ruben and Carmela, but it's Tiffany's brief time at the table that strikes me. Still shy, Tiffany comes by to wrap her arms around her father's neck in a show of affection. If Ruben is deported, Carmela worries about what staying in the United States will do to Tiffany's emotional state. He is, after all, an active part of Tiffany's everyday life. "She is more attached to him," Carmela says gently.

Certainly, Carmela and Ruben are concerned about Tiffany's emotional well-being. Having grown up without a father, Carmela is reluctant to have her daughter separate from Ruben. Stuck in this perplexing and unfortunate circumstance, Carmela still muses on what Tiffany can accomplish educationally and professionally if the family remains in the

United States. She believes that the United States has a commitment to children, especially to their educational development. In contrast, Carmela regrets her own limited educational opportunities growing up in Mexico and sees promise in her daughter's future. Like other parents, Carmela also articulates how class differences would mitigate some of the impact of having to transfer to a Mexican educational context. For many undocumented parents, paying for private education in Mexico is not feasible. Ultimately, as a parent, Carmela wants to do what she can to support her children's opportunities and possible economic mobility in the United States, as reflected in her comment, "We don't want to cut our children's wings." Ruben and Carmela wait for the outcome of Ruben's hearing, but for other families, a parent's deportation takes place, and the ensuing moments become more of a whirlwind that leaves little time for plans.

For some families the deportation of an immediate family member becomes a reality. I knew that Irene had an experience with this. She is a young woman with much enthusiasm for life, service, and community. When I have a chance to chat with her, we talk about the possibility of an interview and, of course, whether or not she is eligible in terms of being part of a mixed-status family. At the time, I was not sure if she had citizen siblings. Irene, I knew, was undocumented. Although she is not a parent herself, her experience demonstrates how young adult children must also take part in mitigating the "illegality" effect on loved ones.

Irene migrated to the United States with her parents at the age of four along with her one-year-old sister. Like many childhood arrivals, Irene now has deferred action but is somewhat ambivalent about her place in the nation. Although Mexico remains a fuzzy and distant memory, at many points in her educational journey, she was reminded that she was an undocumented outsider to the United States. Despite these challenges, Irene made it to college and found support in student groups on campus. As the eldest child in her family, her responsibilities to her family were typical and mostly centered on doing well in school. Very abruptly, however, things changed.

When Irene was in college, she witnessed ICE apprehend and remove her parents from her home. Her family did not have a deportation plan in place, and the deportation occurred so suddenly that there wasn't much time to process what was happening. Irene had seen the

ICE agents at her house, and her parents were quickly taken by these agents. Later in the day, her parents were already in Tijuana. After her parents' deportation, there were family conversations about whether anyone wanted to go to Mexico to reunite with their parents. While in part Irene desired to join them, she ultimately decided that staying in the United States was her responsibility to help manage the family and the finances. At this time, her youngest sibling was also in high school. In our interview, Irene describes this dilemma, "This [deportation] happened and for us to all leave, it just felt wrong. It felt like we would all be giving up or something. So, I just felt like we just needed to stick it through." Hinting at the possible sacrifice she and her family already made to be in the United States, Irene did what she could to help her family through this crisis.

Irene had to quickly take on a number of responsibilities. This entailed spending several days gathering paperwork and adjusting or ending household contracts with certain utilities, and mortgage or business providers. She also had to find a way to make a living. This was a new responsibility because, as she expresses, her undocumented father's salary had been sufficient for supporting a family. Irene had the sudden responsibility to run and financially support a household. She recalls, "You know, it's hard because you're used to your parents doing everything for you even as an adult. So, you're used to your parents having your back, so we actually did not rely on friends or family. I think it was me. We were all pretty prideful about it. So, we just did it." Parents who have not experienced deportation may plan on relying on kin to help care for US-based children. However, it's clear from Irene's narrative that in a moment of crisis, extended family ties may not always be ideal for helping in these situations. Irene did not initially ask for help from family members, and in speaking to me she notes that when she did need help, extended family members who had initially offered support became unavailable. Ultimately, though, she could not harbor any ill will toward these kin because she understood they also had their own families to support.

By Irene's account, because both of her parents were deported so quickly, there wasn't much time to think, much less to make carefully planned decisions about the family's future. Instead, it was eventually understood that the children would remain in the United States for the long term and would finish their educations, and Irene would help take on the necessary roles to keep the household and family running. Families manage as they can, and in Irene's case, her efforts to take on breadwinning and family responsibilities in the aftermath of her parents' deportation highlight how avoiding the cutting of wings means some sacrifice. In her case, taking on this role meant delaying graduate school and putting family needs first. The actual event of a family member's deportation can drastically alter family responsibilities precisely because of the commitment to remain in the United States. Although in this chapter we have learned how parents mostly think about their possible deportations, their articulations about wanting children to fly demonstrate how illegality is something that is managed as a family.

Conclusion

For many Americans, regardless of citizenship status or the status of their family members, accessing educational opportunities is considered part and parcel of achieving the American Dream. For immigrant parents, this represents one of the central motivators for migration in the first place and remains the most frequently highlighted aspiration they have for their children. Unlike the tenets of the deficit model that views Mexican and Latino parents as uninterested in their children's educational pursuits, my research suggests that parents are actively thinking about their children's educational futures. Their investment in this educational future also means that the value they place on it outweighs the emotional stability that may be preserved by keeping a family intact.

For mixed-status families, the experience or possibility of a parent's deportation means children remain in the United States to access US schooling and higher education. In these narratives, undocumented parents discuss their plans for what should happen if they are deported, often pointing out how they would consider fragmentation of the family if it means children could remain in the United States. These negotiations rely on caregiving and kin networks that families depend on to make children's stay in the United States possible.

As seen in this chapter, parents try to mitigate their own illegality and exercise agency in the context of few options and frustrating ambivalence. Parents express that their children do belong in the United

States mainly because they deserve to matriculate through US schools. For parents of undocumented children, this claim is centered on moral grounds and how children are socialized in the United States, while for their citizen children, they articulate a rights-based argument for their children's deservingness to stay. Importantly, this attempt to mitigate illegality is also class-based. Parents view the United States as a country where educational opportunity is possible regardless of one's class status. In contrast, they see their countries of birth as places where class privilege matters a great deal. Further, we cannot forget that parents' own educational experiences shape such decision-making. Their very migration often is embedded in experiences marked by *blocked* education opportunities that are shaped by both time and place. I make no claims that US educational systems or opportunities are better than those in Mexico; rather, parents are exercising their agency to imagine and protect what they believe is best for their children's futures. Parents believe they need to protect the American Dream for their children. Although parents can't control their own status, they can make efforts to better ensure that their children are able to access a quality education, and, as a result, live a comfortable life.

These decisions are not made easily. Talking about deportation with family members can also be taboo, uncomfortable, and emotional. Some parents may avoid broaching the subject with children to protect them emotionally.[49] In my research, some parents noted that Donald Trump's rhetoric got them thinking and talking about possible emergency situations with immigration agents or *la migra*. Indeed, even in an immigrant-friendly place like Los Angeles, some participants' discussion of Trump made it clear that they felt their immigration status could make them vulnerable. Still, sometimes deportation plans are unspoken, sometimes they change, and sometimes they are shared only with partners.

For parents, thinking through deportation is also an experience contrary to narratives of parents birthing children to strategically legalize their status. Immigrants often do not plan to remain in the United States, and primarily do so only because of what they see as the right of their American children to live in their country. While parents hope their children can legalize their status, family planning is not centered on this goal, nor do children serve as anchors in that way. Instead, parents sometimes make or imagine painful futures of family separation so that children are anchored in the United States. As these decisions are emotionally fraught, fathers, too, experience concern and fear. Indeed, narratives about transnational life and family fragmentation run counter to the norms of hegemonic masculinity for Latino migrant men.[50] To some degree, these difficult return migration choices can shape gendered experiences and outcomes.

Certainly, some families collectively participate in return migration. Some reports suggest that about half a million US citizen children now attend Mexican schools.[51] In my research, participants tend to talk about these families—neighbors, fellow churchgoers, and friends—as if they vanished from one day to the next. These family-wide departures do happen and have been referred to by scholars as the "de facto deportation" or "effective deportation" of US citizens.[52] While courts do not recognize parental or family deportation as a violation of citizen's rights,[53] this chapter demonstrates that undocumented parents are doing what they can to protect what they perceive as their children's citizenship rights and future. In this sense, not wanting to cut a child's wings represents a powerful metaphor for how parents manage family illegality and think through where they feel they and their children do and should belong.

Although it is emotionally and financially challenging, family fragmentation can be a practical strategy to keep children in US schools. Research suggests that Mexican American children transplanted to Mexican schools face significant bureaucratic obstacles and resource limitations.[54] Popular accounts suggest that even among co-ethnics in a country of their parents' birth, these children struggle in this new cultural and linguistic environment.[55] Further, many Mexican compatriots stigmatize deportees because they assume deportees were removed from the United States because of criminal activity.[56] There is a fear that this stigma will extend to the children of deported parents. Whether parents plan to have children stay in the United States or leave to a country of their roots, the choice is difficult. Lived reality is not easy either, even when plans are followed, especially when they go awry. As I will show in the next chapter, young adults with intact US-based families still face barriers to accessing higher education, and these young citizens do not necessarily navigate a higher education or financial aid system that is always meritocratic, high-quality, or sensitive to the plight of students in mixed-status families.

About a year after our interview, I returned to Luz's house for Esme's next birthday party. Esme is no longer the only US citizen in her family; she now has a sister. On this celebratory and colorful day, any concerns about the future and legal status are lifted. Under a white tarp in the Southern California heat, the adults sit at tables catching up while waiting to be served food and drinks as children play on a nearby swing set. I catch up with Luz, talking about the familiar pain of loss and the bittersweet subjects of life that make us thankful to see another year. Esme is napping inside, and the deejay sets up as the guests trickle in. A few hours into the night, most of the other guests arrive, and children jostle with each other as the deejay plays renditions of Mexican musical favorites such as "La Chona."

Later into the night, Luz emerges from the house with Esme. Luz, I see, is beaming as she carries Esme on her hip. She points out to Esme her brightly wrapped presents on the gift table and turns the little girl to see her guests. Seeing Luz and Esme together reminds me of the kind of image I remember seeing in my own baby photos: beaming mother balancing her chubby-cheeked toddler. At one point, Luz lifts her birthday girl ever so slightly. Esme's somewhat expressionless face brightens, and I smile to see the innocent joy on her face. Luz gently bounces Esme. The little birthday girl becomes increasingly happy, giggles even. As the music plays, I see Esme as her mother raises her to the sky. I am reminded of Luz's metaphor about not wanting to cut off her children's wings. I look at Luz as she gently bounces Esme into the night air. From my vantage point, it looks like Esme is *flying*.

2

Negotiating Family Illegality as Young Adults

Beneath the industrial lighting of a coffee shop, I meet twenty-four-year-old Alejandra. Originally from a working-class neighborhood, Alejandra is undocumented, and what immigration scholars would identify as part of the 1.5 generation since she migrated as a child.[1] Alejandra is the third child in her family. Her parents and one older sibling are also undocumented. Alejandra's spirit is contagious. So, when she tells me, "I am kind of like a funny, happy person," I believe her immediately. Alejandra is creative and goal-oriented, hoping to establish her career. Her ultimate goal is to open her own business and draw in customers from different walks of life.

Alejandra's DACA application is processing when we meet. The uncertainty she faces is a strain for Alejandra, who is eager to enjoy and pass on the benefits of DACA to her family. Like a sizable number of my undocumented research participants, Alejandra is pursuing the American Dream but is somewhat pessimistic about how the government views her presence in the United States. After receiving a letter indicating her DACA application would be delayed, she was understandably anxious and frustrated. She tells me, "The whole thing is very unfair. I feel they don't want us here." "They," in this case, is the government. While Alejandra's application is being processed, she expresses hope that her GED and career training will make her worthy for some sort of legalized status.

Alejandra describes herself as the emotional rock and caretaker of her family. Since her parents have always worked, Alejandra describes her childhood as one in which she and her siblings were always "raising each other," and she took on the role of helping with housework and raising her younger siblings as the "second mom." Alejandra taking on a lot of housework was not a responsibility she believed her family distributed based on immigration status.[2] Later in the interview, though, Alejandra explains to me how citizenship does divide some other family responsibilities: "I felt kind of jealous of [my sister's citizenship], but she had a lot of responsibilities. She felt like she needed to help our family as much as she could, with you know, paying for rent and stuff like that." I learn later that her sister, Natalia, has also been paying for Alejandra's career training. Before long, Alejandra has to leave our interview, and I realize that Natalia has to drive Alejandra to an appointment, another one of the many responsibilities Natalia holds in her mixed-status family.

On another day, Natalia and I carve out our own private corner in a café usually brimming with local Angelenos. For the next several hours, Natalia tells me about her life, all against the backdrop of stringed lights and candlelit tables that make the large room appear intimate. When I ask Natalia to describe herself, she quickly shares with me how much she enjoys her career. She is clear that having a full-time job is not only a benefit to her alone. Instead, her employment gives her peace of mind because it helps her provide for her parents and siblings. She explains, "Helping my family by knowing I will have a check every month is such a comfort." When she was growing up, Natalia was constantly aware of her family's financial struggles. Her father, Javier, spent his working life in different factories, and her mother, Cecilia, worked a number of "under-the-table" jobs during the day.

Because both of her parents labored as undocumented workers, there was often some economic uncertainty. Yet, as a citizen, Natalia was committed to helping her family, telling me, "I've always felt that someone in my family should offer my mom money, you know, the kids need a lot. I am the second oldest, but the oldest that can legally work here." Noting this, Natalia felt that her citizenship meant she had a responsibility to "do something" to support her family. This support was not always dependent on whether Natalia has access to full-time work either. When she was in college, she would offer her family her financial aid funds to help them make ends meet. As a citizen adult, Natalia negotiates her citizenship privilege—her legal access to wage labor—and the family responsibility her status inspires.

While the previous chapter focused on how parents plan for the future, this chapter narrows in on how citizen children in mixed-status families experience their citizenship as adults. These educated young adults primarily have both parents without legal status. I argue that young adults contend with what I call family illegality by negotiating the family's relationship to undocumented status. These young adults are citizens, but illegality permeates their lives by shaping family opportunities, pressures, and responsibilities. I find that young adults manage family illegality in their lives when they cope with parental deportability, apply for college financial aid, consider the possibility of sponsoring parents for legalization, and participate in family breadwinning.

Children in Mixed-Status Families

There is a substantial amount of research that explains how parents' undocumented status can impact their (citizen) children. For example, parental undocumented status may formally or informally leave minor citizen children "chilled" from accessing social service resources that they are eligible for.[3] Parents may avoid accessing social services and health or developmental programs for their children because they believe such usage may negatively impact their chances of legalizing in the future.[4] Additionally, parents might not be aware of available programs or may be concerned that utilizing program resources may make them vulnerable to deportation.[5] Deportation risk negatively impacts parents seeking support from WIC, a federal food assistance program, particularly when they are part of Mexican mixed-status families.[6] Although strong community networks and immigrant-friendly hospitals and schools can help mitigate undocumented parents' fear of accessing resources, status does matter in how citizen minors access or benefit from state services.[7]

Even as parental status may impact young children in a multitude of ways, children eventually grow older and can help their immigrant families to navigate life in the United States. For example, citizen and undocumented youth often serve as translators for their families in new and long-term immigrant settlement locations.[8] In undocumented families, adult undocumented children may serve as "legal brokers" to help families navigate US legal systems.[9] Financial insecurity also means that some adolescents, including both citizens and undocumented youth, work to provide vital income to the household.[10] Young citizens may also help support their families by sharing credit, accessing loans, and serving as legal guardians to younger siblings.[11]

Parents also help their children. Some research suggests that parents may unknowingly devote more attention to their citizen children's activities, perhaps because they believe these children have better access to higher education and secure career opportunities.[12] If this is the case, we would expect that citizen children, in turn, may then negotiate the expectations parents have of them when they become adults. Such expectations may be reflective of what scholars call the "immigrant bargain."[13] When immigrant parents make sacrifices for children, they expect children to work hard, perform well in school, and eventually return on their investments.[14] When second-generation children do well in school, go on to college, and develop professional careers, these young people have kept their end of the bargain. Such family expectations may be especially pertinent in mixed-status families.

Shifting to how illegality has impacted citizen children, sociologist Laura Enriquez has argued that policies intended to target the undocumented population impact other members of the family who themselves are not undocumented through what she calls "multigenerational punishment."[15] Policies meant to punish undocumented immigrants impact citizen children in aspects of everyday life, such as when families drive, travel, avoid deportation, and when parents seek and access employment.[16] These experiences of multigenerational punishment may continue or change when children in mixed-status families reach adult age. Indeed, legal status distinctions are complex and can deeply shape family experiences and relationships. Illegality is a status, as well as a sociolegal production.[17] Illegality, like citizenship, is a "juridical status" given by the state, but this status also creates meaning and different expectations for members of mixed-status families. Instead of conceptualizing parental undocumented status solely as a variable that leads to an outcome that impacts citizen children, I contend that family illegality is also an everyday negotiation about family survival and planning. In these negotiations, it becomes clear that illegality can also influence how young adults experience their US citizenship.

Accessing and interviewing a mostly educated group of young adults provides essential contributions to our understanding of the immigrant second generation. Researchers investigating the incorporation patterns of the children of immigrants tend to view educational attainment as a signal of US incorporation.[18] Using these traditional markers of success or integration, on the surface these young adults are integrating and working toward achieving upward economic mobility. For the most part, they have some college experience under their belts and are working toward their careers. Yet, as I will demonstrate, family illegality permeates their lives, even for this educated group of young adults.

Citizen Responsibilities and Some Relief

The existing research on mixed-status families reveals that children are often met with limitations that exist because of the punishments directed at their undocumented parents. This inspires the vital question: *What happens when children become adults?* As children transition to adulthood in their mixed-status families, new responsibilities emerge; some fears become better managed and sometimes less salient. For example, young adults, albeit few, report regularly driving for undocumented family members. As adults come of age and become licensed, this new transition allows families as a collective to legally access a reliable form of commuting. Yet when it came to driving, most families did without the *routine* help of adult children.[19] Instead, if parents were unlicensed, adult citizen children sometimes reported taking the wheel during long-distance drives or family trips to leisure destinations. California Assembly Bill 60 allows undocumented immigrants to apply for driver's licenses. Those who were ineligible or decided against this option already had established driving routines that did not regularly rely on children. It is also possible that the nature of parents' work, such as jobs that require visiting multiple homes or job sites in one day, all but require driving on their own or with coworkers. Some parents also had driver's licenses that they had obtained years ago from other states.

As citizen children transition to adulthood, they also experience new tangible benefits of their legal status. When they are children, citizens in mixed-status families often learn that their travel is restricted because of their parental ties or become acutely aware that their undocumented loved ones cannot leave the country for family trips.[20] Young adults later experience relief to have greater mobility, including being able to travel internationally, even if they feel some guilt that they can do so but their family members cannot. Even with this new independence, traveling with their undocumented parents or siblings internationally was largely not possible. Young adults lamented that they could not partake in family trips with parents or other loved ones to mark special occasions, such as a milestone birthday or graduation. Participants sometimes had a lingering dream of being able to take their loved ones on trips near and far, including vacations to Ireland, France, several countries in Latin America, and, most important, their parents' homeland.

Despite the sadness at not being able to take family trips, young adults were comforted knowing that they not only could travel but could do so on behalf of their parents to their ancestral homeland. Some participants spoke to the newfound privilege of traveling, but Robert's narrative of visiting Mexico was the most emotional. In between tears, Robert notes that he initially felt very guilty about going to Mexico when he turned nineteen, knowing that his parents did not have this same privilege.[21] After meeting relatives in Mexico, bonding with them, and sharing stories about his parents, he realized that he had a unique privilege in serving as a link between his parents and their kin. With tears in his eyes, Robert shares: "I am their connection."

Adult Transitions and the Shifting Nature of Deportation Fears

Adult children of immigrant parents often recall childhoods marked by vulnerability when they learn that their parents' status is precarious. I found that the young adults who still had parents residing in the United States had developed ways to cope with deportation fears as they became adults. Part of this has to do with shifting policies that happen to coincide with their transition to adulthood, while other changes were the result of adult children living more independent lives. For many, local and state policies that seek to protect immigrants were a cushion that allowed them a sense of partial relief. For example, when adult children could now see their parents access driver's licenses, the thought of their parents on the road did not have to inspire extreme stress. This was a departure from childhood memories, in which children recall watching parents' body language and driving behavior change when they spotted police vehicles. These retrospective accounts of witnessing parents drive with fear and extreme caution are well documented in the immigration research.[22] Fortunately, as adults, children have the advantage of observing the enactment of new policies that could help their families.

Young adults articulated that they experience a partial emotional reprieve from worrying about parental deportability because they live in a sanctuary city. Even when young adults expressed that they did not follow immigration politics, they had a general sense of local policies that seek to support immigrants or protect them from being detained for deportation purposes. Still, it's worth noting that this sense of relief was always tenuous and did not mean young adults were not fearful. They still knew, for example, that there can be a disconnect between local and federal policies regarding immigration enforcement. Ultimately, they understood that their parents were not safe from deportation, but as adults they had a better sense of the policy and community protections that could support their families. Immigrant-friendly policies coupled with a sense that parents were cautious in their everyday routines also provided another layer of relief for adult children. Thanks to their networks, some young adults also felt empowered knowing about the resources and rights available to undocumented immigrants if they encounter ICE or local police.

Adult children also believe that parents are generally cautious, engaging in strategies to avoid interactions with police or immigration agents. This meant, for example, that parents would avoid areas at certain times or days that were well known for having police/DUI checkpoints. There was frequent mention of avoiding a particular DUI checkpoint in downtown Los Angeles, among other locations. Young adults also felt a sense of safety if they knew their parents were not engaging in criminal activity or were not actively being sought out by immigration agents due to a deportation order. Victor, for example, explains this sentiment quite clearly:

We do have an understanding that those types of things [deportation] do happen because in my first year of high school our neighbors were visited by ICE, and they were deported. My father was getting ready to go to work in the early morning and he saw the ICE agents, so he went back home. He saw what happened. So, we knew about that. But we also knew that our neighbors had an order of deportation . . . we had an understanding that if you have an order of deportation, it's more risky and [ICE] are probably going to come look for you. But for my family, it's more like if we follow the law and stay away from problems and the cops,

we'll be fine. Don't worry about it and we'll be fine. They always try to follow the law. . . . So they always stay away from trouble, especially my dad.
He has a clean record, so he has been doing a good job with that.

Here we see how Victor's fears of his parents being detained and deported are mitigated somewhat because his parents do not have an active deportation order and avoid police. His points echo research with
immigrants who feel they are protected from detention and deportation
so long as they lead crime-free, model lives.[23] Later in the interview,
Victor also offers that his parents' extended time in the United States,
along with local sanctuary policies, a large undocumented population,
and knowing one's rights, are all reasons they may feel a sense of safety:

> They know that if something ever happens, they should talk to a lawyer.
> They understand their basic rights. So, I feel like they are knowledgeable
> about it. Maybe they do have some fear, but at the same time, I think they
> feel comfortable enough because they have been here nineteen or eigh-
> teen years and have not had huge interactions with ICE where they have
> been at risk personally. They know people who have been deported, but
> they know it's because they had an order of deportation or because there
> was a police checkpoint. So, they understand that as long as they stay out
> of those routes, they should be fine. Another thing is LA is a sanctuary
> city so they know a lot of people are undocumented. I know a lot of my
> friends are and a lot of my friend's parents are too. So, I think they feel
> really comfortable and really safe up to an extent.

Victor believes that the precautions his parents take will help mitigate
deportation risk. This, too, was probably a comfort to him as he studied
in a college in-state but still a significant distance away from home.

In the transition to adulthood, young adults also realized that their
routines drastically changed. Most young adults felt their time was often
occupied by their college classes, community work, wage labor, care work,
and/or social life. As a result, they sometimes realize that they have very
little time to see their parents. This was a departure from their childhood,
when they would observe the world through the eyes and experiences of
their parents on a more regular basis. This means that adult children are
inadvertently able to sidestep some of the daily experiences of illegality.

What could not escape the attention of young adults was when media reports of immigration enforcement actions, especially local actions, reminded them of how illegality can be a precarious status. These media observations seem to shake any semblance of safety, at least temporarily. Media reports about increased immigration enforcement can be considered "situational triggers" that inspire fears about parental deportability.[24] Since media observations about immigration enforcement did not differ by immigration status, both young adult children with citizenship and those who were undocumented or DACAmented responded similarly to these triggers. In our interview, Amanda, a DACA recipient, for example, thoughtfully explains how media reports about family separation and immigrant suffering can trigger fears about parental deportability or family separation:

> I feel like it can just impact you in so many different emotional levels. Like you can be sad and then mad and then afraid that [family deportation] can happen to you. I guess it goes back to the sanctuary cities and so you think nothing can happen to you, but then when you start seeing it's getting closer to you, it's very stressful. It's not that I don't care about the people being deported, but you just kind of feel the knife closer to you.

When young adults viewed messages about the Syrian refugee crisis or the 2016 presidential election, they also expressed anxiety about their family's ability to remain together in the United States. Alma, for example, tells me that she tries to avoid watching the news for this reason:

> Right now, from what I've seen—because I don't really watch TV anymore—but everyone is talking about what is going on in Syria and all that stuff and how families are migrating and countries are kicking them out. Maybe that is the most I've seen, but I can relate to that because I've seen Spanish news and it also shows families getting snatched apart and it's like, damn! That's hard. Obviously, hopefully that never happens to me. I hope it never does.

Alma expresses that the election and one candidate in particular were causing stress about the future of her family. She elaborates on how news reports are also complemented by social media posts and memes:

Everyone is posting photos of [Trump] with Adolf Hitler and obviously it's to make the comparison, but to see that going on, it's like, whoa, that's not really that far off. Let's just not pay attention. I don't like paying attention to the news because it just worries me and gets me upset and frustrates me when we should all be the same and live life.

Similarly, another young adult expressed how the possibility of parental deportability feels pronounced when she watches the news: "That always crosses my mind when I watch the news and when a new president comes in. I just don't want a racist president. . . . The first thing I always think about is: don't deport my parents." Members of mixed-status families were concerned about the 2016 presidential campaign because they saw their parents and family members as targets of both nativist *and racist* rhetoric and policy proposals.

There is power in reaching adulthood. The extant research makes clear that minor children experience various difficulties in making sense of their parents' status and the possibility of deportation. Children, in many ways, may feel powerless at not being able to help their parents through the uncertainty that accompanies tenuous immigration status.[25] Even so, young children may feel a desire to help their parents in any way they can.[26] As adults, children may not be able to help prevent their parents' interaction with immigration enforcement agents, but they are better prepared to manage the aftermath of a parental detention or deportation. Young adults can also do the emotional labor of comforting younger siblings about deportation fears. They also reported, for example, that they would "step up" if their families experience an immigration-related emergency. Young adults age into new experiences of family illegality. As I will explore in the next section, these young citizens' transition to adulthood and their entry into the higher education context also represent a new exposure to illegality.

"Little Barriers Are Constructed": Young Adults Accessing Financial Aid

Imagine a university administration building where you are greeted by bright overhead lights and an overwhelming array of tethered black ropes that mark waiting lines. At the end of one wall there are windows indicating "Admissions," "Financial Aid," and so forth. At a large public university, what might be most apparent is the rumble of student noise, confusion, and the groan-inducing sight of excessively long lines. Backpack zippers *zip*, papers *rustle*, shoes *shuffle*, and cell phones incessantly *ding*. For any student trying to get information about financial aid, waiting in line can be a frustrating experience of anticipation. Students can wonder: *Will I get enough aid?* For some college attendees about to embark on their educational journeys, sometimes the question is: *How can I fill out my financial aid documents when my parents are undocumented?* While their college transitions are their own to experience, the financial aid process reminds citizen students of the connection to their undocumented parents.

Eligible college students may access state and federal aid to attend institutions of higher education. Government financial aid includes an array of educational subsidies, including grants, scholarships, and loans. Access to these resources requires students to be US citizens or eligible noncitizens. For those who are eligible, accessing aid begins with filling out and submitting the Free Application for Federal Student Aid (FAFSA), which is submitted on a yearly basis and can involve a lengthy process of gathering necessary details about the student's and parents' personal information. Through the FAFSA, a student receives a report on how much aid they are likely to receive; this information is then provided to the student's university or college.

Many immigrant parents have a rosy view of educational opportunities in the United States, but youth are aware that there are numerous bureaucratic processes to endure to access higher education. These challenges can be daunting for undocumented youth and include ineligibility for federal financial aid and many types of state or private aid. The undocumented student experience and transition to college have been well documented by scholars.[27] This focus is warranted. While privileged compared with their undocumented peers, citizen students in mixed-status families can also face unique struggles when they attempt to access college financial aid resources. For example, filling out the FAFSA as a citizen in a mixed-status family can include unique stressors. The application asks for parents' information, including a valid Social Security number, which many undocumented immigrants do not have. Young adults are hyperaware of their parents' status and what this means for their own educational futures, particularly when applying for financial aid.

When I think of financial aid barriers, I think of Robert, who I meet at a popular eatery. As we sit outside with our coffees, met with the constant rumble of street traffic and sounds of nearby pedestrians, Robert tells me how he successfully finished his social science degree at a California university, but not without an occasional break from school or financial struggles to cover his tuition and living expenses. Although he has now completed his college education, Robert argues that he could only apply for financial aid and eventually finish school because he is goal-driven and considers himself extraordinarily resourceful. Still, the financial aid process brought to the fore his connection with illegality. In applying for financial aid, Robert, a US citizen, explains, he was unsure what to provide for his parents' information, since they do not have Social Security numbers:

> When I was doing financial aid, I was like: "What do I have to do?" and [college counselors, teachers] were like "I don't know." I figured out that you have to put zeros for [parents'] Social. You have to print out the application instead of doing it online. Am I complaining about these little things? Yes, just because they are glitches that contribute and become something bigger. Does it take a lot of effort to print something out? No, but does it take two weeks more to get or for them to process my financial aid? Yes, and sometimes you need your money, you started school. So, they make you wait two more weeks, and the deadline to pay for classes is this week. Now I have to figure out where I am going to get the money. I know I will eventually get the money, but before that I will be stressed.

Robert recalls this moment as a challenging experience. Getting an accurate answer to his question and providing the required paperwork involved multiple visits with college financial aid staff and high school counselors. As the first in his family to go to college, Robert had the usual anxieties about undergoing this important step, but he was also concerned about receiving accurate information given his mixed-status family background. Still, knowing that other young adults in his life do not necessarily have access to financial aid grants because of their status, Robert did feel it was a privilege to eventually receive aid. His concern was that the process should be more straightforward for everyone, especially when these critical higher education milestones should further encourage students like him (first-generation and working-class) to go to college instead of serving as an obstacle. Robert also felt this way because he figured other students might not be as persistent as he was. Robert makes the following point:

> That is where it starts to divide and become a problem where it's just more like: Are we being treated equal or are you putting barriers to discourage people from doing something? Because that is discouraging. It's like: "Oh, fuck! I can't figure out how to do my financial aid, so what do I do?" Some people can't figure it out. It's like: "I don't know what I am doing. I can't get financial aid, so I am not going to school." Little barriers are constructed, and they eventually become bigger barriers and become one big one where people don't know what they are doing, so they think: "OK, I am still working. Let me just pay my monthly bills and when I get the chance I'll go to school," but, no, they might not get the chance.

The financial aid process was an important moment when Robert felt his parents' status was salient. Even though it was not his experience, Robert posits that young adults may be discouraged from continuing their education when they manage parental illegality during this financial aid process. These are the "little barriers" that can add up and deter youth in mixed-status families from accessing their degrees.

For Raúl, experiencing family illegality through the FAFSA process was not so simple, partly because it was a painful reminder of what the state had done to his parents. When Raúl was in high school, he abruptly lost both his parents to deportation. A few years later, when he was ready to think about a career after high school, he had to reckon with a bureaucratic challenge. Raúl's financial aid experience involved a hunt for W-2s and other paperwork that was hard to find since his parents could not hand over these documents to him. He also had to navigate this obstacle while feeling like he was not getting sufficient support from financial aid advisors. He often had to take his questions to supervisory staff to access appropriate information about his case. Even when young adults have older siblings who have successfully matriculated through college, they may not have experience with FAFSA if they were undocumented. This was Raúl's experience. Although Raúl's sister is a college graduate, she did not have access to financial aid and could not necessarily direct her brother to accurate information. Raúl was frustrated about what he perceived as the lack of communication between the Department of Education and government agencies that oversee immigration enforcement. If there was more communication, he assumed the Department of Education would realize that his parents were deported and likely unable to provide requested information:

> I feel like since the government deports your parents or siblings of yours, they should let it be known to other US agencies, so that they can know because then if Department of Homeland Security knows and no one else knows, it kind of messes it up for you. It makes the process of you receiving financial aid so much harder. I have to go through providing constant paperwork and constant appointments, and sometimes I get the financial aid worker that doesn't know what to do, so they get their supervisor, but then their supervisor doesn't know. So, then they have to contact their higher-up. You would think my case would be pretty common, but I don't know. That's where I feel like . . . sometimes it feels like, man! I'd rather be undocumented. It is just so frustrating to go through the process and going through government agencies like that to get some kind of financial help as a citizen. The process is made harder for you.

While Raúl's citizenship status allows him to apply for financial assistance to attend institutions of higher education, existing at the intersection of being a citizen in a mixed-status family can be difficult. Raúl makes a provocative and frustrated comment about sometimes wishing to be undocumented. These words are more likely an expression of the trauma of experiencing parental deportation and the ways he has had to cope since. They can also suggest he may have "survivor's guilt" because he is the only member of his family who has US citizenship and sometimes feels he does not deserve the privileges afforded by it.[28] Unfortunately for Raúl, negotiating family illegality involves navigating the financial aid process without the benefit of his parents' presence and in-person advice, two things that he misses dearly given their close relationship.

Karla, a twenty-one-year-old student at a California college, describes herself as fiercely independent yet family-oriented. She is one of two adult-age children living in a household with undocumented parents who are in their early fifties. Karla described not thinking too much about her parents' undocumented status until she became an adult. In her words:

> I think when I sort of grew up and matured, I realized what it meant for my parents to be undocumented because, you know, it wasn't exactly a big deal. I did know things were easier for me as a citizen, but when I was trying to do the FAFSA I got a little scared. Why are they asking for my parents' information? Is this normal? . . . Like, I sort of knew that I was the one that was going to be paying for school, so why would they need my parents' Social? I was scared, and I guess it also made me uncomfortable to ask about it. If am a US citizen, why are they asking about my parents?

According to Karla, her parents' undocumented status did not become salient to her until she matured. Interestingly, the college process and reaching the legal age to work prompted Karla to realize how her citizenship status is connected to her parents. Although by no means the same, this experience somewhat parallels that of undocumented youth who "learn to be illegal" or become fully aware of their immigration status when they transition to adulthood and begin applying to college or entering the workforce.[29] Karla realized the meaning of her parents' undocumented status when she became an adult. Importantly, her fear about sharing her parents' information is rooted in the possibility that she wouldn't get financial aid, as well as the possibility of disclosing that her parents are undocumented to a government department.

Nineteen-year-old Yoselyn shared a similar fear about outing her parents in the FAFSA application. She recalls:

> Every time I fill out my FAFSA there is a question about your parents. There is something about when they achieved residency or about where they were born. The question is about my parents, and I am always kind of scared to answer it. Whenever I go fill out my FAFSA application, I am

always weary of filling it out. I do worry: What if they find out my parents are undocumented?

Like Karla, Yoselyn argues that her parents' status is particularly high-lighted during the financial aid process. Yoselyn also consults with her parents to ensure her FAFSA information is correct and that her parents are comfortable with her essentially disclosing their status in this applica-tion. Because college students have to risk sharing information about their undocumented parents, the process of applying for college financial aid is a "threat of denounceability."[30] In these situations, young citizens collec-tively "come out of the shadows" by sharing with counselors and financial aid staff that they are part of a mixed-status family so that they can get appropriate help. Even for resourceful students, the financial aid process is when family illegality is made salient and subsequently managed.

Robert argues that the children of undocumented parents experience "little barriers" that can become larger hurdles in the way of accessing financial aid and seeking a college degree. While the citizen youth in this study eventually secured financial aid, these barriers can some-times evolve into blocked opportunities. For instance, two separate legal cases—one in Miami, Florida, and another in Washington, DC—bring to the fore how citizens are denied aid (or in-state tuition) because of their parents' immigration status. In one of these cases, Wendy Ruiz, a US citizen and Florida resident, was denied in-state college tuition because of her parents' immigration status. Under Florida state finan-cial aid stipulations, parental residency determines the residency status for dependent students, thereby making it difficult for students to prove their residency when parents do not have papers. In 2011, with assistance from the Southern Poverty Law Center, Ruiz eventually won her case in the legal matter of *Ruiz v. Robinson*, arguing that the state policy violates her Fourteenth Amendment rights.[31] In another case, a US citizen in Washington, DC, is legally challenging the district's decision to deny her college financial assistance because of her mother's immigration sta-tus.[32] These two legal fights demonstrate how young citizens are com-pelled to manage family illegality. These cases and the stories of Robert, Raúl, Karla, and Yoselyn further demonstrate how citizens' educational opportunities can be structurally discouraged by a policy context that makes parental illegality problematic for college-going Americans.

Legalizing Parents?

Despite the legal legitimacy of birthright citizenship, the children of undocumented immigrants are often portrayed in popular media as illegitimate citizens. Replete with images of pregnant women crossing the border, one strand of anti-immigrant rhetoric focuses on what many conservatives call "anchor babies." This derogatory term refers to the children of undocumented parents who are believed to provide the legal anchor or pathway to residency for their Mexican or Latina mothers in the United States.[33] Despite the anchor baby narrative, having a US citizen child does not provide an easy pathway to legalization, and the data on immigration motivations or immigrant family formation do not suggest that this practice is widespread.[34] In fact, it is often violence or the search for work that drives many Latino immigrants to migrate to the United States.[35] Yet, public officials use this rhetoric to demonize the children of undocumented immigrants.[36] While the image of babies remains central to this depiction, the almost fixed nature of unauthorized status means that a significant number of undocumented parents have children who are now adult age.

While citizen youth can mitigate family illegality by sponsoring parents for their legal permanent residency (or green card, or "papers"), this process is not a viable option for many families.[37] Sponsoring parents is not easy simply because immigration laws regarding sponsorship can be complicated and punitive. It is also a lengthy process. A citizen child who is twenty-one years old has reached the eligible age to sponsor an immigrant parent.[38] Sponsors also need to demonstrate that they can earn 125 percent over the poverty line to mitigate any state concerns that the sponsored family member will need to rely on government support or become what is called a "public charge."[39] This is just the start of the application process, and it does not even begin to characterize the penalties some undocumented parents could face if they hope to become legal residents.

Many young adults had thought about immigration sponsorship at several points throughout their lives and viewed it as a gateway into family stability. For many, it also represented an opportunity to demonstrate love and appreciation to parents who have made countless sacrifices. In these cases, children see sponsoring a parent as an act of being a grateful son or daughter. It was also perceived as a practice in citizenship in which adult children try to end the enduring challenge of illegality. The idea of sponsoring a parent certainly became more pronounced as children transitioned to adulthood and approached the eligible age for beginning the process.

Mario hopes he can give back to his parents by sponsoring their residency petitions. At his university dorm, Mario tells me about his individual and family goals. I absorb a great deal about him just by what he has placed on his dormitory wall: photos of friends and family, as well as images reflective of his social justice passions. He often credits the fact that he is in college to his mother and father. He remembers that when he was growing up, his parents encouraged his educational goals and extracurricular activities such as soccer. "Having a good relationship with my family also gave me the trust to want to help them," he tells me. Recalling the image of his parents sitting by the sidelines during his soccer games, Mario adds, "They would always be there for me, so the least I can do is be there for them as well." When it comes to the matter of immigration sponsorship, Mario tends to think of it as an opportunity to help his parents:

> One thing that my dad always says is, "When our children grow old, they are eventually going to leave us and they are not going to be here for us." That message kind of struck me because I want to be there for them, physically and morally. . . . I know that one of the dreams is when I become twenty-one, I can sponsor their citizenship. I know for them that is a dream, and I want to be there when that happens. I want to help them as much as I can in that process. So, in a way, I would do it as a gratitude for everything they have done for me.

Mario's parents are undocumented, so he is referring to helping them access their legal permanent residency, which is a step that needs to happen before parents can apply for naturalized US citizenship. In Mario's case, sponsorship would represent a dream fulfilled and a responsibility he would take on as a "gratitude." In many ways, aside from the support his parents have given him, Mario feels his undocumented parents have earned their legal authorization after struggling as immigrants. His father, who migrated as a teenager in the early 1990s, spent much of his days working, then would rest in an extended family member's home where he was only allowed to sleep on the kitchen floor. However, his father eventually returned to Mexico, where he met his future wife. Mario's mother also had her share of hardships that centered on the limited economic possibilities for young women in Mexico. Together, Mario's parents would eventually build their lives in the United States, primarily working in sweatshops while raising their three citizen children.

Although Mario recognizes that it would be a dream for his parents to be sponsored, it was not an explicit goal or pressure placed on him since he was a child. For instance, like many others, Mario reports that his birth was not part of a plan for his parents to gain a pathway to residency. Even when citizens are aware that they could find a way to legalize their parents, they are critical of what they perceive as a demonization of their families when they hear public figures discuss anchor babies or otherwise scapegoat or disparage undocumented immigrants. Mario's case represents a departure from citizens who experienced the question of sponsoring their parents as a point of disappointment, contention, or nuanced pressure.

My research suggests that the pathway to sponsoring an undocumented parent can be challenging for families. Perhaps this challenge partly explains why this study is not about legalizing parents. The young adults in the study had not sponsored their parents. For adult children, this sponsorship privilege can inspire anxiety and responsibility about preparing for sponsorship, including saving money for the process and maintaining a clean criminal record. For some young adults, the eligible sponsorship age of twenty-one would come and go without families moving forward with this process after considering all their options— with or without the guidance of a lawyer. Take, for example, Susie, who was raised most of her life as an only child in her mixed-status family. Susie was several years past the age of twenty-one at the time of her interview, but she had not taken steps to sponsor her mother. This was at the request of her mother, who thought that getting papers might not be the right decision. Susie and her mother had not broached the subject in quite some time. Susie describes:

> We are talking about getting her papers years ago, and she said she didn't want to do it because, she said, "The government could sentence me to

Mexico for four weeks to ten years and I won't know until I am there, and I hate Mexico. I won't be able to find a job ever."

Since Susie and her mother did not necessarily agree on whether to undertake the sponsorship process, they did not attend any legal clinics together or consult with a lawyer about their options. Susie, however, used to pass on information to her mother about sponsorship. Susie explains:

You know, I try—she's still undocumented and she's been here since the eighties. I tell her, "Mom, you can do these things!" But a lot of it was like she didn't have the resources or there's a mythology about access to citizenship and how hard it is and being sentenced to Mexico.

Sometimes it is difficult for families to agree on how to move forward. Certainly, financial resources to cover the costs associated with immigration sponsorship are a common concern shared by both adult children and parents. There is much to demystify regarding immigration law, but Susie's mother may have accurately understood that she might have to face a bar, or what she referred to as a sentence in Mexico.

Undocumented parents can claim that their worthiness for legal residency is strengthened by their years (and often decades) in the United States. Still, some undocumented immigrants working toward residency can face a bar once they exit the country. For example, immigrants can face a bar of three years if they crossed illegally and were unlawfully in the country for more than 180 days but less than one year during a single stay.[40] Immigrants who crossed illegally and were in the country without authorized status for one year or more during a single stay can face a ten-year bar.[41] This bar, or what immigrants sometimes call "the punishment," or *el castigo*, is triggered by stipulations in the Illegal Immigration Reform and Immigrant Responsibility Act of 1996. These bars become active once an immigrant exits the country. The catch-22 of this problem is that some undocumented immigrants who are trying to legalize their status may have to undergo consular processing. This process requires that immigrants exit the United States and visit their home country's consular office to apply for their visa to reenter the United States.

Even for parents who are willing to wait out a bar, legalization may not be an option for those who already have a deportation order and/or have a criminal background. Prospects for legalization can also be much poorer for immigrants who arrived without legal authorization as opposed to immigrants who overstayed their visas.[42] In the majority of interviews, I hear about family members who arrived in the United States without authorization. This difference in arrival greatly matters in prospects for legalization. Those immigrants who arrive the "easy way," with a visa, versus the "hard way," without authorization, can bypass the requirement to exit the country, thereby avoiding the triggering of any bars.[43] In other words, immigrants who became undocumented by overstaying a visa are likely to have a smoother pathway to residency than someone who crossed the border clandestinely. Particularly for those who migrated without legal status, the absence of humane and family-friendly pathways to legalization explains why many undocumented immigrants have been living in "perpetual illegality" since the last broad amnesty program in 1986.[44]

Some immigrants may be eligible to apply for a provisional unlawful presence waiver to waive the three- or ten-year bar. They can apply for this waiver when they are in the United States to have a better chance of legally reentering without having to wait out a bar. In 2013, the Obama administration made available a provisional waiver that could extend to immigrant parents of US citizen adults. Even so, "getting a provisional waiver does not guarantee that the individual will be issued a visa and be allowed to re-enter the United States legally."[45] The waiver was expanded again in 2016 to a broader number of qualified applicants. Undocumented parents of US citizen children may apply for this waiver, but parents still need to demonstrate that the bars would be an extreme hardship to their US citizen or legal permanent resident *spouse* or *parent*.[46]

To put this in context, this would mean that Susie's mother would probably need to be married to a US citizen or a legal permanent resident spouse or be the daughter of a US citizen or a legal permanent resident parent. Susie's mother would then have to demonstrate that her extended absence would be a hardship to one of these lawfully present family members. Susie's mother is currently married to an undocumented man, and her elderly mother is similarly without legal status. Unfortunately, it was also largely the case among the families I engaged with that there were grandparents who were undocumented or foreign nationals. Many of the young adults I interviewed and observed did not have parents married to US citizens. Diruhi's family stands as one of the few exceptions to this pattern. Diruhi, who is ethnically Armenian and Mexican, has an Armenian American mother who is a naturalized citizen while her longtime Mexican stepfather remains undocumented. With a US citizen spouse, her undocumented stepfather may have a somewhat easier legalization pathway. However, according to Diruhi, her stepfather had tried unsuccessfully to legalize previously, and he has a deep distrust of the government and lawyers. Diruhi recalls her stepfather sharing a story about an unscrupulous lawyer who took his money and provided harmful advice about applying for asylum. She tells me,

> It was a lawyer. They took off with his money and told him to file for political asylum, and the judge laughed, basically. Like the judged said, "Seriously? You are from Mexico. How are you going to file for political asylum?" You know? The lawyer took off. So, growing up with that, it's always been caution with everything.

As a consequence of this experience, Diruhi's stepfather refuses to move forward with any sponsorship process.

Many mixed-status families had stories about people who presented themselves as competent lawyers or notaries but then scammed unsuspecting immigrants. In the worst of cases, receiving bad legal advice or trusting incompetent professionals was believed to be what had set in motion a loved one's deportation or separation from family. In this sense, the decision not to move forward with sponsorship can be more of an indication of a parent's strategy to protect him- or herself from the possibility of being a victim of fraud or negligent legal advice. For Diruhi's stepfather, being off the government's radar feels more secure or what one participant, Selina, described as being in "protection mode."[47] For some parents and family members, starting the bureaucratic and governmental process of accessing legal permanent residency requires stepping out of this so-called protection mode.

Immigration law is a labyrinth, and as any competent immigration lawyer would advise, every case is unique. Still, in this study, it seemed these waivers would not have been accessible or useful given that immigrant parents largely did not have ties to lawfully present spouses or parents. Even so, I should acknowledge that this does not mean it is impossible to legalize undocumented parents. For example, individuals currently or formerly in the armed forces may be able to request "parole in place" for eligible undocumented spouses, parents, or children.[48] Doing so would mean that the undocumented family member would not have to exit the United States to move forward with their legalization process. Undocumented immigrants who already had a qualifying petition filed for them prior to April 30, 2001, may also have an easier pathway to legalization by possibly forgoing the requirement to exit the country.[49] Unfortunately, to my knowledge, the families in my study did not have these options available to them.

For some citizens, there is an expectation that they will sponsor parents, but such expectations can entail newfound family or economic pressures. Although some children hope to sponsor their parents, they have concerns about the financial aspect of the process, and such financial concerns may be warranted. Based on research with mixed-status couples who have undergone consular processing, one researcher estimated that the cost for attorneys, fees, travel, and lost wages can amount to $7,500 to over $30,000.[50]

When I asked Anita about what her primary responsibilities are as a citizen in her mixed-status family, she responded:

> I was the only citizen for a long time until my younger brother was born. . . . I knew on my end there were things I would have to do to make sure I could apply. Like, I think you shouldn't have a record, which OK, I can manage. But what about finding and paying for a lawyer? Since money was tight, I just felt like all of that would be placed on me. I don't like that pressure.

For Anita, sponsoring her parents has not come to fruition, even though she was twenty-four when we met for an interview. While it is to be determined if she will eventually sponsor her parents, Anita recounts feeling uncomfortable about the possibility of being a sponsor; having this responsibility placed on her represents unwanted pressure. For Anita, this potential sponsorship could have opened up better opportunities for her legalized parents, but since she had other family-related responsibilities, potential sponsorship represented another duty she would have to take on as the only adult citizen in the family. Alejandra, who is undocumented and was introduced earlier, also summed up how her citizen sister would have been unable to sponsor their parents because of the very real financial constraints in the family: "The conversation wasn't really there, but with my two older sisters, we would talk about it. It wasn't really like, 'Oh, let's get a lawyer and do this' because money was never there. Money was always the problem." Financial limitations are a hindrance to legalizing parents. Even when families were able to put money away for this process, it seemed there was always something that got in the way—an emergency such as an unexpected car repair or a health-related bill or other setback—that would deplete any significant savings.

Although young adults knew that sponsoring their parents could be an act of love and vastly improve their family's quality of life, they also expressed some unease about the process or disagreed with parents on how or whether to move forward. This is not to say that children do not want to help their parents or that these hesitations are not fraught with some guilt and ambivalence. As in any family, ties that are already weakened for other non-immigration-related reasons may influence an adult child's willingness to sponsor a parent. Family resentments over a divorce, absenteeism, infidelity, substance, physical, or economic abuse, and any number of conflicts that families face can impact mixed-status families too.[51] And conflict can get in the way of how families respond to a heavily bureaucratic process—such as immigration sponsorship—that requires family cooperation, communication, and financial obligations. Immigration sponsorship, therefore, should not necessarily be considered a harmonious negotiation, even though it can be in some families. Even in very close families, the immigration sponsorship process can be ripe with disappointment. In one interview study, researchers found that only one of their young adult interviewees was able to successfully legalize a parent, while "much more common were hiccups and traumatic disappointments that exacerbated the legal violence at play in their lives."[52]

There is also a sense of disillusionment among some young adults and parents regarding sponsorship. Some families, for example, decide against investigating the sponsorship question more thoroughly because they are wary of experiencing another disappointment. Not moving forward with sponsorship, then, is a preemptive strategy to avoid yet another devastating disappointment and the loss of much-needed financial resources. In Alma's tight-knit and visibly loving family, the conversation about sponsoring parents was initiated by the oldest daughter, a DACAmented young adult. Their mother, however, did not want to move forward with sponsorship or look into the possibility of meeting with an immigration lawyer. Alma, as the oldest citizen child in the family, recalls a family conversation on this topic:

> A: I remember this one time my sister was talking about how I should work on trying to get my parents papers.
>
> C: As a sponsor?
>
> A: Yeah, I guess you can do that at twenty-one. So, I was like OK. My sister tried to talk to my mom about it, and I guess it upset my mom. She's like, "No, it's going to take forever, so what's the point? By the time it gets done I'll be moving back to Mexico." I let her know it's a possibility and something we could try.

Alma notes that immigration sponsorship is not something she would ever deny to her parents if they wanted to proceed with this option. However, Alma and her family did not choose to do this. Within the family, there were also concerns about having to wait out a very long bar in Mexico. Although it is unclear if Alma's mother is fully committed to the idea of retiring in Mexico, sometimes it is the concern about extreme delays or disappointments that deters families from moving forward.

Another consideration for sponsoring parents is ensuring that one does not commit crimes that may make one ineligible as a sponsor or weaken the sponsorship case. This is something that Francisco carefully considered and used as a motivation to stay out of trouble. He explains:

> That's another reason why I ended up straightening up. I want my parents to get citizenship and one thing my dad told me when I was sixteen is that

I can help them get [legal] status. . . . That's why I have to keep a healthy and good record in order to help out my parents become citizens.

Francisco has not been able to sponsor his parents yet, but he hopes it can be worked out successfully. If his family has to wait out a years-long bar in Mexico, however, this would be very challenging, since two of his sisters are minors. As for his record, Francisco shares that it was what he calls an "act of God" that saved him from going down the wrong path after getting into some trouble with the law as a teenager. It turns out that Francisco was saved by a bureaucratic error that resulted in his misdemeanor not going on his record. Francisco intends to do everything he can to keep his record clean precisely because he hopes it can leave some options open for parental legalization.

Family illegality is part of the legalization process, even if families do not move forward with sponsorship. These decisions are a negotiation, and sometimes they can result in pressure and tension, even while adult children ultimately want the best for their families. In some cases, sponsoring a parent is a welcomed act of gratitude. Still, given the realities of immigration law,[53] many families ultimately decide that "the punishment" is too painful to endure when it means several years of family separation for the mere possibility of legalization. In this way, young adults realize that they endure this unique form of punishment and negotiate family illegality as they plan family futures.

Breadwinning Pressures

The transition to adulthood entails newfound responsibilities and autonomy. Young adults may find themselves working their first job and earning a regular paycheck. Still, in the transition to adulthood parents may provide some financial support to their young adult children.[54] The norms about parental support as children transition to adulthood can be different for immigrant and mixed-status families. Other research, for example, has found that undocumented young adults do not have the expectation that their parents will provide them with financial support.[55] Further, Mexican families may exhibit family helping behaviors as prescribed by a cultural adherence to familism, which describes a process by which the needs of the collective family outweigh individual interests.[56] More recent research has found that family-related obligations are gendered, making women's educational choices key to helping their families of origin.[57] Further, Mexican Americans report that helping family members financially is part of Mexican culture, but empirically this appears to be true for working-class families and not necessarily so for Mexican Americans who were raised in solidly middle-class families.[58] Therefore, cultural explanations for family financial contributions may not be as critical as some have previously assumed. While recognizing the crucial roles of class and gender, I find that financial assistance to parents is further informed by legal status.

Although undocumented immigrants are participating in the labor force, they may not possess the legal status documents to allow them access to the formal labor market. As a result, employers who knowingly hire undocumented workers may use their employees' status as a reason to exploit their labor for lower wages—paying them less than the legally required minimum wage or less than they would to a lawfully present worker. Consequently, undocumented immigrants may experience wage penalties in their workplaces or turn to work in the informal sector even though their job experience, credentials, and skills would otherwise warrant much better formalized employment. One study, for example, found that 30 to 40 percent of undocumented parents earn wages below the legal minimum wage.[59] Without a doubt, one of the consequences of unauthorized status is that it places immigrants and their families at greater risk for poverty. The poverty rate for children with undocumented parents, for example, is double the rate for children with US-born parents.[60] For citizens, their Social Security numbers and other "American generational resources," such as English language fluency, allow them accessible entry to the paid labor force.[61] In my study, adult citizen children are keenly aware that their Social Security numbers are the passes to waged labor that are not available to their undocumented family members.

For instance, Sylvia had been working since she was a teenager. Recalling the transition to adulthood, she recalls how she experienced her mother's and brother's immigration status in relation to her citizenship and possession of a Social Security number:

I felt it was easier for me as a fifteen-year-old to get an OK job than for my mom to do that or for my brother, you know? That kind of sucks if you are a teen and you are the one that can actually have a better job than your parents just because you have documentation.

Sylvia's mixed-status family consists of her mother, stepfather, and brother, all of whom are undocumented. As a result, she was the first and only family member to experience legal access to formal wage labor. She started her labor force participation at a young age because there was an economic need in her family. Poverty and some of the stress associated with economic precarity are what Sylvia recalls from her childhood, aside from other traumas. Sylvia is in her late twenties but still feels pressure to help her family financially, especially because she is aware of her mother's low income. Although Sylvia is a citizen with a college degree and is pursuing a professional career, she sometimes feels unable to help her family:

> Now I still feel pressure. I am the only one that can help out sometimes, but even then, I don't have a high-paying job, so I am still struggling myself to just maintain myself with school too and I feel bad because I am done with college, so I should be able to help out more, but it's kind of like—I don't know, I want to, but my brother I think he needs to help too. I shouldn't have to give them money because I work hard too, so I feel a lot of stress.

For citizen children in mixed-status families, their citizen privilege can be experienced as a familial responsibility that can take a toll. These financial contributions do not end when children move out of the home either. Sylvia had recently moved out to form a household with her partner but was still providing financial contributions to her mother. At the time, Sylvia hoped her brother could also contribute financially so that paying the family's bills could be more evenly distributed. This hope was also shaped by her own growing expenses and the realization that her college degree did not yield as much earning power as she wanted. As Sylvia worked toward paying college loans, funding her master's degree, and managing housing costs in Los Angeles, it sometimes felt like money was stretched thin when she was also helping to support multiple family members.

Most adult citizen children in this study reported making financial contributions to their families of origin. These contributions ranged from the regular and substantial costs associated with housing to less regular and large sums to help pay off urgent or unexpected costs, such as a family member's medical bills. Sometimes financial contributions came in the form of buying groceries or covering schooling or extra-curricular activities for younger siblings. Adult children helping their parents and siblings is not unique to mixed-status families, but the citizenship responsibility can be. Here, gender or birth order among adult children matters less than one's access to resources to help take care of the family.[62] Citizen children understand the need to help their families, and undocumented family members may have certain expectations of US citizens because of their access to resources.[63] Still, we see limitations in accessing sufficient resources and how family breadwinning can inspire a sense of pressure.

Other young adults touched on similar issues of responsibility. Benjamin was working two jobs and taking classes at a local community college at the time I learned about his mixed-status family. Benjamin, who always had a busy schedule, also understood that his citizenship meant a special commitment to his family; he knew from his mother's *consejos*, or advice, that he needed to help his family make ends meet. When I asked him if he had any special responsibilities in the family because he is a citizen, he answered:

> Yes, honestly, yés. I know it's my responsibility to help the family with all the bills we have and at least with my papers I can get a job and for the most part the jobs that I get will be stable. My mom, because of her work, you know from one day to the next sometimes she doesn't know if she will have work. Same with my dad. So, I know I have to take on a big role to help with paying our rent and also helping with the stuff for my little brother.

Now, as an adult with legal access to the workforce, Benjamin helps offset some of the financial difficulties his parents have endured as undocumented workers. Since both of his parents worked in unstable jobs, they have no job security or possibility of advancement. Worse yet, sometimes the family endures unexpected job losses or health-related strains. This is nothing new to Benjamin, who has long observed the impacts of his family's low income throughout his childhood. He also witnessed the toll his parents' jobs took on their bodies. As an adult, he feels the responsibility to help his family. He manages family illegality in this way.

Lupita also identified helping her family as a citizenship responsibility. When she was growing up, her parents were not open about their status, but within their family, Lupita's mother, Gloria, shared her migration story. Gloria is an open book to her daughter, who says to me, "She tells me everything!" As Lupita says this, she emphasizes these words with her eyes and a slight roll of her head. Lupita also knows a great deal about her mother's work life as a housecleaner and tells me countless details about her mother's work history, as well as the employers she liked, loathed, and tolerated. Lupita describes her mother as proud of her work and her financial contributions to the family. Her father also provides, but Lupita recognizes that her family sometimes relies on her financially. Lupita's access to formal sector work can protect her mother from having to work dangerous or exhausting manual labor jobs. She remembers the physical pain her mom experienced when coming home late from work. Observing how hard her parents work and the resulting strain on their bodies, Lupita explains, "Maybe I always knew I had responsibilities as a citizen, but it also clicked in my head: hey: step up! You have papers, you have to work so your mom can get some help." Once Lupita was of legal age to work, she started a part-time job at a retail store. About half of her biweekly income went toward family expenses. For Lupita, her participation in family breadwinning was a pressure she imposed on herself, knowing that she can help the family financially and help mitigate some of the more complicated physical consequences of her mother's informal sector labor.

Whereas Lupita's family work through the challenges of hard labor that can characterize the informal labor market, immigrants who work formal jobs also face physical strain and insecurity. Some immigrant parents can access formal employment with "borrowed" Social Security numbers or get jobs at workplaces where employers knowingly look the other way when it comes to immigration status. Often, however, these jobs seemed to lack long-term stability. Adult children can recall the point when these jobs ended for their parents—either because of new background protocols or because the company went out of business, relocated, or instituted mass layoffs. These moments stand out because the job loss represented a break in employment and triggered the fear that new employment would be harder to obtain. Other job losses were catalyzed by work injuries, such as hernias or severe back injuries, that left parents in pain and unable to continue or to take on other work. Worse yet, among the families in my study, job losses also occurred when a working parent experienced detention and/or deportation.

These setbacks mean families often turn to adult citizen children for help. These citizen children do not fear that their Social Security numbers will suddenly be revealed as invalid or that their presence will be punished with detention or deportation. Their fluency in English also means that these young adults can access work that is not necessarily damaging to the body. For these reasons, citizens can feel a family responsibility to financially contribute because their labor generates more income due to their having legal documents. Their access to employment is also more secure than that for DACA recipients because DACA is temporary, needs to be renewed every two years, and is a program that has periodically been under attack. Still, Natalia, for example, sometimes remembered feeling frustrated that her older undocumented sister Dora did not help the family more with financial assistance. Over time, Natalia decided to not hold any resentment toward her sister Dora: "I would ask my older sister to help too and she didn't think it was her responsibility, and in retrospect, I think she was right because it drains you. I mean, it drains me to be worrying about it: like I need to get money somehow so my parents, or my mom, can have it." On the other hand, Natalia also recognized that aside from access to better-paying jobs, being a citizen worker means you are perhaps less at risk for being disrespected at work than are workers who are undocumented. As a result, Natalia shared how she felt protective of her other undocumented sister, Alejandra. Natalia eventually encouraged Alejandra to leave her job because she believed Alejandra was being harassed at work. Natalia recalls hearing about how one of Alejandra's superiors was subjecting her and other undocumented workers to inappropriate and demeaning comments:

> [Alejandra] did work under the table. But I honestly encouraged her not to work because I didn't want her to struggle. It wasn't even physical struggle. When you work under the table, it's not only physical pain you get, it's that constant bashing of your self-esteem. I grew tired of that happening to my sister. I told her, "If I am working, you don't have to be in that situation."

Natalia's access to higher wages and better working conditions is a privilege compared with the circumstances of her undocumented family members, who may be exploited or disrespected at work. Natalia acknowledges that undocumented workers in the informal sector are overworked and undercompensated, as well as experiencing a "constant bashing of your self-esteem." As other research findings report, undocumented youth are confronted with precarious job options and experience harassment, isolation, stress, strain on the body, and hostility from employers.[64] Natalia later articulated an intersectional perspective on what her sister Alejandra might face as both an undocumented immigrant and a member of a racialized minority:

> I think there is a sense—and I will never know this—when you are undocumented, you feel like you are powerless. I felt that she's been or felt powerless. Not only that, but you are Hispanic and you are one of the top minorities that has been attacked recently. So that's a double whammy; you are not also undocumented, but you are also Hispanic.

While recognizing these circumstances, Natalia helped support her sister financially and emotionally. Still, being a breadwinner in her family was sometimes a source of stress and resulted in complicated feelings of responsibility.

Certainly, while being a breadwinner can be experienced as pressure and responsibility, it does not mean that these pressures are experienced in only hostile or conflict-heavy families. On the contrary, among the children of immigrants, resentment and gratitude, as well as fondness toward parents can coexist.[65] Some citizen children certainly can and do feel proud that they can help their families. For example, among newly middle-class Mexican Americans, giving back financially to their families can be a source of joy and a means to repay the "immigrant bargain" that parents already paid with long-term family sacrifices.[66] Even so, the punishments attached to undocumented status and citizens' access to work help shape family breadwinning constraints and responsibilities.

Again, the pressure to be a current and future breadwinner is also shaped by a love for family members. Still, the emotive feelings about providing financial support can shift over the life course and inspire mixed emotions. For Edgar, he admits that when he was younger, he was upset that his father could not be the financial provider he hoped he could be. He recalls:

> I think one of the concerns that comes up is the financial aspect. At some point during my younger years, I felt very resentful about my father not being able to provide more or not being able to get a better-paying job and overlooking the fact that he can't really go out and apply to Target or someplace like that because they will ask for proof of citizenship so that prevents any means of income. That is something that applies to both of my parents.

Over time, and as an adult, Edgar's perception of his father and his ability to financially support the family evolved. Instead of thinking about the financial limitations of his father's earning capacity, he began to respect his parents for their hard work and look to himself as a vehicle for their upward mobility:

> They both work very hard, and I look up to that. That is one of my primary guiding forces in my life as a student. I look to my parents and see how many hours they work each week, and they should be making twice of what they make for the work that they do, but they don't. That's why I am here studying in college to get a better opportunity.

This citizen responsibility informs these young adults' educational journeys and commitment to supporting their loved ones financially. Edgar, for example, sees his time in college as worthwhile because he imagines that after he graduates, he will be better equipped to help his parents live more comfortably. In thinking about some of the comforts experienced by other families, Edgar reflects on how his parents do not have the opportunity to enjoy leisure time or to indulge in middle-class luxuries:

I do think there are many things that I wish my parents could have, or I guess things I wish they could do themselves. I see other families spending more time together on the weekends, going on trips, going on vacation, going camping, or maybe the father going out with his buddies or the mother getting a pedicure for herself or doing something nice for themselves. I realize my parents don't get to do the little luxuries in life. I think my mom probably does this the least in our family, and that makes me very sad. That's why I wish if I were to get a better-paying job many years from now, I can give back to my family.

It is in these ways that citizen adults in mixed-status families negotiate their responsibilities to their parents. Aside from their current financial contributions, young adults hope that their college educations can help their families reach a level of middle-class security. They also understand that their parents generally support their pursuit of higher education. Whether Edgar can give back to his family is to be determined, as Sylvia's experience serves as a reminder that college debt and high living costs can sometimes diminish the socioeconomic contributions and dreams adult children have for their parents.

Young adults are also keenly aware that their breadwinning responsibilities would inevitably increase if one or both parents were deported. Just as mothers sometimes find themselves taking on the primary breadwinner role after a partner's deportation,[67] citizens also know that they must be prepared for the financial realities of a parent's removal. Diruhi perhaps worries more than most about the possibility of her stepfather's removal from the country, partly because her mother depends on him a great deal. Although Diruhi's mother is a US citizen, her health issues mean that Diruhi's stepfather plays an essential financial and caregiving role in the family. In thinking about what would change if her stepfather was able to legalize his status, Diruhi explains:

I think I'd have that relief . . . especially because I am almost twenty-five and I am almost done with school. I eventually want to move out of my parents' house, but I know until [my stepfather] does get his citizenship that I am always going to have that worry because my mom is not going to have us there. . . . It worries me because who is going to take care of my mom? Again, she wouldn't be able to support herself. She works, but she wouldn't be able to do it on her own. If my stepdad were to have citizenship, things would definitely change. . . . I want to stay close to my parents just in case.

For Diruhi, her stepfather's undocumented status shapes her everyday experiences when interacting with neighbors or the police and in planning vacations. In this case, Diruhi highlights how status is implicated in the language of "just in case," referring to the uncertain futures of those who are undocumented and their loved ones, who must prepare financially for the possibility of deportation.

Diruhi elaborates that she would not feel comfortable leaving the area because of the possibility of her stepfather being detained. Should that occur, Diruhi would need to take over more of the breadwinning and caregiving in her family. These decisions also mean that considering lucrative job offers in another state are out of the question for Diruhi. Such matters were weighing on her mind just as she was considering life after college graduation. In this somewhat subtle fashion, young adults may experience limitations to their socioeconomic mobility because of wanting to be near their mixed-status families in case of an immigration-related emergency. Some young adults decide against or hesitate to consider out-of-state college, graduate programs, or work opportunities for this reason. Such decisions seem to align with results of recent research looking at the lives of young adults in mixed-status families in borderland communities.[68] By staying close to home, Diruhi manages family illegality and prepares for the possibility of increased breadwinning responsibilities.

Conclusion

Family illegality is negotiated and experienced differently for children after they become adults. In some ways, adulthood represents positive shifts in which family illegality becomes better managed or less salient. Adult children come to experience newfound international travel and independence. They realize that their fears of parental deportability are better managed based on several factors that they feel keep their families safe from separation. As adults, they also know that they are better equipped to manage parental detention or deportation and use any available resources to assist their families in challenging times. Local immigrant-friendly policies and a sense that parents are cautious serve as protective shields that help keep adult children's emotional stress over parental deportability in check. However, this emotional management is rocked when news of immigration enforcement and policy changes reminds them that their families are vulnerable to punitive state enforcement measures.

Citizens can legally access financial assistance to fund their higher education pursuits. Still, many college-educated or college-going citizens reflected on how their parent's status was a significant and time-consuming barrier that had to be overcome to access this financial support. In more extreme cases outside of California, otherwise eligible citizen students have been legally prevented from accessing in-state tuition or college financial aid because of their parents' immigration status.[69] While young adults in this study were not barred from accessing financial aid, the college financial aid process creates challenges associated with their parents not having papers.

In theory, citizens can sponsor their parents and extend to the family privileges possible through their citizenship status. I find, however, that this citizenship privilege often goes unfulfilled and families remain as mixed-status. Some citizen children look forward to sponsoring their parents as an act of love, yet others may worry about the responsibility and disagree about whether or how to move forward. These two emotional responses are not necessarily mutually exclusive. Naturally, every family has unique strains and bonds that can shift and come to the fore in these family-based negotiations. In either case, both youth and their families find that the process to legalize a parent is confusing, financially prohibitive, and not an option unless parents are comfortable waiting out a decade-long bar in their country of birth. It is in these nuanced ways that families have to manage illegality. Each decision-making process may look different, but it is still families who have to confront delicate choices about their joint futures. Further, the difficulties young adults face in navigating parental legalization further highlight that anchor baby narratives perpetuated in conservative media are at odds with how current immigration laws work in sponsoring undocumented parents.

Young adults manage illegality through responsibilities surrounding family breadwinning. Citizens have legal access to the workforce, which can help them contribute to the family's household income. Still, this citizenship privilege can leave some children feeling like they are shouldering a disproportionate share of breadwinning responsibilities. Although some research suggests that adult second-generation children financially assist their immigrant families,[70] this obligation can feel heightened for an adult citizen child who may be the "only one" or one of the few family members who can legally enter the labor market. For adult children, it is also not always age or gender that determines who bears the responsibility of family breadwinning. This means that working-age citizen children understand the unique commitment to their mixed-status families, regardless of gender. While contributing to family resources is necessary in working-class families, citizens articulate that *immigration statuses* help shape financial commitments to family. This family breadwinning may be especially critical in expensive areas like Los Angeles, where rising housing costs can compel pooling resources. Still, it is important to note that young adults did not report feeling pressure from parents to leave college to work full-time; adult children felt supported by parents in the pursuit of their degrees, and both children and parents viewed higher education as an investment in future stability. Adult children often expressed gratitude for the ways their parents were able to offer various forms of support as the children worked toward earning a college degree or completing career training. However, the possibility of parental deportation was understood as something that could change their trajectory in college because of the possible need for them to assume additional breadwinning and caregiving responsibilities. If a parent was deported, adult children—and especially those with younger siblings or elders who need care—knew it would become necessary for them to take on much more significant financial and caregiving responsibilities.

To be sure, the research presented here and the concept of family illegality do not suggest that young citizens are always in the same proverbial boat as their undocumented parents, siblings, and other family members. Some citizens do voice frustrations, guilt, and mixed feelings about being a citizen in an otherwise undocumented family. For these young Americans, family illegality is a unique experience. Raúl's exasperated comment about wanting to be undocumented is reflective of this. Even so, citizens—including Raúl—do recognize the privileges they have in accessing financial aid. Raúl's words should be contextualized by the family trauma of separation and the complex emotions that the separation inspired. As I have outlined, citizens do have privileges that are made accessible through their citizenship, which include some privileges that are not available to legal residents or young people with DACA. Instead, this research demonstrates that adult-age citizens with undocumented parents must manage family illegality. When citizenship privileges can be shared or extended, sometimes this is done at an emotional and economic cost that results from the punishments associated with illegality. Thus, citizenship is an individual privilege, but families navigate illegality as a collective.

In the absence of immigration reform, it seems unlikely that citizens in large numbers will be able to see their parents' status change in the foreseeable future. As a result, the responsibilities they hold within their families may remain and accumulate as their parents age and as the adult children may begin to form families of their own. Natalia shared her plans for her family. As she drinks her coffee, Natalia imparts that she will be the one to have her aging parents move into her home once they can no longer care for themselves. Natalia explains that the government would not be able to help her parents as they age. Given her parents' undocumented status, they do not have access to Social Security, and her parents do not have a pension or retirement savings. These are difficult choices to manage for any adult with aging parents, but especially so for children who will grapple with the realities of aging parents who do not have papers.

3

Talking Back to "Anchor Baby" and Birthright Citizenship Discourse

Leonardo arrives at our interview in a neon-colored tank top, bright aviator sunglasses, and flip-flops—a colorful look that is matched by his extroverted personality. During the interview, he tells me about his life and how his immigrant parents made the United States their home. Leonardo's family migration story begins in the late 1980s. At the time, the family was grieving a recent loss, and Leonardo's father—then a husband and father-to-be—decided to make a lone unauthorized border crossing to work in California. Not long after, the family reunited in Los Angeles. A few years later, Leonardo was born and became the first US citizen in the family. Since all of Leonardo's family began their migration journey after the IRCA amnesty program, none of his immigrant family members benefited from this pathway to legalization. Leonardo's parents, older brother, and much of his extended kin in the United States are undocumented.

Leonardo is like a lot of young people. He is working toward completing his education, building a career, and living a well-rounded life. However, because he was born in the United States to undocumented parents, some conservative leaders, anti-immigrant groups, and political pundits consider Leonardo an anchor baby unworthy of US citizenship. Anti-immigrant leaders hurl this derogatory term at the American-born children of noncitizen mothers of color. The main assertion of this false narrative is that undocumented Latina mothers specifically birth children on US soil to "anchor" their own legal status in the United States.[1] Another component of this narrative is the claim that undocumented mothers bear American children to access government entitlements. Many Republicans and anti-immigrant advocates use these talking points to argue that children of undocumented immigrants should be ineligible for birthright citizenship. US birthright citizenship guarantees citizenship to children born in the United States based on the principle of jus soli (right of the soil) and is granted by the Fourteenth Amendment of the US Constitution.

Precisely because Leonardo is implicated in these political contestations, I ask him what he makes of the discourse. Leonardo's college classes have helped him understand these narratives:

> I think it's incredible how these politicians are educated and go to great schools—"great schools"[2]—and they still think like an ignorant person that doesn't have an educated background. Obviously, it's unconstitutional, and you can see with their rhetoric what kind of person they are. Rhetoric is all about persuading an audience, and [politicians] are doing a goddamn great job by using these [anchor baby] terms and making these statements about people who have been in this country for a long time. For example, historically there have been Mexicans living here a long time after the Treaty of Guadalupe. A lot of people forget that the US has taken their lands historically, and they are trying to do the same thing to people who have been born here. History is still repeating itself. We are still doing the same thing. It's just evolved into this.

Leonardo understands that birthright citizenship is the law and that he has the same rights as any US citizen. He recognizes that claims surrounding the children of undocumented mothers born in the United States are untrue, despite politicians' arguments. In this way, Leonardo engages in the critical race theory practice of counterstorytelling because he "challenge[s] the perceived wisdom of those at society's center" by questioning the knowledge of lawmakers.[3]

Leonardo also references what I call an ancestral right to land claim by expressing how Mexicans have a long-standing presence in the United States. A substantial portion of the country was originally part of Mexico, including Texas. After the Mexican-American War, all or parts of California, Nevada, Arizona, New Mexico, Colorado, and Utah were ceded from Mexico to the United States, along with some land bordering a few of these states. The Treaty of Guadalupe Hidalgo in 1848 marked an end to the war and granted the option of US citizenship to Mexicans who chose to remain in the newly colonized land. In the following years, the US government and Anglo-American carpetbaggers, lawyers, and merchants used unscrupulous and/or legally sanctioned tactics to displace many of the remaining Mexican Americans from their property.[4] Armed with this knowledge about his history, Leonardo stakes a claim to his citizenship and his right to belong in the United States.

How do Americans like Leonardo—who are depicted as anchor babies—make sense of and respond to anchor baby and birthright citizenship discourse? How do these citizens understand their membership in the United States when they may be bombarded with images, rhetoric, and policies that suggest the undesirability of their citizenship and mixed-status families? To answer these questions, I turn to feminist scholarship. I draw from the research of feminist scholar Lisa D. Brush, who invited mothers on welfare to "talk back" to stereotypes of welfare recipients.[5] Brush used prompts in the context of a nonprofit writing class, where mothers were able to talk back to elected officials, caseworkers, and other social actors who may construct welfare mothers as lazy or irresponsible. Rarely do these mothers get the opportunity to engage with policy makers who make critical decisions that alter their lives. Similarly, mixed-status families are rarely able to participate in this type of public discourse even though immigration debates are ubiquitous. When I met with members of mixed-status families, I asked them to talk back to elected officials who want to deny birthright citizenship to the children of undocumented immigrants, disseminate anchor baby narratives, and are in favor of deporting undocumented immigrants.[6] This chapter will describe how members of mixed-status families engage in family illegality at a discursive level as they respond to undocumented immigration debates, particularly those about anchor babies and birthright citizenship. Leonardo and other young people like him respond by developing different claims that speak to their knowledge and experience. Based on the patterns of the data, I have outlined these claims in table 3.1.

This talk-back practice is also a form of counterstorytelling rooted in critical race theory because these responses draw from the experiences of people of color.[7] According to scholars, counterstories are the methods that people on the margins use to respond to and transform racist or commonly told stories.[8] The people in this chapter share responses that draw from defining features of counterstories by referencing their (or their family's) experiences that have been shaped by the legacies of racism.[9] The power of the counterstory is that it can

TABLE 3.1. Talk-Back Responses

Claim	Description
Ancestral Right to Land	This claim suggests that elected officials who want to amend birthright citizenship probably do not have a more legitimate right to reside in the United States than Mexican mixed-status families. This is because these leaders may also have immigrant ties or may have benefited from colonialism and White supremacy. Mexican Americans using this claim will mention how Natives were the original inhabitants of the Americas, and how California was originally part of Mexico before it was US land. Another strand of this claim argues that politicians, including Donald Trump or his children, are "anchor babies" because of their immigrant mothers/ancestors, and therefore their citizenship would also need to be revoked if birthright citizenship is eliminated.
Disputing	This claim disputes several anchor baby talking points. For example, Mexican Americans challenge the notion that their families migrate to abuse government resources. Some point to foreign policy, violence, financial need, or family reunification as factors that explain migration. Others suggest that if the anchor baby practice is occurring, those cases are probably the exception. Participants also argue that there is a difference in parents wanting opportunity for their children versus parents using children as legal or economic pawns. Many also point to personal observations of family, friends, and coworkers to dispute the narrative. Further, because sponsoring parents is usually not a feasible option, and because adult children have observed how parents of US citizen children are deported, they use these observations to dispute the idea of the anchor baby.
Affirming the Constitution	This claim affirms the legitimacy of birthright citizenship by referencing the US Constitution.
Repercussions	This claim focuses on what Mexican Americans believe are the dire consequences of altering or ending birthright citizenship. Mexican Americans assume that changing birthright citizenship will lead to a population of stateless and deportable American-born people, causing severe economic and logistical problems, as well as racial profiling and human rights abuses.
(Racialized) Contradictions	This claim asserts that elected officials and members of the public would not have a problem with the anchor baby narrative if perpetrators were White. Another part of this claim that is not explicitly racialized also describes how elected officials wanting to remove birthright citizenship from children are pro-life.
Moral	This claim argues that anchor baby narrative/birthright citizenship debates are dehumanizing to immigrants and their families. It also argues that elected officials should focus their efforts on uplifting communities.
Political Tactic	This claim argues that elected officials opportunistically use birthright citizenship debates as part of a political tactic to diminish immigrant or Latino political power and/or to shore up support for their base or election.
Worthiness	This claim emphasizes how immigrants and their children are worthy of residing in the United States because of their qualities or resources, which include US loyalty or assimilation, a work ethic, and economic value.

challenge a majoritarian mind-set, which is the "bundle of presupposi-tions, received wisdoms, and shared cultural understandings persons in the dominant group bring to discussions of race."[10] Mainstream rheto-ric about modifying birthright citizenship is not color-blind, as political pundits talk about mothers coming from the US-Mexico border or mi-grating from Mexico or Latin America.[11] Mexican Americans also did not hesitate to unpack how race or racism is central to these citizenship debates. In their responses, they challenge notions of privilege by draw-ing on layered and sophisticated counterstories that can entail multiple claims. The voices in this chapter reframe debates about their citizenship and the belonging of their families. Before turning to how interviewees respond, I outline the history of the anchor baby discourse.

The History of the "Anchor Baby" and Struggles over Birthright Citizenship

The first time I heard the term "anchor baby" was in 2010. At the time I found myself involuntarily listening to a conservative radio show dur-ing a drive exiting Los Angeles. Californians at the time were concerned with the state's postrecession budget. The radio show host seemed to blame many of the state's pressing social and economic problems on what he called "anchor babies." As I listened in, the host further blamed these babies for the state's economic challenges and for being part of a larger problem of undocumented immigration. This rhetoric also has the appeal of being visual; pregnant mothers are described as running across the US-Mexico border to give birth in the United States.[12] As I continued to listen to the radio, I wondered how babies could be so heavily criticized. In the ensuing years I have paid attention to this dis-course and observed how the anchor baby became a talking point to eliminate birthright citizenship.

US immigration laws, deportation rates, and the extant data on im-migrant families do not support the idea that an anchor baby practice exists—at least not in significant numbers. In other words, there are not thousands or millions of undocumented pregnant women crossing the border in a nefarious plot to access legalized status for themselves, sim-ply by birthing a child on US soil. If this were true, it would be incom-patible with the large-scale deportations of immigrant parents in the twenty-first century. From 2005 to 2013, the United States deported over 3 million migrants, which affected over 1.5 million citizen children.[13] Being a citizen child did not provide a shield against the traumatic circumstance of family separation or living as an exile in another country.[14]

The anchor baby practice is not supported by patterns of undocumented immigrant family formation in the United States. In 2010, more than 50 percent of undocumented immigrants who were parents of citizen children had been in the country at least five years.[15] In more recent years, undocumented migration from Mexico has declined significantly.[16] Despite the stereotypes about Mexican immigrant women's reproductive motivations, women can be ambivalent about having children and carefully negotiate familial and economic factors when considering starting families.[17] The feasibility of the anchor baby practice is also illogical considering current immigration sponsorship policy. Undocumented mothers seeking to adjust their status through a citizen child have to wait until the child is twenty-one years old and meets other requirements in addition to having financial resources. Still, as we saw in chapter 2, this is just the beginning of a process that many families in this study ultimately decide not to pursue.

The anchor baby narrative is also not supported by existing data on immigrants' motivations for migration. In their extensive study with Latino migrants, Douglas Massey and Magaly Sánchez find that immigrants report migrating to the United States for economic reasons, for family reunification, or to escape violence.[18] I have also found that most immigrant parents migrate in search of work. Many immigrants did not want to migrate; it is costly and can be an emotionally gut-wrenching process. Ultimately, however, US policies and business practices make migration not only attractive but sometimes necessary. The militarization of the US-Mexico border that began in full force in the 1990s altered the historically seasonal Mexican labor migration, causing migrants to consider permanent settlement in the United States. Since many of these immigrants are also of childbearing age, some of them produce families.

If this anchor baby practice is not actually occurring on a large scale, what fuels this discourse? The discourse serves a political function by positioning Mexican immigrant mothers as social problems. Anthropologist Leo Chavez argues that Mexican immigrant women's bodies are "ground zero in a war of not only words but also public policies and laws."[19] These women's potentially pregnant or birthing bodies inspire anxiety among those who oppose immigration from the global south and fear non-White demographic change.[20] Indeed, racialized (immigrant) women's reproduction has long been deemed undesirable and/ or controlled by White social actors and institutions. In the 1930s, anti-immigration advocates and eugenicists criticized and brought attention to Mexican immigrant women's birthrates to propel their campaigns.[21] A number of historical cases also point to how Mexican, Puerto Rican, and Indigenous women were coercively sterilized in the United States.[22] Enslaved Black women's reproduction was exploited for enslaved labor, and later pathologized following the termination of slavery.[23]

In part due to an increase in the number of Latina migrants, the renewed concern over the reproduction of women of color immigrants became a political issue in the 1990s, and during this time the archetype of the "problem immigrant" shifted again from gendered male to gendered female.[24] While there was a "welfare queen" discourse that demonized Black women, the racialized and gendered depictions of undocumented women also positioned Latinas, particularly Mexican-origin women, as economic burdens to the state.[25] This discourse contributed to policy changes that sought to prevent undocumented and mixed-status families from accessing state services. Proposition 187 is one manifestation of this discourse.

Proposition 187 was a 1994 ballot initiative passed by California voters that sought to limit aid and social services to undocumented immigrants. The measure would have restricted vital services that are especially necessary for children and families, such as immunization services, childhood education, and prenatal care.[26] While earlier anti-immigrant discourse focused on the trope of immigrants taking away jobs, support for Proposition 187 was garnered through the fear of a growing Latino population that was perceived as an economic drain on the state.[27] Publicly, however, grassroots activists and elected officials in support of Proposition 187 disavowed any racist intent and argued the proposition was a step toward fiscal pragmatism.[28] While it ultimately was overturned, Proposition 187 exemplified a shift in racial politics that targeted Latino immigrant families.

Eventually, discourses on Latina fertility and immigration would also arguably catalyze support for the Personal Responsibility and Work Opportunity and Reconciliation Act (PRWORA), also known as the Welfare Reform Act of 1996. This policy replaced the cash-based federal welfare program Aid to Families with Dependent Children (AFDC) with Temporary Assistance for Needy Families (TANF), a program meant to encourage workforce participation.[29] PRWORA impacted low-income families across the board, but undocumented immigrants were explicitly ineligible from receiving federal subsidies, including TANF, food stamps, and Medicaid.[30]

The anchor baby is made legible from these 1990s-era welfare reform and immigration debates. In the 1990s and particularly in the first decade of the twenty-first century, the narrative began appearing in television news programming, such as Fox News.[31] Along with such programming, magazines and newspapers contributed to a growing moral panic about the children of undocumented immigrants by featuring alarmist images of immigration and non-White babies.[32] Once these narratives began appearing in online blogs, anchor baby talking points reached the public consciousness.[33] In many ways, this kind of discourse has proliferated to the extent that it has through organizations like the Federation of American Immigration Reform (FAIR) and other anti-immigrant organizations with a web presence.[34] In 2010, anchor babies had reached the mainstream, as reflected by the term becoming *Time*'s buzzword of the year.[35]

The anchor baby discourse is used as a justification to alter birthright citizenship. The citizenship clause of the Fourteenth Amendment specifies: "All persons born or naturalized in the United States, and subject to the jurisdiction thereof, are citizens of the United States and of the State wherein they reside."[36] Those who oppose birthright citizenship believe that undocumented immigrants are not subject to the jurisdiction of the United States, while the other side emphasizes how parental immigration status is irrelevant.[37] Regarding the matter of parentage, the US Supreme Court previously ruled in *U.S. v. Wong Kim Ark* (1898) that Wong Kim Ark, a US-born Chinese American, was a citizen despite his Chinese immigrant parentage. At the time, the racial question of birthright citizenship was particularly important because only those who were considered White by the courts could become naturalized citizens.[38] *U.S. v. Wong Kim Ark* is often cited as the Supreme Court decision that parentage should not be a factor in whether a US-born child is considered a citizen.

Since the days of *U.S. v Wong Kim Ark*, there has been no shortage of contestations against birthright citizenship, many of which have occurred in the twenty-first century. These include the US Citizen Reform Act in 2005 and the Birthright Citizenship Act in 2007, both of which proposed making children born to undocumented parents ineligible for birthright citizenship. The Birthright Citizenship Act was reintroduced in 2009 and 2019. In 2011, conservative Arizona politicians presented a bill requiring separate birth certificates for children of noncitizen parents while another bill would have made Arizona citizenship exclusive to children born of at least one US citizen or legal permanent resident.[39] That same year, US senators Rand Paul and David Vitter introduced a resolution to amend the Constitution to modify birthright citizenship, while Representative Steve King introduced the Birthright Citizenship Act to the House.[40] Birthright citizenship was also up for debate during the 2016 elections. Then presidential candidate Donald Trump claimed that he would curb birthright citizenship, arguing that it was a "magnet for illegal immigration."[41] When Trump became president, he announced that he would end birthright citizenship via an executive order.[42] Ultimately, none of these proposals or public announcements impacted birthright citizenship. It is incredibly difficult to amend the Constitution. As a result, these policies and talking points may be more about communicating symbolic messages to an anti-immigrant base than earnest attempts to modify the jus soli basis of citizenship. Similar to Kitty Calavita's argument that citizens voted for Proposition 187 to "send a message,"[43] birthright citizenship reformers may be sending a message about the undesirability of *certain* mixed-status families.[44] It is ironic that Trump and his allies do not seem to mind that he formed his own mixed-status families with immigrant women who birthed American children or that his own mother was also an immigrant to the United States.[45]

According to historian Mae Ngai, the legal and cultural battles over birthright citizenship suggest that children born to racialized immigrant parents are continuously constructed as alien citizens.[46] She elucidates: "The alien citizen is an American citizen by virtue of her birth in the

United States but whose citizenship is suspect, if not denied, on account of the racialized identity of her immigrant ancestry."[47] For this reason, the American children of Mexican undocumented immigrants are arguably a quintessential example of *citizens who do not belong.*[48] Struggles over birthright citizenship have perpetually been about denying citizenship to people of color.[49] Changing birthright citizenship may be a strategic political move to diminish the voting power of children of immigrants, many of whom are part of the changing ethnic and racial demography of the United States. It is perhaps not surprising that calls to modify birthright citizenship also coincided with non-White births outnumbering White births for the first time.[50] Therefore, elected officials may also propose altering or ending birthright citizenship to mitigate the racial demographic changes that migration can produce. Denying birthright citizenship to the children of undocumented parents would disproportionately impact Latino and Asian American families.[51]

Ultimately, policies and discourse construct mixed-status families as unwanted outsiders. In debates about anchor babies and birthright citizenship, mothers and children are usually portrayed as a problem for the United States.[52] Depictions of anchor babies challenge the legitimacy and humanity of both citizens and noncitizens in mixed-status families. Yet, in all of this, we learn of claims made mostly by elected officials and political pundits who have access to public platforms. Members of mixed-status families also have something to say.

Talking Back

Members of mixed-status families learn about anchor baby debates in news media or from family, friends, coworkers, classmates, and teachers. Most participants had some understanding of these debates. Those who were unfamiliar usually consumed very little news or political media but knew of anti-immigrant tropes, including narratives about undocumented women's reproduction being a burden on the state. Regardless of whether participants were informed of the debates, living in an immigrant family provided them with a unique perspective from which to talk back to this public discourse.

Like Leonardo, young Americans in this study respond to anchor baby discourse by making claims about an ancestral right to land that highlights US legacies of colonialism. Susie, for example, had the following response to elected officials who vie to amend birthright citizenship: "I would call them White supremacists. This land wasn't theirs, so why do they feel like they have ownership over it?" Members of mixed-status families point to the forced removal of Native Americans, Mexicans, and other people of color from US lands as an example of how elected officials use rhetoric and policy to dispossess them from their homes.

Mexican Americans also discuss their right to belong in the country based on the widely expressed notion that the United States is a country of immigrants. By doing this, members of mixed-status families challenge the legitimacy of public leaders who probably also have immigrant ties unless they are Native Americans or descendants of enslaved people. Using these logics, Mexican Americans express that if their citizenship is going to be revoked, all descendants of immigrants will need to face this fate as well. This sentiment was expressed by Anahí, who shared the following:

> I would reference the European colonizers that came here, their ancestors. All of them had to migrate here because there were no White people here, so then would [amending birthright citizenship] take away their citizenship too? Are their ancestors citizens? The same would have to apply to them too. It shouldn't just apply to us.

Mexican Americans vie for belonging by challenging the legitimacy of generations that begin with ancestors who had no legal permission to migrate to the United States. These claims allow Mexican Americans to universalize the term "anchor baby," thereby reducing its power as a slur that is commonly directed to Mexican or Latino second-generation children. It is also a counterstory that attempts to dismantle immigrant generational privilege, especially as it applies to Whites, who are commonly constructed and perceived as unquestionably American.[53] The young people in this study do not agree with amending birthright citizenship, but they believe reframing the debate as one where citizenship would be revoked from all descendants of immigrants would mean the end to birthright citizenship discourse and proposals.

Mexican Americans knew that Donald Trump was one of the public figures who was outspoken about altering birthright citizenship. As a result, they sometimes referred to him and his family when challenging ideas about who belongs on US soil. Alondra's thoughts exemplified this very idea when she argued, "I am pretty sure when it comes to Donald Trump, his lineage, [his family] wasn't completely born here. So, if he wants to [change birthright citizenship] he has to realize he would not have been given citizenship. You know? It's not really fair." These claims in particular challenge what are called "majoritarian stories of privilege";[54] in other words, they challenge privileged groups' legitimacy to claim (more) ownership of the United States. In these cases, privilege is not exclusively tied to race even though Mexican Americans think of anti-birthright officials as White, but also privileged in terms of being part of a later immigrant generation and holding political power. As Mexican Americans do this, they challenge their family's non-belonging in public debates about mixed-status families.

Francisco was unable to recall popular citizenship discourse probably because he did not follow news reporting closely. However, this does not mean he is apolitical or apathetic about social issues. He spends his free time volunteering with a community organization in his neighborhood to help his "underprivileged brothers and sisters" because he has the privilege of citizenship. Since he lives in an area heavily populated by foreign-born people, some of his community work necessitates working on immigrant advocacy issues, as well as organizing for safe and affordable housing.

Francisco's politics are also shaped by his upbringing in a mixed-status family. His parents migrated separately without papers and later met and fell in love in Los Angeles. Throughout the years, his parents have worked different informal sector jobs to make ends meet and help support Francisco and his three younger sisters. When I ask Francisco to talk back to elected officials who want to change birthright citizenship, his eyes signal that the question may have caught him off guard. Still, he responds by disputing the claim based on his own family experience and refutes the idea that the anchor baby practice exists on a large scale.

F: What? They want to propose for someone like me to be ineligible for citizenship at birth?
C: Yes.

F: Wow. How would that work? . . . I would say that's not right just because there are probably some examples of those anchor baby situations who are mothers who will do that, but the problem with that is they generalize and say we all do that and for that reason we should not allow citizenship. So that's how they use that against us. That's another stereotype, I guess. That's not the issue at all with immigrant families. For example, with me, I don't think that's what my parents had in mind. What they planned was to come here, work, and make money so that they could help out their families back in Mexico. They just happen to have me and the rest of my sisters and now I just want to help them out. It's not right, basically. I guess if you want to turn this into a deeper conversation, we are all immigrants. This was never our land, so you can't do that to us if these same people were immigrants not too long ago.

While Francisco concludes by mentioning an ancestral right to land claim, most of his talking back is about countering the idea that the anchor baby practice exists. He argues it is possible that some families may be engaging in this practice, but the reality is more complicated. In thinking about his own parents, Francisco knows that his family was not formed in the United States so that his parents could gain legal status.

Tomás and Raúl also dispute the anchor baby narrative based on their family experiences. Both young men had suffered the deportation of at least one close family member, and these deported family members are also parents to citizen children. Tomás and Raúl refer to this family trauma to challenge the narrative, since parents can be deported long before their children reach the eligible age of twenty-one required to sponsor them. Sharing a bit more about his uncle's circumstances, Tomás disputes the narrative on the basis that his uncle had three US citizen children when he was deported. With a tinge of sorrow, Tomás explains how his cousins now live without the presence of their father. Thinking of his cousins, he asks rhetorically, "How are they anchor babies?" Some family histories that contribute to these counterstories are colored by this trauma of deportation and family separation.

Olivia was another member of a mixed-status family who had something to say about these debates. She frowns when I bring up the subject.

She, too, refutes the idea that mothers participate in any anchor baby plot, saying, "I am what you call an anchor baby except I am not because I was not born for some sort of political purpose. I was born because my parents wanted to have a child for a long time, and eventually they had me." Olivia has considered these discourses for several years and remembers students debating the issue in one of her college classes. Although Olivia did not participate in the class discussion, she remembers feeling upset when some of her classmates suggested babies should be sent back to their parents' country of origin. She tells me, "I remember feeling powerless. There wasn't anything I could say that would have kept me from getting too angry or maybe even crying. They were basically saying people like me and my family should be sent back." Olivia regrets not being able to speak her mind in class. "It hits too close to home," Olivia offers as an explanation for her lack of class participation. Nodding, I understand. As I close my binder ready to conclude the interview, Olivia confides in me that maybe the next time she will be prepared to confront these debates head-on.

Olivia's classroom experience points to another important way that Americans like her make sense of the anchor baby debate; they see it as a heinous attempt to garner support for deporting immigrants and citizens alike. This is not accidental. Olivia got this message from her classmates, while others learn of this sentiment from public figures who advocate deporting mixed-status families. Several of the Mexican Americans I interviewed commented on what would be the catastrophic consequences for families if birthright citizenship was eliminated. When Mexican Americans take a stance against anchor baby rhetoric, they also communicate a broader opposition to deportation. Edgar explains how he took on this perspective:

> I think it's absolutely ridiculous. There are a lot of things that go into this than just taking citizenship away. It becomes a question if you were not born here or there, where exactly do they fit? . . . If my citizenship was taken away, I wouldn't have citizenship anywhere. It goes back to the fact that these are people—like you and I—and it makes absolutely no sense to do anything like that. When someone grows up here there is a culture and all of those things that influence us as we grow up. That is simply

something you can't take away from anybody. That would be a violation of human rights. It's like going to another country, picking up people, and taking them somewhere else where they have never been and might not know the language or how to behave. It's just something that is out of the question to me. It's not a possibility.

Edgar describes the consequence of an entire population of young people becoming stateless, which not only is a catastrophe but also violates human rights. Because these ramifications are quite dire, Edgar copes with these thoughts by arguing that such actions are not a possibility.[55] Other interviewees added that altering or ending birthright citizenship is unlikely because of the expense, the logistics, and the likelihood of human rights abuses. Some expressed the concern that excluding the children of undocumented immigrants from birthright citizenship means that state agents will racially profile Mexican- and Latino-origin communities in their efforts to deport American-born people and their immigrant families. If this happened, it would not be the first time in US history that Americans of Mexican ancestry were deported to Mexico.[56]

Edgar also makes moral claims in his talk back to elected leaders. He points out that when elected officials refer to "anchor babies," they create a moral problem by dehumanizing people:

I think people shouldn't look at it that way because I think using that word [anchor baby] turns immigrants into nonhumans. They are not any different from anyone else. They have ten fingers and two eyes, two ears like everyone else. I think it's a term that is just [pauses] very wrong. It's wrong to me.

Here we see how Mexican Americans view the term "anchor baby" as not only a slur directed at citizen children but also a term that dehumanizes immigrants more generally.

Another approach in talking back to anchor baby debates is by referencing the US Constitution and affirming that birthright citizenship is working as intended. Mario makes his point by referring to the Constitution:

[It's] just not fair because according to the law everyone born in the US is a citizen and guaranteed rights. In fact, it would be unconstitutional to deny these rights and if that is what [elected officials] are all about, they are breaking the American system and they are the ones being unconstitutional about everything. I feel like I have a right to be here. I have a right to be a citizen of the United Sates because that is what the law dictates.

Mario views birthright citizenship as a precious legal right. Some legal scholars argue that birthright citizenship was established to serve as an equality principle to prevent a caste-like system for the children of immigrants.[57] In our interview, Yoselyn similarly suggests affirming the Constitution claim by sharing the following response with elected officials:

They just need to not discriminate. If a baby is born here, they have the right to citizenship. That is what the Constitution says. I think they should go by that. Our whole government already has a stance on that, so just because they don't want any immigration or anyone who is different from them being here, that's no reason why this should be changed.

Later in the interview, Yoselyn expresses how these debates are racialized when she identifies those who oppose birthright citizenship are White Americans, who, she notes, dominate the country politically.

In talking back, some participants emphasize how immigrants and their children are worthy of living in the country. For instance, they point to their US loyalty, patriotism, or assimilation as beneficial to the United States. Francisco has made this connection in his response to elected officials: "If we are born here, we grow up here and familiarize ourselves with the American way. It's not like we are going to be anti-American. That's not what we are. We are not anti-American." In this way, Francisco is able to emphasize how children's assimilation and familiarity with American customs are a resource, not a hindrance, to the country. It is striking that Francisco explicitly articulates how children like him would not be anti-American. In *U.S. v. Wong Kim Ark*, US-born Ark won his case affirming his citizenship, but nineteenth-century judges questioned whether Ark would be subject to the "emperor of

China" because of his Chinese parentage.[58] Arguably, Francisco pre-empts this notion that children of immigrants are potentially disloyal to their countries of birth. Although not explicit, Francisco's response can also be read to include undocumented youth who are also socialized in the United States and do not necessarily have a political connection to their parents' homeland.

When Mexican Americans talk back to debates about their citizen-ship, they also sometimes reference their economic or labor contribu-tions to the country. An example is Robert, who is adamant that he and his family are worthy of being in the country because their spend-ing habits and labor are a positive economic contribution, rather than a drain on government budgets as popular anti-immigrant narratives claim. He further explains his argument:

> The way I would put it is that I am actually benefiting your country . . . working multiple jobs and I am consuming many of your products, so to take my citizenship status away is a joke at first, but I am probably going to get mad after a while if I keep hearing it, especially if you are going to call me an anchor baby. Because I am not. I am not taking your resources away.

Robert later shares that if given the opportunity, he would challenge others to live up to his work ethic by taking on his type of low-wage work. He knows that many citizens would not be able to put up with the working conditions. Robert believes attempts to remove citizenship from children like him are absurd and would prove fruitless. Similar to many of his peers, the debates anger him, but he does not believe changes to birthright citizenship are likely to occur.

Aware of debates on anchor babies and birthright citizenship, Lu-pita engages with the (racialized) contradictions in her response: "You know, all of this is really about certain people not wanting America to be a non-White country. I think that is really what this is all about." Like others I interviewed, Lupita considers the anchor baby narrative a problem because the mothers and families are Mexican or Latino, in-stead of White American or White immigrant families. Lupita recog-nizes the racial politics that underpin most of these debates and realizes that amending birthright citizenship would primarily impact families of color. Recalling a conversation she once had with her mother, Lupita disputes the anchor baby claim:

> If a mom is glad that her child is born in the US, what is wrong with that? Obviously, a mom would be grateful that her child can be born here because there are more opportunities and, you know, freedom from violence too. So, no. I think people maybe have trouble figuring out the difference between being relieved a child is born in the US, and I don't know—planning a pregnancy for all of these motives.

Reflecting on the global realities of poverty and violence, wanting a child to be born and raised in the United States can be read as a self-sacrificing gesture on behalf of the mother. This is very much at odds with the anchor baby narrative that paints mothers as opportunistic and having suspect motives. It is much more likely that parents strive to make decisions that will enhance the lives of their children, sometimes at a personal cost.

Next, I turn to Sylvia, who during our interview pulls from several different claims in her narrative. When I ask her about anchor babies and birthright citizenship, I immediately know Sylvia has an opinion about these debates. With a groan, she begins to explain how it is US intervention in other countries that frequently sets in motion migration, not any anchor baby scheme. If Sylvia had her way, politicians would be held responsible for their policy decisions and hurtful rhetoric. With frustration in her voice, she argues, "It's all foreign policy." Without losing a breath, Sylvia continues by noting that when US policies damage local economies in Mexico, it is the poor who are left with few options but to migrate. Sylvia observes that struggling as an immigrant and having to endure culture shock suggest that most people do not want to migrate but end up doing so in order to survive.

When I ask Sylvia to talk back to elected officials who claim that anchor babies are damaging to the United States, she passionately disputes the argument:

> The damage of anchor babies? Please. Most of those people are afraid to go and seek out services, and who is taking most of the social services?

White people. We are always the scapegoats. You really have to look through all the policies that this country develops. I think sometimes it's just plain racism.

As Sylvia disputes the idea of the anchor baby, she worries that the underlying racism of the narrative will make it difficult to have productive and thoughtful conversations with politicians. She asks herself if it is possible to "break through" and reach an understanding with others who push these narratives because she believes racism is at the heart of these issues. Sylvia draws from her experience growing up in a mixed-status family to dispute the anchor baby narrative:

> It's frustrating. I don't think we come here and take jobs. OK, anchor baby, so then my mom should be really good right now. If I am an anchor fucking baby, then my mom would not have struggled as much as she did and she wouldn't be struggling right now. I wouldn't be struggling right now. I still struggle even though I am a citizen and I don't have the privilege [of intergenerational wealth] and just that alone could bring so much security for people. I am not even that well-off or privileged yet as an anchor baby. You think [mixed-status families] are doing really great, but we are not doing really great at all. I don't know what they think, that welfare is buying a good standard of living? I don't understand the whole concept, and they are constantly throwing the anchor baby thing in our faces, like it's somehow helping us a lot.

In highlighting the racial politics embedded in this issue, Sylvia argues that these debates are just another way to scapegoat Mexican immigrants for a number of the country's problems. In this way, Sylvia's words serve as a counterstory that challenges narratives of racial privilege that exist in the public sphere. Moreover, Sylvia uses her own family experience to vehemently dispute claims that anchor babies and their mothers are opportunistic and greedy. Her family has consistently faced poverty, and her parents have been limited to low-wage jobs. As a result, her parents do not own property that they can pass down to her or future generations. Sylvia's critique highlights the importance of intergenerational wealth in creating opportunities for social citizenship. White Americans have more wealth than any other racial group.[59] Many of these discrepancies are shaped by historical legacies of racism and the resulting differences in homeownership by Whites and non-Whites.

Ultimately, Sylvia is against amending birthright citizenship and argues that politicians may only take on anti–birthright citizenship stances as a political tactic to gain support from a White and/or conservative base. However, Sylvia does not believe politicians even care about their White constituents. As she explains, "White people are also poor and struggling. They [elected officials] just want to have that platform to keep dividing people." In this way, Sylvia unpacks the debates surrounding anchor babies as a disingenuous political ploy to garner the favor of White American voters.

Mexican Americans in mixed-status families reframe these debates based on family or personal observations, an understanding of US history and the US Constitution, immigration law, and a number of other logics. In doing so, they develop their own claims and counterstories. Education and family history are powerful tools to protect young people from internalizing this rhetoric or feeling they do not belong in the country. Sylvia explains:

> For me, I think that school helped a lot and shaped my identity and [helped me] feel secure [about my background]. Every time that I hear these things, I don't feel like they are right, and I never internalize them, but I also kind of understand more why it's not true. If I had not gone to college, maybe it would scare me or make me feel powerless, but I don't fear that now and [I don't] think other Latinos should be deported just because I am a citizen. There are a lot of Latinos who are citizens and are anti-immigration. That has a lot to do with being a certain generation because you have Chicanos who have been here and are fifth generation and might not feel so angry when they hear sentiments about anchor babies or might feel like "Oh that's true!" Obviously in mixed families you are not going to have that sentiment that other people should be deported.

For Sylvia, managing family illegality is part of her life, yet her education has provided her with the knowledge to reject anti-immigration discourses. Instead of letting herself internalize harmful rhetoric, she can logically critique the debates and feel secure in her identity. Sylvia's thoughts on generational differences are also substantiated by research that finds a lack of solidarity among later-generation Mexican Americans with Mexican immigrants.[60] Second-generation Mexican Americans in this study attempt to dismantle the privilege of later generations of immigrants. Some of the interviewees, for example, are aware that there are later-generation Mexican Americans who may choose to forget or ignore that their great-grandparents or grandparents arrived undocumented or that these same ancestors could have been accused of producing children who anchor them to the United States. According to Sylvia, this means that Mexicans in mixed-status families cannot always count on the support and political solidarity of other co-ethnics.

Mothers Talking Back

The anchor baby narrative does not exist without the figure of the mother. According to the narrative, undocumented mothers are assumed to be heterosexual and hyperfecund, opportunistic, and neoliberally inept. These characteristics do not begin to describe the mothers I interviewed, nor do these narratives do justice to women who may need state support, have large families, or are financially secure. Mothers in this study reported they did not start families with the intention to gain legal residency or to use state entitlements. Immigrant mothers took issue with narratives that disparage their fertility or motherhood, noting how their reproduction is perceived as problematic and analogous to that of animals. Mothers dispute these debates seen in the media by comparing them with their own experiences. In their responses, I found that mothers, similar to other members of mixed-status families, view these debates as wrong and illogical. They argue against the narrative by drawing on moral claims about how healthy societies need to support children. Reflecting on the moral and logistical quandary that could be the elimination of birthright citizenship, mothers are unable to imagine creating a group of children who have no country to call home. This dilemma is particularly upsetting for mothers who tend to acknowledge they may have a tenuous claim to US membership, but express that their American-born children have a precious, legal birthright to claim membership in the United States.

Emiliana was eager to respond to these debates about her mother-hood. As the undocumented mother of three children, she knew the anchor baby myth, as well as other media narratives about Latino immigrants. From her lived experience, she found no grounds to support the narrative, telling me, "I would say in my case it's a lie. I don't see it that way." Emiliana communicates the discrepancies between what she sees in news reports about immigrants and her reality as an immigrant working mother:

> When I hear on the TV or on the radio that mothers come here to have babies so those babies can help support them, I am wondering who they are talking about, you know? Because I didn't come to this country so that my children can maintain me. If I did, I wouldn't be here breaking my back working. I would be lounging around.

Emiliana is quick to note that these narratives do not make much sense because she recognizes that government assistance is unlikely to be enough to cover all of a family's living expenses. She argues that it is much more likely that mothers use government assistance on a temporary basis during hard times. Emiliana's thoughts on government support match the difficult experience faced by Paloma, a mother of three who shared an important perspective in response to these debates:

> I know the US thinks that because I am a woman, I came to pop out children so they could get benefits. That was not my goal to have children here so that they use benefits or to benefit myself. I came here for one reason, which was to work and send money to my sick father, but oh well, I had children and made this my home.

Covering medical expenses for her ill father was the catalyst for Paloma's migration journey. As a single woman, Paloma migrated and later married and began a family in the United States. Several years after migrating, Paloma needed temporary financial assistance when her husband was imprisoned for charges related to driving under the influence of alcohol. Suddenly losing the family's only breadwin-ner meant she and her children became homeless. Since Paloma did not have papers or family networks in the United States, she could not draw from these resources for housing. So, in a moment of crisis, Paloma "went and asked for help." Although undocumented immigrants are blocked from accessing many government programs, Paloma was able to get some financial assistance to cover almost half of her $700 rent, which was later reduced when she found employment soon after.[61] Paloma's experience adds important and much-needed nuance to popular debates about immigrant mothers accessing government assistance. Paloma's decision to ask for temporary help was born out of an unexpected family crisis that propelled her to do whatever she could to secure her children's safety.

Paloma's life revolves around the needs of her children, all of whom are US citizens. She considers the United States to be her home but is even more troubled that political leaders would try to deny her children their citizenship. She tells me, "I don't understand because they are born here, and in practically any country that means you are from the country you are born [in] even if your parents weren't." Paloma conveys how debates about altering birthright citizenship are actually terrorizing for mixed-status families:

> We are here to strive for better lives. Sometimes you get scared, actually it creates terror because you get to thinking that one is not from here and neither are the children, but then the children wouldn't be from anywhere else either. Where would the children be from? They couldn't be US citizens and they can't be from Mexico or Guatemala or X country.

For Paloma, creating a population of stateless children is ludicrous and alarming. Undocumented parents recognize that they have a country to return to, whereas their children, at least for a period of time, "wouldn't be from anywhere." Furthermore, if children born in the United States to undocumented parents are suddenly ineligible for American citizenship at birth, Paloma worries that racial profiling will be used to enforce this change. She notes that White undocumented immigrants may pass as American, but this would not be the case for many Latinos.

On another day, I meet Fátima in an almost empty nonprofit waiting room. By then most of the mothers there had left the room except for about two women waiting for the few remaining children whose sessions with volunteers ran long. Fátima, clad in a floral top, was with her daughter playing with a colorful bead-maze toy resembling a roller coaster. Fátima struck up a conversation with me by inquiring if I was waiting for my own children. When I explained my purpose for being at the nonprofit, I was surprised at how quickly Fátima said, "Oh, well, you can interview me!" We agreed to an interview the following day.

Fátima tells me about arriving in the United States fifteen years ago with a visa. She had enjoyed her life in Mexico and describes it as relatively comfortable. She only migrated at the insistence of her sister, who was a transnational mother working in the United States while her daughter remained in Mexico. Distraught by this arrangement, Fátima's sister felt she could no longer bear the separation from her young child, and Fátima was tasked as the person to help reunite mother and daughter. Fátima recalls that her family arranged the visit, which was planned as a short trip but transformed into permanent settlement. "While in the U.S. [my family] put the idea in my head that I should stay. My sister was telling me I could study and work here. My sister was telling me I could do all these things while also helping my mom. Well, she convinced me, and I stayed." Before long, Fátima found work, married, and had children.

As mothers confront anchor baby debates, children are also privy to anti-immigrant discourses. Fátima sees firsthand how her US citizen children are impacted by news of anti-immigrant policies. As a result, she no longer watches the news, but the damage has already been done. When I ask Fátima about media representations of mixed-status families, she becomes somber as she recalls one particularly difficult moment:

> Well in that regard, a few months back my children and I were watching television and there was a news story about how a family was separated by deportation. It was something very hard for us, but very hard, because the children started crying and yelling for their dad. My kids don't see their dad and I don't know if that has something to do with it, but it was such a hard moment especially for my daughter because she started crying and was crying for her dad to come back and she said that she didn't want her dad to be deported, even though I am not sure if she knows what that is. Afterward, I stopped watching the news. I stopped watching

altogether. Now whatever is going to happen is going to happen. I talked to my daughter and told her that is not going to happen to our family. I told her we will always be together, but it's so ugly for our family to see that on TV. We see little babies who have nothing to do with this and are separated from their families.

Fátima had been in the country for over fifteen years at the time of our interview and has two US citizen children. Her family stopped watching the news after what felt like a recurring trauma at seeing families separated. Yet, Fátima's family sometimes catch moments of news during commercial breaks when watching other television programs. Fátima wants to be informed, but much of what she and her children hear or see in the media frightens them. The messages are constant reminders to her American children that they are vulnerable to family separation and threats to their citizenship. It is in this way that children consume messaging about their belonging in the country. To cope, Fátima encourages her children not to worry and to "leave it in God's hands."[62] Since her separation from her husband, she has relied more on her faith to overcome challenges.

Like the young citizens I interviewed, these mothers and children recognize birthright citizenship debates as intertwined with the issue of deportation. Fátima shares that she has conversations with her adolescent son about these topics. She recalls one particularly poignant conversation with her son:

He says [deportation] is unjust but I tell him those are how the laws are. I tell him what I think is unjust is that they would try to take away his [birthright citizenship]. I think, and I tell him, "OK, maybe I am here where I shouldn't be and I don't have documents or permission, so this I understand, but you all, the children, no, this is too sad."

As we learned from the comments of young citizens, deportation and birthright citizenship are viewed as inseparable political issues. Mothers may see their place in the United States as tenuous, but they find it morally difficult to accept that their children's citizenship may be challenged. Reflecting more on birthright citizenship, Fátima "talks back" to birthright reformers:

> I would say that the sun rises for everyone. I think those people must be egotistical. I say this because they have jobs and so can us immigrants. We also contribute. Immigrants also create businesses and create jobs for communities. We come here to work and to push our children to succeed and so we don't come here to be a burden. We come here to succeed.

Fátima believes that everyone deserves an opportunity. However, even if we are to believe that birthright citizenship debates will not result in any actual policy change, Fátima's everyday family life suggests that they are "getting the message" about their undesirability in this country.

Finally, I turn to Karina, who is not an undocumented mother but was born into a mixed-status family and later formed a mixed-status family of her own. From this dual perspective, Karina is the daughter of formerly undocumented parents but also observes her daughter's experience of having an undocumented father. When we first met, I did not know Karina's partner is undocumented. Karina learned about the details of my research when we met at a public event where she introduced herself to me as a possible resource to recruit families through a connection she had with a local nonprofit. It was several months later that Karina disclosed her own story to me. Karina's undocumented partner, Arturo, was detained when we scheduled an interview. Even though Karina and her partner have a US citizen daughter, that does not protect her partner from being detained or possibly deported.

I was not surprised Karina was familiar with the subject of anchor babies, since she closely follows immigration-related news. During our interview, Karina becomes noticeably upset as she grunts, "Oh, those famous anchor babies." Karina elaborates that the original anchor babies were the children of European immigrants and colonizers: "At one point, there was a person in their family that was an immigrant, and they had kids and those were their anchor babies." Reflecting on her intimate familiarity with detention and her partner's previous deportation, Karina adds:

> If we look at our immigration system and our undocumented individuals, most of them have kids, and that doesn't mean they get any special treatment. They are still undocumented, and having kids doesn't give them any legal leeway here, so I really disagree with that anchor baby term.

Look at my child; her dad has a US citizen child, and he can't [legalize]. Many people have kids, three or four kids, and they still can't fix their legal status based on this anchor theory, so I definitely do not agree with that term at all.

Having experienced immigration enforcement in her family life, Karina knows that the anchor baby theory is not based on reality. If it were true, she posits, her daughter Lana would be able to legalize her father or protect him from the continued terror of immigration enforcement. Karina had already "talked back" to her colleague who recently brought up the subject of anchor babies. During our interview she relays her counterstory:

I would say look at the statistics and the data on undocumented immigrants having children. So, tell me, where is your anchor baby theory coming from indicating that if you have kids, you have priority here? There is no priority here. . . . I just had this conversation with one of my coworkers . . . who told me: "I really dislike that people come to this country and have anchor babies and take opportunities away from other people." I said, "That's not true. How many individuals live here with kids? All grown kids? And that has given them what kind of benefits? No benefits." She said, "Well, I'm fifth generation. My great-grandmother migrated here." She's Caucasian, and I told her, "So, you are telling me your parents' parents were the anchor babies." And she just looked at me like I guess it hit her. I don't know. She changed the subject. I think everybody forgets because they are not in that situation anymore.

European immigrants also had children who served as family links to the country. Karina finds that people stop caring about immigrant families when their own family migration histories are generations behind them. Karina, like other members of mixed-status families, was quick to point out that since European Americans cannot be native to the United States, they operate with the privilege of a kind of amnesia about their immigrant ancestors' migration history, including the fact that some immigrants arrived without any formal authorization or before some restrictive immigration policies were in place. Members of mixed-status families have a sense that those who are now many generations past their immigrant roots forget about their family origins and then oppose support for contemporary immigrant families. Karina's family, however, cannot forget. Karina was eventually able to reunite with her partner, but in the months that ensued, her family relocated and did what they could to protect Arturo from deportation.

Conclusion

A significant aspect of citizenship is membership. The state creates legal categories of inclusion and exclusion along citizenship lines, but citizen members also participate in the enforcement of who does and does not count as a citizen.[63] Confronted with anchor baby narratives, members of mixed-status families use counterstories to claim belonging for themselves and their families. These counterstories rely on personal histories and observations, as well as historical and legal examples related to US racialized violence and nation-making. With their complex and overlapping claims, the voices here simultaneously reject the term "anchor baby" and universalize its application to all descendants of immigrants. Arguments made in talk-back claims illustrate that the young adults in mixed-status families are not passively consuming anti-immigrant rhetoric. Clearly, young adults' knowledge and observations of family, friends, and coworkers served as a protective shield against believing and internalizing this harmful rhetoric.[64]

Mothers who saw themselves depicted in the media as opportunistic breeders did not find their realities reflected in these debates. They drew from moral claims, as well as those that dispute the narrative or focus on the repercussions of restricting birthright citizenship, to talk back to mainstream discourse about their motherhood and families. For mothers, anti-immigrant debates sometimes had heavy consequences. They feared the outcomes of such debates, especially as this discourse impacted their children. Mothers described their children reacting with worry, anger, confusion, and tears. This occurred in conjunction with broader reactions from children who watched television news coverage of family deportations—such news stories elicited the most emotional responses among children. Children's reactions cannot be carelessly dismissed. Exposure to anti-immigrant rhetoric has deleterious health impacts on Latino children.[65] Mothers, who already had many responsibilities on their plates, were met with the added emotional task of comforting their children.

Even as I believe that some of the public debates about birthright citizenship aim to create spectacles and not necessarily policy change, these political issues must be considered with caution. As I collected data in 2015–2016, members of mixed-status families feared a Trump candidacy, but few actually believed a reality TV star with no political experience would win. Further, although birthright citizenship has not been eliminated or altered, elected officials running on campaign platforms against citizenship for children in mixed-status families have won reelection.[66] This would suggest that there is some popular support for restricting birthright citizenship. On a global scale, citizenship has been up for debate, and various countries have successfully restricted birthright citizenship in recent years.[67]

Further, the ways in which mixed-status families are under threat take on different forms across various states and locales. In Texas, undocumented parents were prevented from obtaining their children's birth certificates. The issue arose in 2013 when local officials told parents that they would no longer accept the *matricula*, or Mexican consular identification, in the process of obtaining a birth certificate.[68] This presented a problem for undocumented parents who are unlikely to have US government or state photo identification. In effect, this roadblock presented very real bureaucratic problems for mixed-status families and US citizen babies who were obviously much too young to request their own birth certificates. Eventually, several immigrant parents took the matter to the courts and won their legal battle to use Mexican voter identification cards to access their child's birth certificate.[69] Parents from Central America were also able to get acceptable identity documents from their local consular office.[70] This outcome, however, does not rectify the several years families had to be without a child's birth certificate or the more concerning problem about how individual states may enact their own indirect challenges to birthright citizenship.

The individuals that conservative elected officials refer to as "anchor babies" eventually grow up to become adults who can advocate for themselves and their communities. Contrary to what some elected officials publicly argue, these young Americans are not born because their parents are trying to find a pathway to residency, even as many parents do hope that legal pathways will become available to them. The counter-stories of mixed-status families provide evidence to dispute damaging political myths, and these families' histories and knowledge remind us to embrace the depth of the human experience. Perhaps their counter-stories remind us that our political efforts are better spent on supporting all kinds of families and breaking away from historical cycles that only repeat disenfranchisement and pain.

4

Moral Boundaries and the Right to Belong

I often find myself taking new bus routes to the next interview or event. These bus trips offer me a literal window onto the streets and local economy of Los Angeles. On a late afternoon bus ride from Malibu, I was distracted by the expansive view of the Pacific Ocean, but I also noticed that most riders were Latino laborers, probably returning home from jobs in exquisite private estates or fine dining establishments. On other days, looking out the bus window at the orange trees in the San Fernando Valley made me think of the Mexican and Japanese immigrant agricultural workers who likely planted them.[1] Heading east to Pasadena, I sometimes fall for the romance of its Victorian and art deco architecture that transport me into an old black-and-white Hollywood movie. However, these nostalgic sights also reminded me that Southern California was also home to sundown towns—places where African Americans and other non-White groups were barred from living, but not working.[2] White residents and business owners still needed laborers of color during the day, hence the exclusionary restrictions once the sun went down.

Eventually, with the introduction of fair housing policies, such practices became illegal, yet histories continue to touch our current day. As it was decades prior, the siren song of Los Angeles is possible because of workers—predominantly (immigrant) workers of color—who cook the food in the restaurants and clean the hotels that make other people's leisure and business possible. And, of course, there are workers who make the lives of residents feasible by caring for their children and their elderly, remodeling their homes, and maintaining their impeccable lawns.

Many of the immigrants I interviewed and observed were participating in the labor force. Aside from working in what has been called "brown-collar jobs,"[3] or jobs with a high concentration of Latino immigrants, many immigrants found themselves in gender-segregated workplaces. Undocumented men whom I interviewed worked in landscaping, construction, electrical repair, factories, restaurants, and auto repair. Undocumented women labored in domestic/care work, in factories, in the sewing trade, in sales, and in restaurants. Youth with DACA typically had access to jobs at nonprofits, legal services, schools, and universities.

How do members of mixed-status families—particularly undocumented parents—experience and articulate their belonging to the United States? What is their vision for immigration reform? Without legal authorization to reside in the country, there are a number of ways undocumented immigrants might construct their membership in the United States, the country that is their longtime home and their children's homeland. Members of mixed-status families claim that undocumented immigrants are worthy of being in the United States primarily because of their economic and social contributions as laborers and because of their distance from criminal archetypes promulgated in the public imagination. They further use these logics to express eligibility and hope for an eventual immigration reform.

I address how undocumented immigrants emphasize their labor and economic contributions. Immigrants argue for their right to be in the United States because their removal inspires a critically important question: *And who will do the work?* Variations of this sentiment position undocumented immigrants as economically necessary to the nation-state and to their local contexts. Researchers have captured how contemporary undocumented immigrants articulate their worthiness of residing in the United States by emphasizing their labor contributions and work ethic.[4] Such claims also are rooted in a long history of Mexican labor in the United States. Even when Mexicans in the United States had citizenship in the years following the Treaty of Guadalupe Hidalgo in 1848, they de facto experienced various forms of exclusion, segregation, and land theft. Their US membership, in other words, was contested. Mexicans in the Southwest in the later part of the nineteenth century and into the twentieth century relied on their labor to make citizenship claims. Glenn explains:

> Mexicans acted on and articulated an alternative understanding of membership in the American community. Workers based their claims to belonging on their having labored in the United States. They pointed to the

toil and sweat Mexicans had expended in growing food that fed Americans, reclaiming agricultural land, and building railroads and other structures that were the source of American wealth.[5]

Such alternative claims were partly necessary because both Mexican immigrants and Mexican Americans were segregated, pushed into coercive wage labor, and de facto excluded from American citizenship.[6] Similar claims are still adopted by undocumented immigrants, although claims of belonging can also be based on logics shaped by family, cultural values, and human rights perspectives.

I find that undocumented immigrants often make economic and neoliberal arguments to express their belonging in the United States. Their claims involve the family mainly when immigrants are making a connection between economically supporting their children or when they are claiming they are raising children to become productive, economically self-sufficient members of society. It is in this way that undocumented immigrants in mixed-status families make claims of cultural citizenship. Without formal inclusion within a nation, cultural citizenship is still a way marginalized people can make claims about their belonging by centering their own experiences and contributions.[7] The promise of cultural citizenship is that it allows communities to seek respect, dignity, and rights.[8]

Pro-immigrant labor-based arguments often go hand in hand with a claim that immigrants are not criminals. Immigrants do commit crimes at lower rates than do US-born citizens.[9] On an individual basis, some undocumented immigrants emphasize their worker roles while also highlighting their clean legal records as reasons they should be able to gain a legal pathway to citizenship. On a larger scale, when members of mixed-status families envision a future for immigrants, they often propose a pathway to citizenship that can be open to immigrants who have been working, raising families, and following the law.

"And Who Will Do the Work?": Articulating Worthiness through Labor

In a Los Angeles home, I chat with Renata about her family history of migration. Renata is a naturalized citizen who can trace her Mexican family back for generations. Many of her relatives had been farmworkers across the United States. Some of these ancestors participated in the Bracero program, a government program (in effect from 1942 to 1964) that formalized a system by which temporary workers from Mexico could work seasonally in the United States, mostly in agriculture. Over the course of more than two decades, five million legal Mexican migrant workers participated in this guest worker program.[10] This policy was instituted during a time when migration from Mexico was waning. By the time that program was formally terminated, the system had already set a foundation that relied on Mexican migration and would subsequently encourage a flow of Mexican labor migration—legal or otherwise.[11]

Decades later, Mexicans and Mexican Americans remember stories of grandfathers working as braceros, or unauthorized workers, tales of family loss, and triumph in the face of tremendous adversity. When Mexicans and Mexican Americans tell me these stories, they beam with pride remembering the contributions of their ancestors, although their affects become somber when they recall stories of loss and exploitation. Mexicans and Mexican Americans also have stories of family separations forced by the state, and they remember how working fathers and grandfathers were deported. Mexicans have long had this labor-migration relationship with the United States. In this sense, migration for wage earning is nothing new. What has changed is the increasingly fixed and criminalized nature of undocumented status today. Although Renata was able to eventually obtain US citizenship through family ties, her husband, Pedro, remains undocumented after residing in the country for more than two decades.

As Renata and I talk, Pedro enters the living room wearing a black shirt and gray cap. He had been in the front yard finishing up an oil change on Renata's car. With distressed and oil-stained jeans, Pedro swiftly excuses himself, noting he will need to get washed up before our interview. Noticeably refreshed, but still looking tired, Pedro later returns and is ready for the interview. Like many Mexican undocumented men, Pedro has held various jobs doing manual labor and service work. After a brief stint working at a restaurant, he started working in construction. As of late, he has been working in kitchen remodeling but expresses that, now in his fifties, he feels increasingly worn out.

Pedro is surprised I want to interview him. I don't find suspicion in his voice so much as a disgruntled sense of curiosity. "Why would you want to interview *me*, or immigrants like me?" When I tell him that I am interested in how members of mixed-status families experience belonging in this country, he grunts at my explanation, takes off his cap, and responds:

> Well, immigrants, we are here for what we can say is a matter of circumstance, economic need, fate maybe. In any case, we are here to work, and this is why we should be able to stay here. One day, I would like to have my papers. I am a good worker. If they deport us all, just think about that. Think about what that means. We are the workers. We are the ones that help keep this country going. So, maybe I don't have the right to be here in this country, but I know why I am here and why I should be here.

Pedro ostensibly tells me that he does not have a legal claim to belong in the United States, and yet his labor is the vehicle by which he makes a case for his right to be in the country. He does not foresee a future in which he will get papers unless there is widespread amnesty. While Pedro waits for that possibility, the public rhetoric on immigration is not lost on him. "They say . . . we [immigrants] do not belong here. So, they want to kick us out. My question to them is: And who will do the work?" Pedro sighs, slapping his hands on his knees, and it seems that he doesn't want to keep talking about this topic. Renata later tells me he had a hard week. His mother—who is in the United States—is very ill. Pedro already has a lot on his mind.

Undocumented immigrants who emphasize their labor and economic contributions sometimes contrast themselves to American Whites, perceiving them as less hardworking and/or unwilling to do the difficult jobs Mexican undocumented immigrants perform. When I think of how undocumented immigrants place their contributions in relation to others, I think of Emiliana. When I meet Emiliana, she immediately discloses to me that she talks too much. Her daughter warned me of the same issue, but I tell Emiliana that for an interviewer, that is not a problem. Emiliana is in her fifties and has been undocumented in the United States for over twenty-five years. She wants a pathway to citizenship, so I ask her what kind of policy change she would propose, and she responds as follows:

> People always try to maximize the negative on the news, but you never see anything good. The good news is minimized. So, I listen to the news, but when they are talking about immigrants, they don't talk about the good we do or how we contribute to the country. I don't feel like I am a problem for the United States because I am working to eat, not asking for food. I am proving myself with my job. I don't feel like I am also taking a job away from an American because with this job that I have, I don't see American women doing it. You understand? So, I am not taking the job away from anyone. I don't see Americans wanting my job. They just don't. So, I don't feel like I am taking anyone's job.

While Emiliana does not outline a possible policy for immigration reform, it is evident the public discourse on immigration weighs on her mind. She provides a critique of the media's representation of immigrants, while also challenging a long-standing anti-immigrant narrative about how immigrants take jobs away from Americans. As a house-cleaner, Emiliana performs work that has long been relegated to women of color, including immigrants.[12] Geographically and historically, there has been some variation, but the job was usually not deemed appropriate for White middle-class women, nor was it work White women generally wanted, especially when factory or office jobs became available to them.[13] In Los Angeles, Latina immigrant women are channeled into this labor.

Importantly, as an immigrant mother of three, Emiliana has work that challenges the raced and gendered narrative of the Latina immigrant woman as a welfare drain. Emiliana's reference to "working to eat, not asking for food," is a direct response to this stereotype that views immigrant women as abusing state services and resources. Even when she was pregnant, she made it clear that she did not want to apply for or receive any government financial assistance for prenatal care. Emiliana recalls that even as she refused financial assistance, she was confused about why health care staff insisted she apply for a program that could cover some of her medical costs. Her critique continues as she positions herself and her community as contributing members to society:

We, the Latinos, are good business for the economy. We do the cheap jobs that no one wants, and we create jobs through our families and if we are good parents—and many immigrant parents come to this country to advance themselves and their families and not because we want to be stuck—so the majority do our best so that our children get educated, seek good careers, become good people, benefit society, and involve themselves in productive community efforts. In the news, all they show is gangbangers and rapists and killers. Where I live in my building, we see everyone in the parking lot because we are leaving to go to work! The majority of us are going off to work. It's rare the mother who stays home because she has an infant or young child. Everyone that I know here and everyone that I see, they work. The older kids go to school or they go to work too. So, the majority are working. . . . The majority of families that we know are productive people.

By contrasting what she sees on the news with her reality, Emiliana argues that she and other Mexican immigrants are contributing to US society. Further, she contends, immigrants not only contribute, but they are not in competition with Americans, since they perform the labor or take "cheap jobs that no one wants." Based on the number of workers in the building where she lives, Emiliana knows that many immigrant mothers are not afforded the luxury of staying home to care for infants but instead must go to work. Emiliana also positions immigrant reproduction as economically and socially productive by arguing that parents raise children who become educated professionals and participate in "productive community efforts." In this way, she can do the symbolic work of distancing herself from some of the more harmful depictions of Latina immigrant motherhood.

Similarly, Berta, another immigrant mother, views undocumented immigrants as crucial to the American economy. To her, it seems nonsensical that those who oppose undocumented immigration fight so hard to challenge the belonging of these immigrants. When Berta heard in the news that Donald Trump, at the time a presidential candidate, was proposing mass deportations, she thought the idea did not make any sense. I ask her what she would say to Trump in response to his policy plan of deporting undocumented immigrants, and she responds as follows:

We all have a right to something. Just because we are Latino doesn't mean
we don't have rights. We are the ones that work. We help this country a lot
because a White guy isn't going to start doing all the gardening work or
go work in the fields. We do all these jobs. No one has the right to demean
people. I would say other things, [laughs] rude things.

Even though part of Berta's framing of undocumented immigrants'
belonging is partially family-based, she highlights how the country depends on immigrant labor. Recognizing the concentration of Latino immigrants in fields like gardening and agriculture, it is clear to Berta that
no "White guy" is clamoring to fill these positions. Employers also partake in the relational assessing of workers by viewing Latino immigrant
workers as more appropriate for agricultural labor than African Americans, White Americans, and second-generation Latinos.[14] Importantly,
even though Berta does not have legal authorization to reside in the
country, she advocates for herself by saying she still has rights—which
can include civil and human rights. Perhaps more critical is how Berta
asserts that her rights should not be diminished because of her racialized identity as a Latina. It is also certainly true that even as Berta advocates for undocumented immigrants, she, like many of her co-ethnics,
views immigration debates and policies as a reflection of anti-Latino
sentiment. For Berta, some of the policies on the news are very much
about denigrating Latino immigrants and Latino communities in general. Ultimately, undocumented immigrants are privy to how Latino or
Mexican identity and illegality sometimes are constructed as one and
the same, making matters of immigration a deeply racialized issue.[15]

When immigrants claim they help the country by doing the jobs no
one else wants to do, they emphasize that they are not belittling honest work. For Paloma, the topic of denigration struck a chord. Paloma
wants her children to become professionals, but she worries that they
will forget their roots and, worse yet, look down on her for being undocumented or for being employed in the service sector. As an undocumented working mother, she begins to explain her thoughts on this
matter and how it intersects more broadly with labor and privilege:

Some people would say that immigrants without papers deserve the
worst jobs. A lot of [people] say that they should do jobs that are con-

sidered denigrated. I would not say that because people need to sustain their families. Someone born here isn't going to do work that an immigrant would do. Citizens don't want to work in fast food. Nobody wants a job washing the floor or toilet. You may even think to yourself: I don't want this kind of job either. But it's work, and who else is going to do it? Who else is going to want this work? I wish more people would think about this. There are professional people who can leave a job when they want. Good for them because they worked so hard for their degree. These professionals hire people to clean their house or maintain their yards. So, if you are [a] professional, but if you didn't have the person that helps you, what would you do? My point is that we need immigrants. We need people to do this work because citizens won't want to do it. For me, my children [are] citizens, and I wouldn't want them to do menial work. I am not denigrating that work because [thanks to] that person you have clean clothes and [a] clean house, or your worker took your kids to school.

Paloma's point centers on her worth as a worker and argues for a sense of honor for work that sometimes is denigrated. Paloma insists her labor is important and valuable, but it is also difficult work that she does not want for her children. Researchers and poets alike have captured this painful dilemma; while immigrant mothers seek dignity for the labor they perform, they hope that their children will not follow in their occupational footsteps.[16]

Without outsourcing caring, cleaning, and home maintenance work, Paloma wonders, what would professionals do? Paloma's point gets to the heart of a feminist debate about middle-class women's increased labor force participation and a failure of the state and/or women's male heterosexual partners to provide solutions for care and domestic work. As dual-income households became the norm, institutionalized childcare options were limited, and extended families often were unable or unwilling to provide childcare for families with working mothers. Consequently, middle-class families turned to outsourcing care and cleaning labor. In Los Angeles, middle-class working families hire Latina immigrant women to pick up the slack at home.[17] As feminist scholar Grace Chang has argued, undocumented Latinas became the new "employable mothers" in the 1990s.[18]

It is within this context that Paloma's claim to belonging in the United States is based on her labor and her understanding that she "does the work that makes all other work possible."[19] This is a familiar claim made by immigrant and workers' rights advocacy groups as well as pro-immigrant employers, media, and public officials.[20] Participants in my study favor economic claims because they strongly believe them to be true and feel other claims, such as family-based ones, are less persuasive. Members of mixed-status families sometimes shared that they used these economic claims because they believe Americans can be less sympathetic about the circumstances of undocumented immigrants but are more likely persuaded by the financial or labor gain extracted from immigrants. In thinking about her undocumented partner, Karina shares, "I know this country runs on money. When they do policy, let's talk about money. Let's not talk about someone's feelings or what is right or wrong. Let's talk about money. . . . Let's look at the taxes these [undocumented] individuals contribute, and all of their labor." Contrary to popular belief, undocumented immigrants do pay a wide range of taxes, including annual income tax. Paying taxes, further, is often viewed as a prerequisite for being an American, as well as a quintessential American duty.[21]

As immigrants center their belonging on their economic contributions, they also discuss how having a clean criminal record makes one worthy of residing in the United States. Further, they blame other immigrants with criminal histories as perpetuating the stigma that the larger undocumented community faces. We cannot understand how social actors mitigate stigma without understanding how stigma is produced in the first place.

Moral Boundaries and Deflecting Stigma

Without a legal claim to belong in the United States, undocumented immigrants claim their worthiness by arguing against popular narratives that concern them. For example, they manage the looming stigma of criminality that follows undocumented immigrants. Sociologist Erving Goffman, has written extensively about stigma, and defines it as "the situation of the individual who is disqualified from full social acceptance."[22] Undocumented immigrants are stigmatized, even in the language applied to them—the words "illegals" and "aliens" imply a designation of undesirability, nonbelonging, and criminality. Goffman elucidates that when a person is stigmatized, they are "reduced in our minds from a whole and usual person to a tainted, discounted one."[23] Further, illegality is often racialized Mexican, requiring Mexican undocumented immigrants to deal with the suspicion of illegality or the consequences of stigma one way or another.

This stigma is perpetuated by strands of the popular media that promote a "Latino threat narrative" that constructs Mexican immigrants as economically draining the state, taking jobs, and changing the demographic and cultural landscape of the United States.[24] Threat narratives include maritime metaphors that describe immigrants as floods and disasters, discursively marking undocumented immigrants as threatening.[25] Alongside these discourses, federal and some state immigration policies increasingly shifted toward criminalizing undocumented people. Across the country, 287(g) agreements partnered local law enforcement with ICE agents to detain and apprehend undocumented immigrants—a move that further criminalized immigrants just by their continued presence in the country. After the terrorist attacks on September 11, 2001, immigration affairs were transferred to the Department of Homeland Security, and unauthorized immigration discourses centered on protecting the country from criminals and terrorists.[26]

In this context, undocumented immigrants were criminalized as lawbreakers. Still, there is also a discursive difference between people who break immigration laws and people who are undocumented and commit other offenses. When former president Obama announced on November 20, 2014, his plan for DAPA, he made a distinction between law-abiding and criminal undocumented immigrants and promised to deport only those with criminal pasts:

> Even as we are a nation of immigrants, we're also a nation of laws. Undocumented workers broke our immigration laws, and I believe that they must be held accountable—especially those who may be dangerous. That's why, over the past six years, deportations of criminals are up 80 percent. And that's why we're going to keep focusing enforcement resources on actual threats to our security. Felons, not families. Criminals, not children. Gang members, not a mom who's working hard to provide for her kids. We'll prioritize, just like law enforcement does every day.[27]

Obama's speech marks undocumented immigrants as lawbreakers, and yet, he also makes stark distinctions between felons and families, gang members and mothers. His rhetoric creates boundaries that construct criminality and family ties as mutually exclusive; one is either a felon or a family member, a gang member or a mother who works hard for her children. Importantly, Obama's speech is somewhat reflective of the boundary work immigrants also adopt. Indeed, DAPA was explicitly promoted as a program only for deserving immigrants.

However, DAPA never became accessible for any families. Even when a Texas judge issued a preliminary injunction on the deferred action program in 2014, DAPA remained a possibility for families until the Supreme Court blocked the program in June 2016. After the death of Antonin Scalia, the eight-person Supreme Court was deadlocked in a 4–4 decision on whether the program should be accessible. Former president Obama described the news as "heartbreaking for the millions of immigrants who have made their lives here."[28] Undeniably, the heartbreak was legible. I heard parents' deep disappointment. One mother exclaimed between tears, "I feel impotent. What gives me hope now are my children. I am not eligible for DACA. . . . My only hope was DAPA. One comes here to better themselves and not to be criminals like some say." While DAPA was not made possible for families, DAPA-eligible parents still saw themselves as deserving of such a program because of their family ties and nonexistent criminal records.

Donald Trump began his presidential campaign by explicitly blaming Mexico for sending to the United States its rapists, drug dealers, and criminals. During a presidential debate, Trump justified his plans for securing the border by claiming that "we have some bad *hombres* here, and we're going to get them out."[29] In these and other statements, Trump discussed Mexican immigrants explicitly as criminals. Throughout his campaign and again while in office, Trump made connections between immigration and crime. As president, he flipped a common antideportation refrain about keeping families together by arguing that undocumented immigrants tear American families apart when they murder citizens.[30] Mexican undocumented immigrants feel stigmatized by this rhetoric and deflect this stigma by engaging in boundary work to position themselves away from Trump's claims. In other words, Mexican immigrants claiming their belonging in a moment after Trump's infamous election speech pushed them to express *what they are not.*

The stigmatization of undocumented immigrants is undoubtedly powerful. Undocumented youth who have been raised in the United States view and experience being undocumented as a stigma.[31] In a study with immigrant families, sociologist Joanna Dreby found that Mexican American children learn that immigrants are stigmatized, even if immigrants are lawfully present.[32] While children can be proud of their parents' ancestral roots in Mexico, in her study they conflated immigration and illegality, which was harmful to their sense of self. Some Asian undocumented students also try to emphasize their legal entry to the states to deflect stigma and distance themselves from border-crossing Latinos.[33]

Marginalized groups often assert their worth and deflect stigma by engaging in boundary work. For instance, in Michèle Lamont's classic study of working-class men, they constructed themselves as moral because of their dedication to working hard.[34] Boundary work is also accomplished among young women of color who manage gendered and raced risk narratives about their reproduction and sexuality. Young women of color who are not pregnant or parenting create "identities of distance" to uphold themselves as responsible and independent women.[35] In doing so, they participate in a politics of respectability by policing themselves and their peers, and stigmatizing their pregnant and parenting counterparts. Middle-class Latinos also partake in similarly situated boundary work. For example, middle-class Latinos employ discursive strategies to combat the everyday racism they face by making statements such as "I'm not your typical Latina/o."[36] This previous research attests to how individuals cope with their marginalization and demonstrates their sense-making around dominant discourses—even if such strategies create additional boundaries of worthiness that leave others out. For immigrants, this boundary work allows them to vie for recognition and personhood. Research on Latino immigrants in Phoenix has shown that immigrants are actively fighting against their criminalization by presenting themselves as moral people who are against lawbreaking.[37] Such processes are adopted by immigrants and encouraged by governments, since they sometimes reward immigrant "good" behavior by granting legalized status.[38]

Historically marginalized groups—from Black civil rights leaders to gay and lesbian organizers—highlight the image and needs of normative, respectable individuals at the expense of those who fall outside those bounds (e.g., those with criminal pasts; those who live queer, nonheteronormative lives) as part of a political strategy to gain acceptance from the mainstream. By adhering to respectability politics, a marginalized group tries to "demonstrate their compatibility with the 'mainstream.'"[39] Therein lies one contradiction; undocumented immigrants commit crimes at lower rates than US-born citizens.[40] The undocumented population as a whole is actually already quite respectable. However, by learning about this population's efforts to resist their marginalization and boldly claim their belonging, readers will learn how undocumented immigrants construct themselves as worthy while distancing themselves from imagined criminal immigrants. It is these criminals who are considered unworthy for legalization and the source of blame for the stigmatization of their ethnic and immigrant community. However, immigrants in my study do not think all crimes are considered equal. Some immigrants believe that crimes that facilitate access to labor—driving without a license to get to one's workplace and using a fraudulent identity to access employment—are sometimes an unfortunate but necessary risk if individuals are to financially support their families. Violent or dangerous crimes, on the other hand, are strongly denounced. Thus, immigrants create their own subjective hierarchies of deservingness for solidarity and eligibility for a future immigration reform.

Por Uno Perdemos Todos/Because of One, We All Lose: Deflecting and Reproducing Criminal Stigma

To immigrants, anti-immigrant rhetoric is painful to hear, particularly when such discourses are manifested in policies that criminalize all undocumented immigrants. Immigrants distance themselves from immigrant peers who commit violent offenses, often referencing the kind of crimes Trump said that Mexican immigrants commit in the United States, such as rape, murder, and dealing drugs.[41] As immigrants deflect the stigma of being undocumented, they emphasize their clean criminal records or the moral reasoning behind some of their choices. While doing so, they also demarcate immigrants with records as harming the prospects of all undocumented immigrants. In this way, undocumented immigrants use variations of the phrase *por uno perdemos todos*, or *por uno pierden todos* (because of one, we/they all lose), to highlight how the actions of a few can have negative consequences for an entire community.

Hernán has been in the United States for over twenty-five years and at first felt out of place in his new country. He experienced the initial migration and settlement in the United States as a culture shock. Hernán recalls being a young man, navigating the bus system and his new home as best he could. Initially afraid of *la migra*, with time Hernán came to feel more comfortable in navigating public space and laboring as an undocumented immigrant. He no longer lives with much fear in carrying out everyday activities because, as he puts it, he is "doing right and being right." He hopes there will be an opportunity to eventually obtain legal status. Still, he believes that the actions of other immigrants or co-ethnics can shape his experience of belonging and his access to eventual legalization. When I ask Hernán to discuss immigration reform, the plan he describes leaves out some immigrants. He suggests, "I say it's not fair to give permission to . . . delinquents, criminals. Because of some, we all lose. Some criminals make us look bad and they sort of ruin it for the rest of us. People think 'Oh, he's Latino' so because of a few, we all lose." Hernán views Latino immigrants with criminal backgrounds as producing the stigma that Latinos are criminals. Consequently, he shares that it is harder for immigration reform to be accomplished if members of the public have this image of Latino undocumented immigrants on their minds. Even as the perception of Latino immigrants as criminally prone persists, it is not supported by research on Latino immigrants and crime. Criminologists, for example, have long noted what they call a "Latino Paradox" because the presence of Latino immigrants actually helps reduce crime in neighborhoods, despite many of them living in underserved urban communities.[42]

Fátima and Hernán share a similar view. Fátima does not feel like she can rightfully call herself an American, but she does consider herself part of the country. She tells me, "This country has given me so much and in a certain way I do love it. I am grateful because I have been here a number of years and my children were born here and I consider myself Mexican, but I love this country." Fátima wants to eventually access US

legal permanent residency and citizenship, but she is concerned that the
public imagination has a negative view of Mexican immigrants:

> I guess there are some immigrants who are selling drugs, killing, and
> raping, so I am on board with punishing them, but people see a Mexican
> doing that and they think we are all the same. Well, no, in reality there
> are many of us that came here to work and to give it our all to earn a little
> more for our families.

Fátima places the onus of blame on other criminal immigrants who
make law-abiding immigrants look bad. She also underscores how ethnicity becomes an indicator of generalizing all Mexicans as criminally
prone. Certainly, Fátima, Hernán, and others were critical of these racialized associations. Part of the issue is that the media perpetuates the
notion that the Mexican body is a lawbreaking body,[43] but Fátima also
blames individual lawbreakers who confirm the stereotype. Fátima,
then, thinks immigration reform is harder to accomplish when the hegemonic image of Mexican immigrants is that of drug dealers, murderers, and rapists.

Fátima and Hernán are certainly not alone in advocating for a reform
that excludes immigrants with criminal histories. Members of mixed-
status families who were not or no longer undocumented also expressed
similar eligibility criteria for citizenship. Renata, a naturalized citizen,
suggested the government delineate which immigrants deserve amnesty
by including a background check that excluded immigrants who have
committed violent crimes.

> C: Ideally, in terms of policy, what do you want to see change? What
> kind of immigration reform would you suggest?
> R: Well, that the president gives papers, but that they check for those
> who do deserve them. For example, people say that we come here
> to rape and murder, but no, the government could check on this.
> There is a saying about this. They should check for the people that do
> deserve it because they have been here so many years working. There
> are people that come here truly to do bad things, but we are not all
> bad. I would ask that they pass the laws to make this possible, but I
> would ask that they check to make sure that the people deserve it.

Renata also had to undergo a similar process for applying for her green card, and later for naturalized citizenship. She imagines a similar process for her husband if amnesty becomes available. Later, almost forgetting myself, I ask Renata what saying she had been thinking of earlier. "Oh, yes!" she responds, and she says something that essentially translates to "because of one, we all lose."

Amanda, an undocumented young adult, has lived in the United States for over half her life and recently became a DACA recipient. She had hoped that there could be a program, such as DAPA, to protect her mother and older sister. In the long term, she wants an amnesty program for her loved ones so they can live securely. In thinking about a broad reform, Amanda laid out her vision by expressing how undocumented status should not automatically imply criminality:

> I understand the concerns that the government has about criminals and the fear of giving them residency, but I think it is important to realize the difference between undocumented people and criminals. There might be some undocumented people who are criminals, but you don't have to be a criminal if you are undocumented. There is a line between those two categories. At least for DACA when you apply you have to submit so many items, like you have to finish school and submit records and stuff like that, you get fingerprinted. So, things like that can help us narrow in on how to go about doing a reform.

Part of the reason DACA applicants get fingerprinted is for a background check. Undocumented youth who meet educational eligibility requirements for DACA are ineligible if they have certain crimes on their record. In the early years of the undocumented youth movement, youth activists wore graduation caps and gowns to emphasize their moral worth, educational perseverance, and other frames reliant on respectability politics.[44] Segments of the undocumented youth movement, but especially allies and elected leaders, framed young peoples' worthiness by arguing that they migrated through no fault of their own—thereby implicitly constructing their parents as lawbreakers.[45] Such an approach created boundaries between "good" Dreamers and "bad" criminalized immigrants, but it was also an effective strategy in persuading those on the fence about immigrant-friendly policies for undocumented youth.[46]

Yet, years into the movement, some undocumented youth moved away from such so-called Dreamer narratives, particularly when their parents and communities continued to be criminalized, targeted, and deported.[47]

Not All Crimes and Infractions Are Considered Equal

The boundaries between good immigrant and bad immigrant are not clear-cut. When immigrants reference other immigrants damaging the reputation of the immigrant community, they sometimes highlight heinous crimes, such as rape and murder. Immigrants who may actually have criminal records or a history of committing crimes or infractions also discuss an immigration reform that should be available only to immigrants with clean records. Even so, immigrants describe their reasoning behind these hierarchies or the justifications they have for certain crimes.

Rosario has been undocumented for twenty-eight years and has been working her entire adult life. During her twenties and thirties, Rosario was a single mother supporting her family. Now in her forties, she is married and has a young child and also an adult daughter from a previous relationship. Her husband is also undocumented. We do an interview during her lunch break at a fast-casual restaurant in Southeast Los Angeles. Since Rosario is on her lunch break, I find her in the restaurant easily. She wears a black apron and visor that signal employment in food service. Rosario works as a promoter of food products across Los Angeles County. She is a people person, which is probably a helpful quality in her line of work. She is also generous and offers to buy me a chicken teriyaki bowl for my lunch. After we sit down, Rosario starts the interview by telling me about her life and values, which include her critique of sexism in Mexico and her struggles with finding appropriate support for her autistic toddler. She already thinks of the United States as her home and sees herself as an American. In between bites of chicken and broccoli, she shares, "I feel like I am more a part of the US than part of Mexico. For me, this is my country. This country has given me a lot. This country has given me my children and opportunities." Despite not having papers, Rosario expresses that she is already too acclimated to life in the United States to want to live anywhere else.

Like many immigrants, it is also evident that Rosario's feeling of Americanness is tied to a belief that the American Dream is possible— that the *opportunity* for economic advancement is there. She is fiercely dedicated to her work because she sees it as the key to family advancement, especially for her young child. Even with all her efforts to achieve economic security and family well-being, Rosario can't help imagining a world that would be radically different for her if amnesty became a reality. However, she notes that immigrants who commit violent crimes might delay amnesty and stigmatize all undocumented immigrants as criminals. As she explains, "You know the saying that because of one, everyone pays?" Rosario, like many immigrants in the United States, is resentful of the image of immigrants as criminals. However, she believes that most undocumented immigrants are not breaking any serious laws. According to a Migration Policy Institute Report, only about 6 percent of the entire undocumented population have been convicted of a felony or serious misdemeanor.[48]

Not all crimes are deemed unacceptable, as Rosario admits that being undocumented sometimes necessitates technically illegal acts, such as driving without a license. These are acts Rosario justifies, explaining, "I am not supposed to drive because I don't have a license, but I mean, I don't go around driving drunk. That would be serious. I don't go to parties. I drive because I have to and my job requires it." In California, driving without a valid driver's license can be a misdemeanor offense.[49] Public transportation options in the urban sprawl of Los Angeles are time-consuming and unreliable, making driving necessary. Rosario is an experienced driver and thus does not see her infraction as something that is irresponsible or even done in the pursuit of pleasure or vice. Instead, she justifies her driving as a harmless, necessary requirement to be gainfully employed. A contradiction of illegality is that, while the country depends on undocumented labor, the necessary preconditions to carry out paid labor sometimes compel immigrants to partake in unlawful behavior such as driving without a license or using false documentation.

Many undocumented immigrants are blocked from accessing legal employment because they do not possess valid Social Security numbers. Some of them circumvent this problem by using documents or Social Security numbers that are not their own. This is something Socorro admitted doing, but she recognized it was a thorny issue. She tells me, "The bad thing is some people use fake papers and do bad things, like take out a credit card and buy things and don't pay. So, I know why people get mad when people use someone else's Social Security number. I did it only to work, so not to abuse it. Just work, and I paid taxes." For a brief time, Socorro used another person's Social Security number to access employment at a factory. She believed this decision wasn't right but considered it necessary only because she used it to gain employment. As she explains in our interview, "I think a lot of people have a negative view of immigrants because maybe some do take advantage of it and used it to get into debt and all that, but not all of us. Not all of us do it to do fraud, because many of us do it to work." As Menjívar and Abrego describe, "The various laws at federal, state, and local levels today seek to punish the behaviors of undocumented immigrants but at the same time push them to spaces outside the law."[50] These actions are born out of necessity to economically support families, not as an effort to purposefully break laws.[51]

Rosario's and Socorro's explanations allow us to see how boundaries are drawn between certain crimes and infractions. Rosario's reasoning about driving without a driver's license was not uncommon. Because she drives safely and mainly to get to her work sites, Rosario believes this makes driving morally acceptable. These logics also help immigrants feel safer if they are stopped by the police. Esteban, for example, no longer fears getting pulled over by the police. Since he views himself as a good, perhaps reformed, immigrant who drives for work purposes, he believes he can justify his driving to law enforcement. When I ask Esteban if he feared getting stopped by the police, he shares:

E: Before, yes. And I'll tell you why. Before I used to drink, so that's why. You know there is a law against drunk driving? So, one way or another I was scared of them, but not now. Now if they stop me for a simple ticket, they just ask to see my vehicle papers and nothing happens. The other day I got stopped and nothing happened because it's been over five years since I've had a drink. I think it has a lot to do with how you present yourself. It's been over five years since I have had anything to drink, so there is no concern.

C: And they accept your [Mexican identification card]?

E: Yes. Yes. The day they stopped me it was because I was going ten miles over the limit and I told them I'm sorry. They looked at my car and saw all the supplies in the car and I told them it was for work. They asked what I do for work and I told them. They said I shouldn't be driving without a license but I told them I have to drive to get to work and that I have to provide for my family. They got my ID and let me go.

At the time of the interview, Esteban had begun the process to obtain his driver's license. Previously, Esteban shared that when he was caught driving under the influence of alcohol, the police would impound his car, but this has not happened in recent years because of his sobriety. In a sanctuary city like Los Angeles, immigrants can feel shielded from the possibility of detention and deportation if they perform as good drivers and citizens. My findings are consistent with other research that finds some immigrants in Los Angeles participate in "moralizing regulation" by performing and positioning themselves as respectable immigrants.[52]

Esteban is critical of how undocumented immigrants are perceived in public discourse. "It's not like what this man says that all Mexicans are drug traffickers, you know, Donald Trump. It's not that they don't exist, but the majority are coming here to work than the ones that are here to sell drugs." Esteban has been working since he was quite young and is proud of his ability to work in an occupation he finds gratifying. Esteban and his wife are hopeful that eventually he may be able to become a legal permanent resident. He suggests that an amnesty should become available to immigrants who meet certain requirements: "A program that includes people who meet the standards. I know that there are certain requirements that need to be met, such as being here a while, working and paying taxes, obviously no criminal record. You have to be someone who is benefiting society." The challenge may be that Esteban does have something on his record. At the time of their separate interviews, Esteban and his wife, Tania, are both hopeful that perhaps DAPA—the program that would have provided temporary protection to undocumented parents—would become accessible. However, Tania expresses uncertainty about DAPA given her concerns about Esteban's eligibility: "I am hoping his case can be expunged. I really do have hope. Obama did stress in the executive order that people that had criminal records would not qualify, but I am thinking it's more about drug dealing or killing someone or something like that." Esteban and Tania attribute his sobriety to their renewed commitment to religious faith. Tania further shares that their family relationship had vastly improved after Esteban completed character-improving classes organized by their church. With these changes, they hope that Esteban can become eligible to change his immigration status.

Changing Esteban's status to legal permanent resident, and eventually citizen, may better match the American identity he wants to fully possess. When I ask Esteban if he considered himself an American, he shares his mixed feelings about the subject:

> Yes and no. Yes, because I feel I have adapted to the systems here. No, because you do feel that rejection. For example, I do feel like an outsider from the system because of not having papers. Sometimes you feel it. For example, I work with a lot of Anglos and I talk to them and they say: "Oh, the ones that migrate here come to do this and that, bad stuff," and I tell them, "Well, I am one of those immigrants" and they'll say, "Well you are different!" Anyway, you still feel the rejection.

It is clear that the criminal narrative that is being applied to immigrants is not coming just from the media but also from others who probably also consume these pervasive discourses. Helping immigrants feel a sense of belonging in the United States is going to mean shifting attitudes about their assumed criminality, as well as, perhaps, a more nuanced understanding of criminality and redemption. Still, formal legal status can probably go a long way in helping Esteban feel that he is no longer rejected in the country he considers his home.

Stratified Belonging

In talking about immigration reform and DAPA with mixed-status families, I realized that the eligibility requirements of these policies or programs could leave a lot of immigrants out in the proverbial cold. Undocumented immigrants who have less than model pasts not only can be barred from current legalization pathways but also may be less likely to benefit from any future amnesty programs. Importantly, depending on their criminal pasts, some immigrants are also marked by some of their co-ethnic immigrant counterparts as responsible for the stigmatization of all undocumented immigrants. This is a heavy burden to bear.

I came to know Arturo after his partner generously allowed me to observe their small mixed-status family. Over the course of several months, I learned about Arturo's life and his perspectives. Having migrated at the tender age of four, he was socialized in the United States and had no recollections of Mexico. Despite being undocumented, Arturo told me that he does see himself as an American. One evening he shared with me his relationship to the United States: "This land saw me grow up. It gives you opportunities and it's up to you if you want to take them or not. . . . I have a love for this country. It saw me grow up to the person that I am now." It is difficult to point out what being an American means. However, Arturo's extended time and coming of age in the United States, as well as his English language fluency, US family ties, and volunteer community service all point to markers of American identity.

What makes Arturo different from most of the other immigrants in this chapter is that he has been involved with the criminal justice system and has already been deported. At the kitchen table, Arturo explains his story to me. Previously, I had picked up bits and pieces concerning Arturo's detention and deportation from his partner, Karina, but there were still many missing details. I came to understand that Arturo had been involved with gangs as a teenager, something that he now regrets. He explains to me how his gang involvement started:

> You have to be really strong to avoid it. Like I said, your friends. Let's say you have friends from elementary and middle school and then one of your friends joins [a gang] and it's not that you have to join, but if my little crew enjoyed surfing or hung around people that surfed, I am pretty sure I would have become a surfer and would have liked that. I think it was more of that was the thing to do, I guess. When you are young, you don't think . . . obviously gangs were there before you were even born so they start implementing this thing in your mind that you have to protect your street and you are young and they feed you this crap and you believe it.

It was Arturo's previous gang involvement that catalyzed his contact with the criminal justice system and, later, with immigration enforcement. At first, I didn't know how his deportation unfolded, other than it had happened. This is a topic I had avoided asking about while I had been visiting their home because I had sensed that it might be too sensitive. Eventually, Arturo shared with me how his deportation occurred:

> I was deported once already. I guess I'll explain everything. After 9/11 they really started hitting hard on immigration. So, I think at that point they started looking into everyone's legal status and decided that everyone that is not doing something good needs to be sent back to their country. Obviously, gangs were the main targets. By all means, yeah. I never said, "Why me?" or "Why?" when it came to my deportation. You know what? There are people that want to come here and do good and there are people that want to come here and do bad, so that's fine. There are a lot of gang members, and that's fine. Those are the people that should be sent back, not when they separate families and all that. . . . I don't have any violence on my record, but due to that one time that I was incarcerated fighting my case, due to that [immigration agents] went to go look for me.

In his late teens, Arturo had been incarcerated while waiting out his court dates to clear his name for a felony charge. He was later found not guilty but felt that his time in jail made him a target for law enforcement or immigration authorities, who probably see him, as he put it, as "a punk [that] got lucky and beat the system." Following his release from jail, Arturo was mostly homebound because of the heavy gang presence in his neighborhood. He worried that even walking down his own street would risk problems with the police. Sometime after his release from jail, Arturo was removed from the United States and found himself in Tijuana, Mexico. After one failed attempt, he crossed clandestinely again to the United States to reunite with his family.

Knowing Arturo's full story, I realized that he probably would not be eligible for DACA or DAPA. During our interview I ask how he felt about these programs, since he would not be eligible, and he responds, "I think it is a good program, DAPA and DACA. I think it is. I know sometimes my partner and I talk about stuff and how it's not fair, but I can't sit around here and say I was an angel when I was a teen." Like other immigrants, Arturo ultimately thinks the parameters of eligibility for programs like DACA should remain as they are: "I think those programs are good. All the requirements, they should be there." As we talk further about these programs, I learn that he appreciated there being possible options for other undocumented immigrants in his extended family. Like many others in Los Angeles, Arturo has formed his own mixed-status family but also is part of a larger, extended web of mixed-status families. Most people in his family of origin are undocumented, but he explains that his siblings have also formed their own mixed-status families with their partners and US citizen children:

> Like I said, there are plenty of people that do come here to make a difference and they do deserve to get a chance to be here legally and not have to worry so much. My parents and my brothers have been here a long time, and they pay taxes even if they have to pay back, and they've never hurt anyone or committed a crime, so it's good that [programs] like that [DACA and DAPA] are passing.

Arturo ostensibly believes that legalization programs—however temporary or permanent—should have certain requirements that would probably leave him out. Based on his history, Arturo may not exemplify the idea of the model immigrant, even though now much of his time as an adult is dedicated to what many may consider respectable endeavors, including actively caring for his daughter, working full-time, and participating in voluntary community service.

Arturo's case exemplifies that there is not just one way to be American or undocumented. Unlike other undocumented parents who migrated to the United States as (near) adults, Arturo arrived as a young child and identifies as American. He is also less likely to benefit from immigration reform than some of the other undocumented immigrants portrayed in this chapter. His experience of a previous deportation and return alongside his gang and incarceration history not only mean it would be harder for him to change his status, but he is also more at risk of experiencing deportation again. For these reasons, in our interview and observations, I noticed how Arturo's family sometimes had to live under the radar and restrict some of their everyday activities. Arturo mostly limited his driving to getting to and from work as a strategy to avoid detection from authorities. At the same time, his driving was also a source of emotional stress on his partner, Karina, who I would sometimes see anxiously checking her phone when Arturo was slightly late returning home from work. Despite living in an immigrant-accommodating locale, he and his family had to live in the shadows.

Conclusion

This chapter has focused on how members of mixed-status families, particularly Mexican undocumented immigrants, claim their membership in the United States. Because undocumented immigrants are unable to claim US citizenship based on their birth or legal documentation, they choose alternate frameworks to argue for their inclusion. Here, the work of family illegality involves the discursive work of claiming one's right to be physically present in the United States. These claims are often economic or neoliberal and rely on respectability politics, but they are also shaped by an immigrant desire to achieve the elusive American Dream. As immigrants rely on labor-based claims, their narratives are a form of cultural citizenship as they express their right to belong in the United States despite their undocumented status and racialized identity.[53] Embedded in Mexican undocumented immigrants' narratives is an understanding that Mexican identity and illegality are deeply connected in anti-immigrant sentiment. This means that even with the promise of eventual citizenship, some racialized stigmas will not dissolve.

As immigrants construct their worthiness, they counteract the trope that immigrants contribute at the expense of American workers. For this reason, Emiliana and others highlight their labor that is sorely needed because Americans are unwilling to do the work. Immigrants' claims point to what some economists have been reporting all along: immigrants and their labor are in fact good for the economy.[54] However, these economic-based claims may not be effective in swaying registered voters on undocumented issues.[55] Immigrants relying on labor-based claims can also contribute to a rather insidious dilemma; positioning oneself as a laborer makes one vulnerable to the unpredictability of capitalism. In other words, placing one's value on labor can appeal to a capitalist sensitivity, but it is only valuable when labor is in demand. This is a problem when immigrants are perceived as threats during economic downturns and times in which unemployed Americans are willing to take jobs previously filled by immigrants. The claim that immigrants do the work Americans do not want to do does not necessarily ring true when job options are severely limited. This has serious ramifications for immigrant workers. Migrant men of color are deemed disposable, and therefore more easily deportable during a recession when their labor is no longer in demand.[56]

Furthermore, placing your worth on your ability to labor is risky. Being physically able to participate in paid employment is not guaranteed. It was not unusual for immigrants aged forty to more than sixty to share with me concerns about their deteriorating health. Both citizen and undocumented youth described witnessing their parents' declining health after years of hard labor. Adult children worried that their parents' bodies would not be able to endure the physical toll much longer. Severe back, leg, and knee pain; arthritis; and throbbing varicose veins were some of the health problems immigrants attributed to the decades-long wear and tear of working in jobs like construction, factory work, and housecleaning. If undocumented immigrants' value is based on their labor (and typically it is very hard labor), then what is the physical toll? Decades of hard labor have robbed many immigrants of their health and bodies.

Participants' claims to belong in the country are not inclusive to all undocumented immigrants. Undocumented immigrants (and their family members) mitigate stigma by emphasizing their fit as "good immigrants" while simultaneously constructing "bad immigrants" as undeserving of immigration reform. These less than model immigrants are also positioned as responsible for perpetuating anti-immigrant and anti-Mexican stereotypes. Therefore, undocumented immigrants can make claims about their belonging, but in doing so they create boundaries for those undocumented counterparts whom they believe *do not belong*. It is in the phrasing of "because of one, we all lose" (or slight variations on that wording) that immigrants place the onus of blame for their stigmatization on immigrant co-ethnics. Further complicating these boundaries are the gray areas of what immigrants may consider more justifiable crimes—specifically those that facilitate access to employment. Yet, these hierarchies are subjective and messy.

I found that youth activists in Southern California were often intentional about creating space and support for immigrants who did not fit the strict boundaries of respectable or normative worthiness. Such work is not easy. Even organizations supporting criminalized immigrants must work to undo the divisions migrants make between themselves based on immigration status and criminality. Moves to broaden spaces for all immigrants may partly be a product of a broader shift of undocumented youth movements to move beyond respectable images of high-achieving college students to fight for pro-immigrant policies. However, respectability narratives still exist and can be adopted by people who are not undocumented themselves, such as by journalists and elected leaders. For example, respectability narratives were common in the public discourse responding to the 2017 DACA rescission announcement. Undocumented youth subsequently critiqued these discourses as marginalizing their parents.[57] Although immigrant youth activists were past creating boundaries of "good" and "bad" immigrants, those outside activist circles do not always engage in a politics of inclusion.

Certainly, the narratives provided here have some important implications. What happens when workers can no longer work? What happens when immigrants do have a criminal record? And, of course, what about the immigrants who do not fit neatly into the box of "good immigrant"? While immigrants are mitigating the stigma they feel, arguably, the pitfall of the "we are not criminals" argument is that it leaves little room for good immigrants to make human mistakes. In fact, the circumstances of undocumented illegality sometimes push immigrants to become criminalized by engaging in everyday nonviolent activity. Further, even while immigrants feel blamed for the actions of drug dealers, murderers, and rapists, few immigrants personally know co-ethnic acquaintances, friends, or loved ones who fall into these categories.

I present here some hurdles to reform and activist organizing. Many immigrants and the families I spoke with suggested a comprehensive immigration reform that left out immigrants with criminal records. To be fair, this policy plan is not uncommon. A similar stipulation was included in the IRCA program, and governments across the globe have also rewarded "good" immigrants with a path toward legalization. What's more, immigrants with records that would probably make them ineligible for DACA-like programs also believe these eligibility restrictions should exist. This leaves more questions than answers on how to envision an inclusive reform that honors the diverse experiences of immigrants in mixed-status families. After some time in the field, and particularly after my observations and interviews with families, I can see how everyday lives are deeply complex. Is there, for example, redemption available for immigrants who have a criminal record or for undocumented fathers, like Arturo, who in his youth temporarily participated in gang life after living in a dense, poverty-stricken neighborhood with a heavy gang presence? Or for Esteban, who is now sober and years past his infractions? These histories are the kinds of infractions that were not made in the service of finding gainful employment. Yet, structural inequalities influence an immigrant's relationship to criminality. As immigration scholars have argued, "While some migrants do commit serious crimes, their lives are influenced by structural forces outside their control, including transnational political-economic inequalities, war, and racial dynamics in U.S. urban spaces."[58] Supporting undocumented and mixed-status communities may mean a commitment to abolitionist movements that are already doing incredible work to support criminalized communities and call for addressing the broader inequalities that underlie crime, such as poor housing, substandard education, and limited jobs and health services.[59] For undocumented communities, creating opportunities to access legalization actually makes everyday activities suddenly legal—activities that lawfully present people may take for granted, such as lawfully driving or having the valid documentation to get a job or access a trade license.

Ultimately, immigrants and mixed-status families with records or criminal histories not only must manage ubiquitous stereotypes in the media that denigrate all immigrants, but also must recognize that their fellow immigrants and co-ethnics sometimes participate in their denigration. Worse yet, it is these immigrants and their families who are most at risk for deportation. It is in this sense that the claims for belonging and solidarity can be deeply stratified.

5

Navigating Racialized Belonging in Segregated Los Angeles

When I met with research participants across Los Angeles County, I viewed a variety of sights and sounds of both Mexican American and urban life throughout the area. I would be on my way somewhere and suddenly hear a familiar trombone and accordion introduction to a popular Mexican ballad, passed storefronts with signs promising to fix immigration problems, and delighted in the sight of laughing Latino youth walking home from school in a sea of white polo shirts and customary uniform pants. I also walked sidewalks interrupted by abandoned and noticeably distressed mattresses, took a familiar orange Metro bus home with mostly working-class and elderly Angelenos, and sometimes caught a lucky ride even if it was through the almost inevitable bumper-to-bumper traffic. This description of Los Angeles might not be the image typically highlighted in films and television programs, where the city's image is a distorted patchwork of ritzy Hollywood homes and majestic beach communities.[1] However, the working-class Latino and Mexican communities that make up this expansive metropolis are part of Los Angeles too.

On one of these days, I took an overcrowded Metro bus to meet Juan Carlos, who suggested we meet at a nearby eatery that he insists will be quiet enough for an interview. As it turns out, he was right. As we sit with our food, Juan Carlos tells me a little about himself. At nineteen, Juan Carlos seems old beyond his years and is a proud Angeleno, but he admits, "Let's not fool ourselves. LA has its problems." When I ask him about being American, he shares the following:

> You know that anxiety you feel when you are at the border and immigration asks you if you are a US citizen? You know, because I am Mexican, I am already thinking they might think I am not a citizen. Every time they ask me, I get worried I am going to say the wrong thing or somehow forget. I get real [sic] nervous. So, it's like every now and then that sort of happens.

Juan Carlos talks about the distinct discomfort of being a Mexican American at the US-Mexico border, knowing his physical appearance marks him as suspect. The experience is not uncommon, as previous research has documented how immigration authorities routinely accost and racially profile Mexican Americans.[2] Later, Juan Carlos equates the border with experiencing racism in White areas of Los Angeles when he has been employed as a tutor and in food service. He elaborates, "People are going to throw racial slurs at you, calling you wetback, and calling you illegal. It's not going to happen often, it really doesn't. But when it does, I am in these really White areas of LA." For US citizens like Juan Carlos, the experience of belonging rests on the question of *where*. Because he grew up living in Latino communities, his citizenship is not challenged until he finds himself in predominantly White and wealthy locales in Los Angeles.

In this chapter, I discuss the limits of citizenship that Mexican Americans experience as they navigate the county of Los Angeles. For undocumented immigrants, navigating space entails efforts to avoid contact with police and immigration authorities. Most immigrants I interviewed and informally spoke to generally remained within county limits. San Diego is the quintessential example of a location to avoid for mixed-status families because of its proximity to the border. Young adults recalled feeling disappointed when they were younger because they could not visit popular destinations in San Diego, such as Sea World or the San Diego Zoo. Parents explained to children that these locations and destinations outside the United States were restricted to them. Giovanni, for example, recalls that San Diego was a city his parents told him they were not able to visit because, if they did, they might not be able to return home. As a child, Giovanni did not always understand the nuances of undocumented status, but he knew that certain places were off-limits to his parents, and therefore off-limits to him. Differences in travel access are among the ways children understand differences in legal status.[3] Now that he is an adult, Giovanni's mobility is not restricted. With their own driver's licenses, adult routines, and decreased dependence on parents, young citizen adults get to move through Los Angeles without the immigration-based restrictions directed at their immigrant family members. Only when these young adults are with their parents do they travel with family illegality in mind.

Most interviewees live in or were raised in co-ethnic neighborhoods—this is not surprising given the racial and ethnic segregation in Los Angeles.[4] Undeniably, Los Angeles qualifies as a "minority-majority" locale representing a majority non-White Angeleno population.[5] In total, Latinos constitute a significant portion of the Los Angeles County population at 48.3 percent, followed by Whites at 25.9 percent, Asians at 14.6 percent, Blacks at 7.8 percent, and American Indians and Native Hawaiians/Pacific Islanders each at 0.2 percent.[6] The highest number of Latinos in the United States can be found in Los Angeles, where many of them are also of Mexican origin.[7] Mexican-origin Latinos have long represented a significant part of the Angeleno population. Still, Los Angeles is a paradoxical place of both belonging and rejection for Mexican Americans.

Los Angeles represents a beacon of relative freedom where Mexican Americans feel *almost* accepted as community members. In fact, despite the racism that exists in this world-class metropolis, Mexican Americans regularly perceive Los Angeles as much less racist or xenophobic than other regions both near and far. Research participants describe Los Angeles as liberal and diverse, and its people as kind, open-minded, and respectful, often noting how much more welcoming Los Angeles can be to immigrants and Mexican Americans than in neighboring Orange County. Outside of California, participants identify Arizona, the Midwest, and the American South as more hostile to their ethnic communities. Still, interviewees expressed their nuanced and honest view of Los Angeles. Robert, a longtime Angeleno, stated, "At the end of the day, we always face racism on a daily basis."

Many pointed to not feeling like outsiders because a significant number of locals are immigrants or part of immigrant families in their neighborhoods. Mexican Americans are also aware of the long history of Los Angeles as being both an immigrant gateway and a settlement location for generations of Latinos, particularly for Mexicans and Mexican Americans. However, for Mexican Americans in Los Angeles, their sense of belonging is spatial. They feel a sense of belonging in their local, mostly Latino contexts but see themselves marked as racially unwanted when they navigate to White spaces in Los Angeles.

Mexican Americans experience citizenship as a tenuous social belonging that partially rests on whether members of the citizenry accept them. They feel a sense of belonging in their local contexts, where they interact with co-ethnics and other people of color in their neighborhoods. It is in their Latino neighborhoods where their American citizenship is largely not questioned in a confrontational manner. When Mexican Americans' citizenship is questioned in Latino spaces, these interactions are often not hostile and suggest a subtle sense of solidarity, as I will later describe. On the other hand, in predominantly White areas, Mexican Americans experience microaggressions and feel their citizenship is questioned in a hostile or offensive manner, however subtle.[8] Over two-thirds of citizens of all ages in this study report experiencing racism, discomfort, and microaggressions in predominantly White spaces. Since citizenship is not something that is physically marked, it is Mexican American identity that makes these citizens vulnerable to racism and microaggressions. While the racism Mexican Americans experience occurs in interactions with individuals, this does not mean they do not experience institutional racism at work, at school, and in other settings. They do. However, individual interactions are also part of a systemic pattern of indignities that are directed at Mexican Americans. Since Mexican Americans in Los Angeles experience belonging spatially, I move now to discuss the power of space.

Residential Segregation and Spatial Inequality

We are very diverse because LA has been very good at mixing people . . . but everybody kind of just runs back to their neighborhood. . . . Latinos live here and the White people live there.
—Raúl, US citizen

Understanding spatial inequality begins with unpacking segregation. A person's residence shapes their employment opportunities, public safety, and environmental exposure, and it correlates with health outcomes and other factors that can impact economic opportunities and quality of life.[9] Using locational attainment models, researchers examine how demographic factors such as race, class, and nativity shape access to desirable neighborhoods.[10] According to other research, White Americans have access to the most desirable neighborhoods, while Latinos and Blacks tend to live in more impoverished communities.[11] This finding is not surprising considering the substantial amount of research documenting racially and linguistically discriminatory housing practices.[12] Specifically, Los Angeles is an epicenter of hypersegregation for Latinos.[13] Further, when documentation status is accounted for, undocumented Latinos are living in the least desirable neighborhoods, faring worse than native-born Latinos and Blacks in Los Angeles.[14]

The segregation between Latinos and other racial/ethnic groups across the United States has increased in recent years.[15] For instance, in long-established Latino immigrant destinations like Los Angeles and New York, segregation for Latinos has intensified.[16] While some evidence suggests that Latinos in Los Angeles prefer co-ethnic neighborhoods, this is only true among recent arrivals with limited English language proficiency.[17] This might explain why increases in Latino and Asian immigrant populations contribute to greater segregation between these two groups and White Americans.[18]

Spatial inequality research is also attuned to the qualitative nature of how navigating space is not a neutral endeavor. Sociologists in this research area are attentive to how space contributes to inequalities.[19] Participants shared their meanings attached to space and their experience within and through it as they interacted with others. Neighborhoods are primarily places of social contact.[20] Following other scholars, I conceptualize space both as a specific geographic setting and as "relational units that organize ideas about places and implicitly or explicitly compare locations."[21] Here, I explore how social actors construct *meaning* concerning space in Los Angeles. Spatial boundaries are constructed by edifices or physical parameters and by social actors and their power relations that govern who belongs within the boundaries.

Citizenship as an Experience of Racialized Belonging

In recounting lived experiences, Mexican Americans portray space as a form of inequality wherein White strangers in White communities do not freely accept their presence or associate their identities with foreignness or illegality. Since citizenship is a form of membership that requires the consent of other citizens, this policing of local space is critical to how Mexican Americans experience US membership. When this group navigates Los Angeles, citizenship is a spatial experience colored by racialized boundaries.

While the literature on spatial inequality highlights how space serves as a distributor of life chances, I bridge spatial inequality with theories of membership. Citizenship is constructed and experienced as a category of membership—and one that is enforced by the state and by laypersons.[22] The cross-fertilization between theories of citizenship and space, in some ways, could not be more complementary. Citizenship, by definition, demarcates inclusionary and exclusionary boundaries.[23] Similarly, space also "embraces some things and excludes others."[24] The ways Mexican Americans experience urban space can illustrate how this group experiences citizenship.

While US citizens can make a legal claim to belong in the United States, it is unclear if they are accepted as members of their local and national community when membership can be policed and contested. Specifically, when Mexican Americans navigate White spaces, they report feeling like outsiders based on their racialized or ethnic appearance. Alongside microaggressions, Mexican Americans experience a variety of racisms meant to denigrate and subordinate their existence. Thus, how Mexican Americans *navigate* and *create meanings* around space is a central aspect of making sense of their citizen membership. However fractured, Mexican Americans' sense of belonging also demonstrates their resilience and their resistance to marginalization. They fight their contested citizenship with full agency by relying primarily on self-presentation and linguistic strategies to promote their American identities.

Setting the Context: Los Angeles County

Participants hailed primarily from Central Los Angeles, East Los Angeles, Southeast Los Angeles, and the San Fernando Valley. Central Los Angeles includes the city's downtown business and political headquarters and a patchwork of surrounding communities. Participants from these areas were living in or had grown up in parts of downtown, East Hollywood, Echo Park, Westlake, Pico-Union, and Koreatown. Participants who grew up in Central Los Angeles described the area as home to small, cramped apartments, with sounds of a bustling, dense city and street vendors selling Mexican and Central American street food.

Like most regions, Central Los Angeles is highly segregated by class and race. Participants who call Central Los Angeles home, for example, were not living in the Hollywood Hills or feeling nostalgic about large, gated, idyllic homes and gardens. Instead, participants primarily call the eastern and southeastern parts of Central Los Angeles home. Despite the ongoing issue of gentrification, other communities on the eastern and southeastern sides of Central Los Angeles also reflect the large Latino populations found there. Walking on Sunset Boulevard in Echo Park, one might come across restaurants that make a nod to Los Angeles's Hollywood and its eccentric history. However, one can also see, for example, a remarkable hot pink mural honoring the Chicana and Mexicana heroines Frida Kahlo, Dolores Huerta, and Selena Quintanilla-Pérez.

East and Southeast Los Angeles have long been home to Mexican and Asian immigrants. The racial demographics of this region are not coincidental. In the early twentieth century, officials pushed immigrants out of the downtown Los Angeles area to help construct an image of the city as a White metropolis.[25] As Mexican immigrants were pushed out, they established strong-rooted neighborhoods and their own community and civic organizations.[26] Today, Mexican-origin communities represent the majority population in communities like Boyle Heights, Maywood, Downey, and South Gate.

Boyle Heights is known for its large Mexican American grassroots effort to address gentrification. Located just over two miles east of downtown Los Angeles, the community is considered a prime area for real estate development. Despite battles over real estate and concerns about specifically White, middle-class and wealthy gentrifiers, the community remains largely working-class, immigrant, and Mexican-origin. The small community is primarily Latino at 73 percent and is home to about 50 percent US citizens and 50 percent foreign-born residents, 17 percent of whom lack legal status.[27]

People who live in East and Southeast Los Angeles described these communities to me as impoverished, friendly to Spanish speakers, majority Mexican, and home to large populations of undocumented immigrants. In the words of college-going Enrique, "Here in East LA . . . everyone is like you," referring to himself as being both Mexican and undocumented. Enrique, who now is seeking a degree at one of the University of California campuses, notes that in East LA "everyone has broken English, people have accents . . . you are still here in the ghetto. You are still here in the hood. You are still a minority but everyone around you is a minority."

Similarly, much of what residents describe in East Los Angeles can be said about Latinos living in neighboring Southeast Los Angeles. The Southeast's proximity to the Los Angeles River and the railroad made the region an ideal location for the city's industry. The region is a base for manufacturing household items and thus is populated by workers who have established vibrant working-class communities of color throughout the years. In addition, Southeast Los Angeles communities include industrial cities like Maywood, where driving by warehouses and intimidatingly large semitrailers is not uncommon.

Participants who lived in Southeast Los Angeles were from communities such as South Gate and Maywood. South Gate, like many of its bordering cities to the north and east, is predominantly Latino at about 95 percent.[28] These numbers complement one participant's perception of South Gate, which she describes as "99 percent Hispanic and maybe one Black person." With about a third of South Gate's population, Maywood is also predominantly Latino at 97.4 percent.[29] Even though my first time in Maywood was when I met with a research participant, those census numbers seem to reflect the population based on my few times there. I went to meet with a Maywood-area Latina eager to participate in the study during the winter holiday season. Before our interview, I ran a few errands, zigzagging through retail parking lot while vendors asked me if I wanted to buy seasonal Mexican drinks. Later in the day, after completing the interview, I made a quick stop at a local Mexican chain supermarket carrying my basket of mangos, avocados, Mexican hot chocolate, and snowman-decorated wrapping paper, all while Vicente Fernández serenaded me over the store's sound system.[30]

Some thirty-odd miles from Southeast Los Angeles and northwest of downtown Los Angeles is the San Fernando Valley. "The Valley," as it is colloquially called, is a sprawling postwar suburban region. Though perceived as less metropolitan than Central Los Angeles, the region has become more urbanized and is almost as racially diverse as the rest of the county. Over the years, the Valley witnessed an increase in Latino residents and the flight of White residents leaving for the outskirts of county limits. By the 1980s, there was an understanding that Latinos were increasing in numbers and in their political presence, rejecting the popularized image of the Valley as "lily-White, mostly blonde."[31] These shifts, however, still did not suggest racial or ethnic integration. By 2000, many White Valley residents were concentrated in the southern and western neighborhoods of Sherman Oaks, Encino, Studio City, and Woodland Hills.[32]

For decades, pockets of the Valley were heavily Mexican, notably Pacoima and San Fernando. These communities remain primarily Latino at about 86 percent.[33] Aside from these two communities, participants lived in Arleta, North Hills, Panorama City, and Sylmar. In these areas, it is not unusual to catch yourself being stared down by a mural of the popular actor and entrepreneur Danny Trejo or walking by a residential gate painted with colorful images of horses, charros, and the Virgin of Guadalupe.[34] While the Valley has some neighborhoods that are also largely White, Raúl summed up the San Fernando Valley by telling me matter-of-factly, "Everyone knows you find *Raza* in the Valley."[35]

For some students, the Valley is where they were bused to school from their homes in other parts of the county. For some parents, the Valley was a desired destination for setting roots after living in high-crime neighborhoods closer to the Los Angeles city center. Despite comparisons of the Valley being more tranquil than other parts of Los Angeles, some parents called their own neighborhoods *caliente*, referring not to temperature but to their perception of high neighborhood crime. On one evening, I was welcomed by Elena, who was standing in front of her San Fernando Valley apartment with outstretched arms and offered me the greeting, "Welcome to the ghetto." I had smirked at her half-joking words; *if these were homes in the ghetto, I had lived in the ghetto my whole life.* Ultimately, even while outsiders may see the Valley as generally suburban and White, this image does not represent the entire San Fernando Valley. Whether participants lived in the Valley or other parts of Los Angeles County, what is certain is that most lived in Mexican or Latino neighborhoods and were surrounded by co-ethnics *and* immigrant families.

Contested Citizenship and Racism in Los Angeles

In the blinding heat, I face a bulky metal gate to a modern gray apartment complex. I need a code to get into the building and realize I came unprepared. Thankfully, a grinning child of about eleven walks out of the building with his scooter and lets me in. I meet Teresa after she arrives home, carrying several crimson tote bags that bounce with each step, along with the curls of her dark brown hair. Since she is wearing a T-shirt displaying the acronym of her alma mater, I am reminded that Teresa is coming home after her morning class. She meets me by a fountain at the center of her apartment complex and offers me a tentative smile as she leads me up an outdoor steel stairwell to her family's apartment.

Inside, we are met with an apartment overcrowded with boxes and cardboard crates of food and water bottles. "Excuse the mess, we are moving," she explains. Teresa lives with her mother, stepfather, maternal half brother, and occasionally her six-year-old paternal half brother. One day Teresa hopes to have her own place with her fiancé, but for now, the family is moving up the street to another housing unit.

Teresa is part of a blended Salvadoran-Mexican family and is an American-born citizen. She works two jobs and struggles financially to help her mixed-status family and her undocumented fiancé as much as she can with emotional and financial assistance. Alternating between Spanish and English, Teresa uses Spanish-language musical genres to denote the mix of Mexican and Salvadoran influences in her life. "My friends are all Mexican. So, I have *cumbias* and *merengue*, but I also have *bandas* and *norteños* and *corridos* and all that stuff in my head. That is my *ambiente*."[36] This is her environment, she says.

Teresa was born, raised, and currently resides in a part of the San Fernando Valley that has a long history of Latino settlement and remains overwhelmingly Mexican. She is comfortable in her community and feels she fully belongs there. This is how belonging can be place-based; even when feeling ambivalent about American identity, young adults can feel a sense of belonging in their local communities. Teresa's American citizenship is not often questioned in her neighborhood or in other Latino spaces. When it is questioned in these areas, these interactions are not experienced as uncomfortable or alarming. For example, when young adults attend Latino dance events or other cultural gatherings popular among immigrants, they are sometimes asked which *rancho*, or ranch, they are from because co-ethnics assume that they are also immigrants from rural areas. To Mexican Americans, these questions are not microaggressions when they occur in these contexts because the question is not born out of White or racist aggression. Instead, the question is asked to forge connection.[37]

When Teresa's citizenship is questioned in White settings, she experiences hostility. For example, as she recalls, one childhood memory regrettably left a lasting impression:

> T: When I was younger, we went to Costco at Burbank, and my dad was waiting for a parking spot, and he saw another one free up, so he went over there, but there was another guy who was coming for it. I guess my dad beat him to it, and this guy started calling us a whole bunch of racist names. He harassed us. He screamed at us . . .
> C: So, you were in the car when this happened?
> T: I was in the car, and then we started walking to Costco, and he kept saying things . . . he just kept insulting us and saying, "Go back to your country. . . ." I felt like I was a target. I guess that makes me kind of biased or judgy with them.
> C: With who?
> T: With White people. Because I am always expecting them to say something, like a rude remark or assume that I am not legal. I know they are not always going to ask me directly.

Teresa's childhood experience in a city that is majority White demonstrates how Latino citizens experience unbelonging.[38] In Burbank, a city known for film and television production, Teresa and her family were harassed with anti-Latino and anti-immigrant slurs. Her direct discussion of being told to "go back to your country" indicates that she knows she can't be considered American. To this day, she believes that White Americans wonder if she is legal. Thus, while citizenship is not a physical attribute, Teresa experiences her identity as a Latina—a racialized category—marking her as an immigrant when she spatially navigates predominantly White communities.

Twenty years later, the moment continues to shape how Teresa constructs belonging and moves around in various spaces. Beyond the plans of urban planners or developers, space is lived in subjective ways by people moving through it. As the French philosopher Henri Lefebvre notes, space "bears the stamp of conflict" that can begin from moments in childhood.[39] Therefore, people can experience racial microaggressions that continue to color their perceptions of space and belonging.

Teresa feels most welcomed and free from subtle and explicit racism in Latino or racially mixed neighborhoods and spaces. She attends a racially diverse university and tells me, "I love [my university] because it is very diverse and at the same time there are a lot of Latinos there, so I feel very comfortable there. So just having, you know, people that you know are Latinos around me kind of like boosts my self-esteem." In White spaces, Teresa looks for other people of color as a source of solidarity. "I feel like if I go to Thousand Oaks Mall and see another Latina, I want to smile at them because it's like: "Hey! We are sticking in there. We have each other." While Teresa feels comfortable at her university and in Latino neighborhoods, many recreational activities like shopping or dining mean navigating White space.

Like many young adults, Teresa enjoys the occasional evening out when she can unwind from work and school and have dinner with her fiancé. However, she has to take into account certain considerations when deciding where to go for leisure or entertainment. Although she and her fiancé like to dine at restaurants in Thousand Oaks and Westlake Village, Teresa is disappointed that White patrons often give them "weird stares." She interprets these stares as hostile interactions. "They are just staring at us like: *Why are they here?*" Thousand Oaks and Westlake Village are predominantly White communities, and are known for their high-priced shopping and dining options.[40] Thousand Oaks rests just outside of Los Angeles County in Ventura, while neighboring Westlake Village, formerly part of Thousand Oaks, is located within the western border of Los Angeles County.

Place-based belonging implicates Latinos' perception of their inclusion in space. Sometimes the comments they receive are explicit, akin to racial and anti-immigrant slurs. At other times, microaggressions are subtle and include stares, such as the kind Teresa describes as silently

asking: *What are you doing here?* For instance, Diego, another participant, admittedly does not venture outside his local neighborhood very
often and generally believes he does not experience discrimination.
Yet, he recalls microaggressions experienced in largely White cities and
comments, "I do get the sense that Anglo-Saxon White people, White
Americans, they do tend to see me, I guess differently. Like, racial profiling. You do get treated differently." Incidents of racism or perceived
racism in predominantly White areas were not uncommon for Mexican
Americans.

Robert tells me he experiences a sense of having second-class citizenship in White spaces. For Robert, being a person of color in these
spaces is a burden of experiencing slights that he suspects are racially
motivated. Robert remembers:

> R: As a person of color, even in Santa Monica when I was fresh out of
> high school, I was like: *everyone is staring at us.*[41]
> C: You and your family or you and your friends?
> R: Me and my friends. We are people of color. Is it because we are
> young? Maybe. Is it because we are brown? Maybe. Like I said, we
> always question it. That question is always on our minds. It's always
> going to be in the back of my head because I am a person of color.
> Why are you staring at me kind of thing. Am I overreacting? Maybe,
> but I have a right to because our society is so corrupt, and you made
> me internalize that I am not wanted.

Robert lives with the lingering question about his acceptance. He
questions how people look at him in White spaces because he believes
he is unwanted there. Robert and many other citizens report feeling
uncomfortable (or made to feel uncomfortable) in White spaces. The
glares and comments extended to Latinos in White spaces can be described as "moments of denied belonging."[42] However, the subtlety of
some of these moments is sometimes difficult for Mexican Americans
to process. Participants sometimes question if their experiences can be
considered racism or microaggressions by expressing that maybe "it is
just me" or noting that they were relying on "feelings" or "vibes." Indeed,
unwanted or out-of-place feelings are difficult to articulate when these
experiences are embodied, and the perpetrators of microaggressions are

subtle. Ultimately, Robert decides that his experiences are likely racially based microaggressions and aims not to internalize any messages about his nonbelonging.

Maggie's subjectivity of American identity also implicates others who enforce the boundaries of citizenship. When I ask if she considers herself an American, she responds:

> Ha! Well, yes, sometimes, but not all the time. How can I be an American if sometimes I am not considered an American? So how does that work? With my clients and my friends and family, yes, there is no doubt I am an American. With strangers, it's still pretty obvious, I think, because I speak English, so no-brainer. And then I go over to Sherman Oaks, and it's like people tell you: "Go back to Mexico!" so what does that make me? Not American, apparently. If you want to be treated like an American, sometimes that means you just have to be Anglo or White.

These types of accounts describe Maggie's and other Mexican Americans' experiences of belonging that is place-based. In her words, it is hard to be considered an American when others do not acknowledge your citizenship. While generally Maggie feels a strong sense of belonging in Los Angeles, she feels less accepted because being a citizen usually means being "Anglo or White." Her nonbelonging is acute in areas where she experiences direct racial harassment, such as in Sherman Oaks, a neighborhood that is 71 percent White.[43] This is an area Maggie tries to avoid.

On the other hand, racially mixed or predominantly Latino neighborhoods are spaces in which Maggie knows her belonging or presence will not be questioned. "That is where I can be myself and not have to worry so much," she notes. While Latino neighborhoods are not utopias of co-ethnic solidarity, Maggie feels most comfortable in these spaces.[44] As she explains, "At least I know I won't be discriminated." This is how place-based belonging operates for the Mexican Americans I interviewed.

Skin Color and Spatial Change

In spatially navigating Los Angeles, Mexican Americans can find themselves in areas where their citizenship is questioned or where they feel unwelcome. These experiences of space can be shaped by skin color, which continues to be an important factor in Latinos' life experiences and opportunities. For Latinos, skin color is a physical marker of being perceived as a foreigner; it impacts employment and legal outcomes, and the likelihood of experiencing discrimination.[45] Being marked as a noncitizen in predominantly White spaces is not shaped exclusively by skin color. In my study, both dark and light-skinned Mexican Americans describe being questioned about their legal status, American citizenship, and other such microaggressions. However, it should be noted that these experiences surrounding skin color would likely be qualitatively different for Mexican Americans who are construed as Black and/or identify as Black or Afro-Latino/Afro-Mexican.[46] Teresa notes the importance of skin color by comparing her experience dating a lighter-skinned man as compared with dating her darker-skinned fiancé:

> [My ex-partner] was lighter than I am. I would walk with him through a mall, and it was fine. Then I would walk with my fiancé through the mall. He's way darker, and we get looks. If it's like Glendale or Thousand Oaks Mall, people kind of stare at us. Those are not typically Latino malls.

Teresa's experience illustrates how skin color racializes daily life for Latino participants. While White strangers have challenged Teresa's citizenship, she acknowledges that darker-skinned Latinos—and perhaps young dark-skinned Latino men in particular—face unique struggles over perceptions of their legal status, assumed criminality, or both.[47] In other studies, darker-skinned Mexican American men report higher instances of discrimination than lighter-skinned co-ethnics and all women co-ethnics regardless of color.[48] In conducting interviews and fieldwork, I, too, picked up on how Latino men were subject to policing in ways that women did not experience or disclose. Women sometimes shared how their brothers or male relatives have been racially profiled while driving.

Skin color becomes a marker for foreignness when US citizenship is so often imagined as White. These sentiments were echoed by participants who discussed how their skin color was often read in White spaces as an indication of being an immigrant or undocumented. In thinking about how she navigates spaces as a Mexican American, Yoselyn offered some thoughts on how she might be construed by strangers on the street: "I think their first thought of me is 'she's definitely from another country,' because of my skin color." Similarly, Alondra made a somewhat similar observation when she noted, "People kind of look at me, and they look at my skin color and assume that I don't have any papers." When asked to elaborate, she says that "people" or "they" typically means Whites in these contexts.

Skin color matters, but perhaps given the long-standing presence of a heterogeneous Latino community in Los Angeles, light-skinned Mexican Americans can still be identified as Mexican and subsequently experience microaggressions.[49] For instance, Susie is a petite, light-skinned woman with black hair and brown eyes. While Susie and her undocumented mother are very light-skinned, strangers have questioned their citizenship and their legal right to reside in the United States. For Susie, this was blatantly clear as she describes an incident at her former workplace: "A person came into the restaurant and was yelling at me, asking me for my green card. . . . I feel like every day I still experience microaggressions from White people." Although light-skinned, Susie is still marked as Latina and subsequently is the target of racial microaggressions. Perhaps especially in the case of Mexican Americans, a confluence of factors sometimes shapes how people are identified racially or ethnically—skin color, eye and hair color, accents, and last names can be cues of Mexican or Latino identity.[50]

Susie's experience also highlights how assumptions about skin color miss the complexity of how Mexican Americans are racialized.[51] Skin color, while often thought of as fixed, can also be perceived differently across space and place. In other words, meanings assigned to race and skin color are deeply contextual. Susie, for example, remembers what it was like to move from the Mexican community of East Los Angeles to the predominantly White community of Thousand Oaks to live with her Mexican American father. She tells me, "There was this weird thing for me where I went from being the Whitest-looking kid in my schools in East LA to being one of the only brown people in Thousand Oaks, people of color in my classes." Spatial context, according to Susie, seems to matter a great deal in experiencing race. Even with the privilege she carries with her as a light-skinned woman, Susie's life is punctu-ated by moments in White spaces when she is the sole person of color and considered a possible foreigner without a green card. Susie's sense of citizenship, then, clearly implicates how others—particularly White Americans—can police the boundaries of membership for Mexican American residents of Los Angeles.

For Sylvia, the changing demographics of a neighborhood can mean going from feeling part of a community to feeling like an outsider. Sylvia witnessed the start of gentrification in her mostly Latino neighborhood in Echo Park. This shifted her sense of belonging. Sylvia had always lived in Latino neighborhoods in Central Los Angeles. She shares with me how she began to not fit in her neighborhood:

> S: I think I started to feel like that when we moved to Echo Park . . .
> it's very gentrified, and back then, it was just starting. So, I did feel
> uncomfortable. I was like: there are so many White people here.
> I felt weird. I don't know why, but I didn't like it. You just kind of
> feel like—I don't know. It just felt uncomfortable. I didn't like being
> around so many White people.
> C: That is interesting because that is not an experience shaped by
> immigration—
> S: But I am Latina! Visibly I am brown. You can say some of that is
> internalized racism for me. I felt othered. I felt like I was out of place.

Sylvia's discomfort is not about expressing animosity toward White Americans but about anticipating or experiencing a sense of being oth-ered or "out of place." This feeling of being "out of place" both signals a lack of belonging and clearly articulates how place itself circumscribes membership. When Sylvia tells me her story, there is something not lost on me. Sitting in a café in a now popularly gentrified and formerly Latino community, we appear to be the only people of color in sight for the almost three and a half hours we are there.

For others, the changing demographics of a neighborhood means a welcome change from feeling like an outsider to feeling more secure. Yvette, for example, remembers seeing a demographic change in places she frequented as a teenager with her now husband. Yvette recalls spend-ing time in Gorman and the general Antelope Valley area:

Y: Back in the day when I was growing up, we would get a lot of looks from White people. They would tell us, as teens, tell us to turn down our music and spit out racial slurs. You know what I mean? As of until recently, I've been feeling, not safer, because it's not safer, but just like I belong there more now.

C: What has changed?

Y: There's more Hispanics and Latinos there. I don't feel, you know, threatened with Black people there either. You know we do have high crime over there, but I don't feel like somebody's going to shoot me because I am Mexican.

C: You did feel kind of like that before?

Y: Yeah! It's a sense of not feeling welcomed.

For Yvette, feelings of belonging are certainly place- and group-based, as she was explicit in identifying areas that she was wary of visiting because of the explicit racial microaggressions she experienced growing up. Her experience of space notes the changing demographics of the location. Yvette felt unsafe but now feels more welcomed because there are more Latinos in the area. She turns mainstream conceptions of safety on their head. While some non-Black Americans may avoid visiting Black neighborhoods because of biased assumptions they make about Black criminality, as a Latina, Yvette's perception of safety doesn't mean distance from people of color. Safety means being free from racist violence.

Just as Angelenos understand where ethnic and racial groups reside, Mexican Americans also attach meanings to particular places as unsafe, not in terms of general crime but in terms of possible hate crime. Antelope Valley, where Yvette spent a lot of her leisure time as a youth, has a history of being home to hate groups and is the region in Los Angeles County with the highest incidence of hate crimes.[52] Yvette shares her memories of mostly White establishments she knew to avoid at all costs:

There are certain places where you don't go. Like there are bars that are near liquor stores. Since that bar was next to a liquor store, you really couldn't go to that liquor store because, you know, there were Caucasians at that bar. People—we did hear that people would get shot if they were over there, somebody of color.

While no signs indicate an establishment is for "Whites only," harkening back to a Jim Crow era, there continues to be an understanding of spaces where Latinos or people of color do not belong. In this case, the implicit threat of physical violence is what marks a place off-limits for people of color.

Yvette's citizenship does not imply full membership in the United States. She is a naturalized citizen who grew up in the care of her legal resident father after her undocumented mother was deported. Yvette ostensibly does not feel comfortable calling herself an American, telling me, "I don't feel like people consider me American. So how can I consider myself an American if they don't see me as an American?" She elaborates, "The citizenship, they [the government] are telling you, you are an American. However, the feeling is different. It's not—you are not treated like an American." Indeed, for racialized others, their non-White identities can mark them as "forever foreigners" and outsiders in their own country.[53] Particularly with ongoing immigrant replenishment, Mexican Americans can be physically marked as foreigners, even when they are light-skinned.[54] When Mexican Americans navigate segregated Los Angeles, they see the limits of their citizenship.

Strategies for Belonging in Predominantly White Areas

While belonging is a place-based ideal, Mexican Americans engage in resistance strategies to express their American citizenship. While their apparent identity in predominantly White areas marks Mexican Americans as possible foreigners, citizens use several strategies, particularly linguistic strategies, to proactively claim their belonging. To a much lesser extent, citizens might carry or memorize information about their legal status to concretely prove it to others. In some cases, citizens with children or younger siblings prepare loved ones for the possibility of racist interactions or have follow-up conversations with them after an incident. These strategies are still place-based, since they are used when Mexican Americans encounter White spaces. Further, the strategies highlight the agency used by these citizens to deal with their contested belonging.

For a small number of participants, carrying proof of citizenship is one strategy they use for their protection. Robert tells me he has memorized his Social Security number specifically to be able to recite it to police officers. He explains, "That is because if I am ever stopped [by the police], I need to know my Social. Like I said, as a person of color, we have to live a different life. If I am ever stopped, my immigration status will be questioned because I am a person of color, because I am Latino." Robert also makes comparisons to his White coworkers, who do not feel the need to memorize their Social Security numbers, something he believes signals their White privilege. This "different life," as Robert describes it, particularly in terms of negative or hostile interactions with police, was also discussed by some of the other young men in this study.

Except for engaging directly with bureaucratic processes to seek work, find housing, or travel beyond the state, very few citizens explicitly discuss carrying or memorizing their Social Security number to prove their citizenship to police. Most citizens rely on more subtle cues to prove their American identity. Teresa relies on linguistic strategies to demonstrate US citizenship. While individuals of all legal statuses can speak English, Latino citizens believe having English language fluency can nip in the bud any automatic perceptions about their legal status and possibly combat anti-Latino racism. When she and her fiancé are dining at restaurants in Thousand Oaks, Teresa relies on a dual linguistic strategy to emphasize her American identity without shedding her cultural pride. After sharing with me how she and her fiancé are stared at in restaurants, she says, "I tend to feel more comfortable even if the person is racist, if they are of color. I feel more comfortable with people of color. So, I guess I kind of get defensive in those moments. If our waiter speaks Spanish, I will talk to him only in Spanish." Teresa then goes on to explain that if the waiter is not a Spanish speaker (or is non-Latino), she will talk to her fiancé exclusively in English. Teresa explains her reasoning behind these code-switching choices: "I feel like that is me being defensive because it's me trying to demonstrate that I can speak English, that I am very fluent and very educated, but I can also speak Spanish and I am not going to hide it." Speaking in Spanish to a Spanish-speaking waiter is Teresa's strategy for demonstrating ethnic solidarity.[55] However, speaking English with her fiancé or to non-Latino servers is a proactive strategy she hopes can help prevent her from being the target of racial microaggressions. This linguistic strategy, I find, is also used by others who want to be proactive about asserting their American identity and their right to respect. Unfortunately, though, these strategies are only deemed necessary because of systemic racism and nativism. Racist and nativist logics have subjugated Spanish-speaking Latinos across the United States to harassment and violence.[56]

For Natalia, doing her best to claim belonging and respect in White spaces includes being especially cognizant of how she expresses herself. To do what she can to avoid racism, Natalia tries to speak slowly and enunciate her words when she is around White strangers. She does this because people treat her differently if they pick up on an accent. She tells me:

> [Whites] think I don't know what I am talking about. I felt like that a lot in places where the majority was White. Every time I spoke to someone who was White, I would consciously try to speak slower because I tend to speak quickly and then I enunciate. You just know they would—mostly I try to sound confident and the way I do that is by using big words. Then they'll be like: "OK." It's also an effect of how the country is right now.

Natalia uses these careful communication strategies to ward off racial microaggressions and stake out her right to be treated with respect. As non-White Americans, Asian Americans also employ similar language strategies to assert their American identities.[57] Interestingly, while Natalia is fluent in English, these strategies are meant to disguise her accent. Natalia feels her language strategies are especially important in a time when she believes there is an alarming rise in anti-immigrant sentiment.

Similarly, Diego uses his fluency in the English language to assert his belonging in unfamiliar White spaces. He engages in this strategy because he believes he is read as non-White and subsequently not deserving of acknowledgment, or service. As a result, like Natalia, he is intentional about how he speaks English:

> There are certain areas that are mostly White. . . . Maybe, sometimes you get the feeling like if you give off a stranger vibe. Like you are not part of the town, even though, you know, I speak English. It depends on the person, but I get the feeling sometimes you are not welcome and they kind of ignore you. When I do talk to them, I speak to them in full sentences in English, and that helps them to think: Oh, OK, he speaks English.

Like the language work that second-generation youth employ to translate for their immigrant parents, speaking English is a strategy to access social citizenship.[58] These resistance strategies are practical responses. Other research suggests that Whites aggressively disrupt and denounce Latino strangers who are speaking Spanish in public places.[59] For undocumented Mexican immigrants in hostile contexts, of course, the stakes can be much higher: not speaking Spanish is a matter of survival to avoid suspicions of lacking legal status.[60] Although Mexican Americans are citizens, their racialized identity makes their linguistic actions a strategy to claim membership in their country.[61]

For some citizens, strategies to combat racism might not be intentional at all. For example, Edgar, a nineteen-year-old who grew up in Koreatown, does not believe he faces much racism. Despite the names and extensive display of Korean lettering on storefronts, Latino residents make up 58 percent of the population in Koreatown.[62] For Edgar, adhering to a sort of unconscious respectability politics in dress and language deflects racism:

I kind of hold myself in a way that wouldn't seem to somebody else that I am from [Koreatown] or [that] I do drugs or something or stereotypes that people have of Latinos. I think I unconsciously made myself that way to prevent that kind of discrimination. I kind of never thought of that until now. The way I dress or speak maybe shields me from that. Some people might be surprised that I speak so well or that I go to college, but I never give it much attention.

Edgar's self-presentation of English language fluency and his manner of speaking are unintentional strategies to prevent being subjected to racism. Dressed in a neat, tucked-in polo shirt, Edgar presents himself as contrary to a host of Mexican American stereotypes, such as drug user or gang member. Certainly, refuting stereotypes through dress can be a strategy employed by both Mexican American and Mexican immigrant men. Other researchers similarly found that Mexican undocumented men dress with "legal passing" in mind and think carefully about choosing clothes not associated with gangsters.[63] Mexican American men of all legal statuses also manage a variety of raced and gendered stereotypes, including assumptions about being drug users, sellers, or gangsters, and may respond with strategies based on respectability politics.[64]

On the other hand, others attempt to dispel similar stereotypes in a contradictory fashion. Unlike Edgar, Robert sometimes goes out of his way to dress like he is "from the hood." He does this to deconstruct Latino stereotypes about what a college graduate looks like. "I want people to question it. Like: Who is this brown kid walking in? Sometimes I wear a tank top or muscle shirt. Can you see all my tattoos? Definitely. Sometimes I go to a college campus to see how people react to it." Robert predicts that if he visits a college that has a significant Latino student population, not many people will react to his presentation of self. In contrast, if he visits his friend at a predominantly White campus, he imagines people are uncomfortable with his presence. Noting the power in his presentation, Robert passionately proclaims, "I want people to feel uncomfortable because we feel uncomfortable." Whether adhering to respectability politics or not, Mexican Americans rely on linguistic and self-presentation resistance strategies to ward off racism and subvert stereotypes.

On another day, I meet with Ximena, a US-born citizen. For her, the issue of language is not so much a strategy in addressing racism as it is an indication of how she is perceived. Ximena does not remember many racial microaggressions from when she was growing up but recalls not interacting with many White individuals throughout her childhood. With the exception of teachers, she didn't interact with many Whites until she was in middle school and accompanying her mother to clean houses in the majority White and affluent community of Pacific Palisades. She reflects that now as an adult with children, she believes others perceive her as an immigrant:

> I see a lot of people just trying to speak to me in Spanish. If I'm out or at a store shopping and people will approach me and speak to me in Spanish. Sometimes they are talking to me in a broken Spanish and they are struggling so I will respond in English and people will tell me, *"Oh my gosh! You speak perfect English!"* because of what they see in me they are expecting me to only speak Spanish. I get that a lot. I'm like, wow! That is really crazy! Sometimes I look at myself in the mirror and I think: *How Mexican do I look?* [laughs].

Ximena is surprised when strangers assume she cannot speak English. She equates assumptions about her language fluency to physical markers of being Mexican. Ximena's description of a stranger's response to her English language fluency was delivered with exaggerated praise and a noticeable flair of condescension. Ximena's interactions with individuals who assume she speaks only Spanish are a textbook example of a racial microaggression directed at Latinos in the United States.[65] No matter the intentions of the executor, these microaggressions send the message that the recipient is not American.

Ximena's way of combating racial microaggressions involves complicating assumptions about her body by responding to Spanish-language comments or questions in English. Further, fighting racism involves her children. Ximena admits that her children are "sheltered," mostly because they live in a quiet suburban Mexican American community. Although the family does not travel much, she is aware of how she and her children are treated in White spaces. Identifying places she has felt unwelcome, Ximena suddenly remembers:

> You know where we get that a lot? In museums. We love museums. If we go to the Getty [an art museum] we get that a lot. Not so much the Natural History Museum because it's so diverse, but when we go to the Getty people follow us and I tell my children—and it's like ugh! I really don't want to make them aware of this, but then I tell them or I prepare them. I tell them, "If you ever feel this, or if you ever hear this, you have the right to get away from that situation. You don't have to tell the man or the lady off, you just stay away, be respectful and stay away and know that that happens."

Ximena enjoys exposing her children to new cultural and cross-cultural activities but is displeased that some of these spaces are not as diverse as they should be. Visiting art centers can be empowering and uplifting, but arts programs can be oppressive when people of color are made to feel like outsiders in these spaces. Ximena prepares her children for racial microaggressions they may face by coaching them on how best to handle the situation. This strategy is arguably a form of racial socialization, which teaches children how to react during racialized experiences.[66] By encouraging her children to be respectful and not "tell the man or the lady off," Ximena teaches her sons to engage in a sort of "politics of respectability" to defend themselves against racism.[67] This strategy is also used by Black middle-class mothers to protect their boys against harmful gendered and raced stereotypes.[68] Notably, Latino young men in another study in Los Angeles described experiencing racial microaggressions during field trips, with one participant expressing, "Everywhere we went, the White people would just stare us down, like, 'What are you doing here?'"[69] Combined with my research, these findings suggest that some field trip sites, such as museums that draw majority-White patrons, are spaces that need to be more diversified so that all guests are actively welcomed.

Other than museums, Ximena admits that she and her children are unfortunately followed around in stores. However, these experiences are also place-based because they do not occur in Latino neighborhoods:

> Sometimes I tell [my sons], "Put that down, we are going to leave right now" because I'll see people watching us, and it doesn't happen often, but sometimes it happens. We live in the Valley, so it depends where we go, because if we are in the Van Nuys area, it does not happen, but if we are, for example, somewhere in Woodland Hills.

Van Nuys is a predominantly Latino neighborhood (61 percent), whereas the Woodland Hills population is mostly White.[70] Ximena describes what can be considered "shopowner tailgate," which is when store clerks and owners suspiciously surveil customers, and is a common discriminatory practice directed to Mexican Americans.[71] However, interviewees did not often report having these discriminatory experiences in Latino or Mexican American communities. Instead, these incidents overwhelmingly occurred in predominantly White cities and locales. In these situations, Ximena immediately left with her children and talked about the incident as a family once they got home. While Mexican Americans in Los Angeles experience racial microaggressions meant to belittle them and mark them as non-Americans, these citizens also rely on various strategies to proactively avoid or retroactively cope with these identity-based indignities.

Conclusion

Mexican Americans can reflect on childhoods marked by some restrictions to spatial mobility. They learn that they may have the ability to travel but that their undocumented family members cannot. Even within the state and Los Angeles County, children are aware of spatial restrictions encountered as a family. As adults, however, their relationship to family illegality changes somewhat when it comes to spatial mobility. With their citizenship and age, their newfound independence allows them to move more freely throughout southern California. In addition, parental illegality becomes more of a consideration when adult children are with parents, typically celebrating a joyous occasion or searching for the occasional weekend recreational activity. For the most part, participants find that spatial mobility entails other concerns about the politics of race and space.

Mexican Americans are experiencing their American membership in a place-based way. Spatially navigating segregated Los Angeles means they are traveling through Latino and multiracial spaces where their citizenship is largely unchallenged and their experience of being a citizen in a mixed-status family is not all that unusual. Since participants grew up in predominantly Latino communities, these neighborhoods are spaces of belonging. On the other hand, when citizens discuss instances of racism or microaggressions, they do so in the context of White spaces where mostly White Americans are telling them to "go back to Mexico." These racial microaggressions include assumptions about their English language ability and citizenship—these microaggressions demonstrate that Mexican Americans' US citizenship is challenged based on physical markers of race or ethnicity. In this way, these Americans can experience place-based belonging and still feel excluded from other parts of Los Angeles (and the country).

For Mexican Americans, their experiences in White spaces point to the limits of their citizenship. Their identities are marked by illegality even in an immigrant and multiracial metropolis. Skin color, their own and that of their loved ones, can increase their susceptibility to microaggressions. Still, light-skinned Mexican Americans are also marked as foreigners alongside their darker-skinned counterparts. These findings are consistent with other sociological research with Latino millennials.[72]

Although darker-skinned Latinos experience greater discrimination than their lighter co-ethnics, lighter-skinned Latinos still do not escape discrimination.

Further, these findings are rooted in the setting of Los Angeles, but the spatial patterns I uncovered are not exclusive to this locale. Researchers have documented similar patterns of Mexican American or Latino residents experiencing racial microaggressions in urban and rural areas.[73] These patterns of racial microaggressions in White spaces are also found in research with middle-class Latinos.[74] Together, this research suggests there is a broader issue of anti-Latino racism across the United States that urgently needs to be addressed.

Evelyn Nakano Glenn's research points to the significance of citizenship theory to address how citizenship is a category of membership.[75] This membership is policed by the state but also by other members of the citizenry. In my research, "other members of the citizenry" is not an amorphous or homogeneous category. For example, among co-ethnics and in largely multiracial spaces, Mexican Americans do not feel their citizenship is questioned in a hostile way or meant to demean them. Yet, in White neighborhoods across Los Angeles, citizens can be made to feel unwelcome, making their belonging only a place-based ideal.

Since Mexican Americans know that their citizenship is not a physical marker that might fend off possible racism directed toward them, citizens move through space with resistance strategies to protect themselves. Some citizens carry documentation as proof for this reason. Other Mexican Americans rely on their English language ability to demonstrate their American identity, yet they sometimes speak Spanish to Spanish-speaking Latino strangers to demonstrate ethnic solidarity. This code-switching is a way to strategically prove citizenship and an effort to avoid threats directed at immigrants and Latino-origin people. No one wants to be ignored, patronized, policed, and brutalized. Even while living in a multiracial and immigrant gateway like Los Angeles, Mexican Americans deal with insidious anti-Latino and anti-Mexican racism.

These citizens, too, are at risk of symbolic forms of violence because they are marked as outsiders. Latinos, especially Mexican Americans, are routinely racially profiled as undocumented immigrants by immigration authorities and police.[76] Across the country, Mexican American US citizens, have been unfairly detained and deported.[77] From a mental health perspective, racism has deleterious consequences for people of color, and managing racial microaggressions certainly compels Latinos to expel emotional energy on resisting stereotypes.[78] Mexican Americans' spatial experiences in LA, then, are consequential.

In moving through segregated Los Angeles, citizens rely on proactive and reactive strategies to help their children or loved ones cope. Citizens like Ximena teach younger children to prepare for the possibility of racial microaggressions in White spaces. These strategies are important, particularly because some citizens realize their children, siblings, or loved ones might be "sheltered" by being exposed almost exclusively to co-ethnic or people of color multiracial spaces. Somewhat like the strategies used by Black mothers who are raising Black boys, some Latino parents carefully teach their children how they might be viewed by others and instruct them on how to best manage these raced and gendered perceptions and interactions.[79] While these conversations can be difficult for parents and family members, they are one strategy for managing racism in segregated Los Angeles. Still, it is worth explicitly articulating that these strategies shouldn't be placed on the shoulders of people who experience microaggressions and that, instead, these subtle and not-so-subtle forms of racism should be curbed by the perpetrators themselves.

Irrespective of how citizens see themselves in the national community, Mexican Americans report feeling welcomed and rightfully considered citizens in their local, largely Mexican American communities. However, Mexican Americans are confronted with racist interactions in largely White communities. Over two-thirds of participants reported experiences of racism, discomfort, and microaggressions in White spaces. While these interactions are between individuals, they are no less consequential or systemic. However momentary or bygone microaggressions are, they leave their mark on Latinos, who represent 48 percent of the Los Angeles County population, most of whom are also of Mexican origin.[80] With these resounding numbers, Los Angeles would not be LA without Mexican Angelenos, but belonging is an ideal yet to be achieved in all areas of this segregated place.

Conclusion

Uncertain Futures

Shortly after I collected the data for this book, the heartbreaking experience of one mixed-status family went viral. The cell phone recording captured a daughter's perspective as she watched her father being arrested in the Highland Park neighborhood of Los Angeles. Her crushing sobs and the image of a father in handcuffs illustrate a family's worst nightmare. Romulo Avelica-Gonzalez and his wife were dropping off their daughters at school when two unmarked cars approached their vehicle. Avelica-Gonzalez was swiftly detained by ICE agents as his wife and daughter watched from inside their vehicle.[1] Following his arrest, the public would come to know Avelica-Gonzalez's story through public outcry and learned he is a Mexican national who has lived in the United States for twenty-five years.[2] In that time, Avelica-Gonzalez and his wife had four daughters, all born in the United States.[3]

Avelica-Gonzalez's experience is striking for its visual representation of what has happened and can happen to countless immigrant and mixed-status families. Reflecting on the incident, Avelica-Gonzalez's thirteen-year-old daughter shared in an interview with CNN, "I never thought I would have to experience something like this in my life . . . on my way to school."[4] As a researcher, perhaps I am most struck by how the Avelica family seems so much like the people I interviewed. Seeing the video of Avelica-Gonzalez's arrest just outside of his child's school reminds me of Ruben and Carmela's story and how ICE agents similarly arrested Ruben while he was walking Tiffany to school. The Avelica family—headed by undocumented parents who have been in the United States for a quarter century, with both adult and minor citizen children—are very much like the families that participants in this study were part of. They, in many ways, represent the millions of post-IRCA mixed-status families that live in the United States.

Throughout this book, I have argued that what I call family illegality can seep into the everyday lives of Mexican mixed-status families. They manage illegality together, even while family members have a different relationship to undocumented status based on their immigration status and age. For undocumented parents, managing family illegality entails their being educational guardians for their children. This means that despite popular myths that Mexican parents do not care about education, I found that parents go to great lengths to ensure that their children can continue on their US educational pathways. Just as the Avelica family was carrying on with its regular routine of dropping off children at school, Mexican undocumented parents are dedicated to their children's educational futures on a regular basis. Families do the labor of managing family illegality because they hope their investments will pay off; a better economic future for the family is the goal, although economic success is not guaranteed.

While economic futures are to be determined for countless immigrant and mixed-status families, what is clear is illegality is dynamic and ever-shifting for all who are connected to it. Examining family illegality with adult children is one way we can see how the consequences of illegality can shift for Americans who possess legal status and are no longer minors. While I sought to explore how members of mixed-status families—in particular adult citizen children—experience belonging in the United States, this book is also about the broader question of what it means to be part of a mixed-status family and the different ways one can be an American. Adults who have undocumented parents manage distinct responsibilities and challenges, but their childhood was already marked by the constraints placed on their parents. As adults, however, we also see positive shifts. Although young adults can experience pressures and ambivalence about commitments they hold for their families, there can be a distinct pleasure in supporting their loved ones. Notably, these young adults are not always hampered by the constant fear of parental deportation. Deportation and family separations do happen, as was the case for several people who shared their stories for this research. Adult children who do not directly experience familial deportation develop ways to manage their fears around this urgent issue.

Popular depictions of the transition to college may include hopeful undergraduates moving into their dormitories with youthful enthusiasm. The young adults I interviewed had a zest for their academic pur-suits, but they also felt the weight of family commitment. For them, the transition to college represents some new experiences of family illegality and a commitment to balance financial breadwinning. Ultimately, they also see their college goals as tied to future financial stability. This goal is not unique to citizens in mixed-status families, but it is one placed on their shoulders precisely because their access to opportunities is at the very least not blocked by their immigration status. We know that un-documented students face harsh structural barriers to higher education and formal wage labor, but their citizen counterparts—while compara-tively and undoubtedly more privileged—also manage family illegality. Undocumented youth "learn to be illegal" once they become adults and newly navigate bureaucratic institutions.[5] In some ways, citizen children in mixed-status families also understand what it means to be tied to il-legality when they become adults. The FAFSA application is especially illustrative of this new adult relationship to illegality. Furthermore, even while adult children have a better hold on their fears about detention and deportation, they still have the lingering worry that something may happen to their parents. Despite their best efforts, these worries some-times distract them from their college coursework.

Young citizen adults' plans for mobility are often also met with the harsh realities of their social positions. Even while seeing college as the path to upward mobility, some college students and graduates realize at some point that these institutions were not built with them in mind. Moreover, once equipped with their degrees, some young adults find themselves still helping their families financially but are not in the fi-nancial positions they had hoped to reach by their age or with their credentials. Therefore, even as young adults manage family illegality and are seemingly on the pathway to success, they are still living their lives in the context of the high cost of living in Los Angeles and sometimes significant student debt. These realities are compounded by limited or sometimes relatively lower-paying professional postgraduate jobs, par-ticularly in fields like teaching, social work, and the nonprofit sector, where some of my interviewees hope to make a difference in their com-munities. This study, then, offers qualitative insights to sociology—a field that has been particularly interested in researching the incorpo-ration of the immigrant second generation, especially the children of

Mexican immigrants. We see the complex, and sometimes subtle, ways family immigration statuses impact the mobility and sense of belonging among this critical subset of the Mexican second generation.

Once citizen children are young adults, they find that they must also sacrifice for the family and live out their parents' educational dreams. Since parents have a dual frame of reference, the goals they have for their children seem feasible, but unlike parents, children do not have a dual frame of reference for making sense of opportunities. Although immigrant parents may have a rosy view of US educational opportunities, their children who have already navigated K-12 and at least some higher education know that these institutions are not always meritocratic or even as superior as parents imagine.[6] For this reason, many children are caught between two worlds: their parents' expectations and the American context where youth can face marginalization as working-class students of color. Carola Suárez-Orozco and Marcelo Suárez-Orozco argue:

> The children of Latino immigrants become the repositories of the parents' anxieties, ambitions, dreams, and conflicts. They are frequently vested with responsibilities (such as translating and caring for siblings) beyond what is culturally expected for children at their stage of psychosocial development.[7]

While this study does not focus on young children's psychosocial development, it is certainly true that children are the "repositories" of parents' hopes and dreams, and that when children are adults, they must learn to manage family responsibilities shaped by legal status differences.

"Illegal" Americans with Citizenship?

I heard from Americans who had a sense of defiance, frustration, or heavy disappointment as they bore witness to the public demonization of their families. In public debates, they see themselves depicted as "illegal" or contested Americans. Such explicit rejections of Mexican Americans' legal citizenship are deeply problematic because citizenship is a shared understanding of membership among the polity. A fundamental aspect of citizenship is belonging and the acknowledgment of social membership.[8] I find that Mexican Americans talk back to elected officials debating anchor babies and birthright citizenship by relying on a number of sophisticated claims. By referencing historical cases and the racial politics of citizenship and immigration, Mexican Americans provide a compelling counternarrative to politically produced rhetoric about mixed-status families.

These narratives also provide empirical answers for questions circulating among legal scholars and social scientists. As scholars debate the origins of the birthright citizenship clause or examine public discourse on anchor babies, there remains uncertainty about how individuals marked as anchor babies may experience these debates. In *Anchor Babies and the Challenge of Birthright Citizenship*, Leo Chavez analyzes anchor baby narratives in the public sphere. At the end of his book, Chavez argues:

> It is difficult to assess the toll on one's psyche of being the subject of vitriol anchor baby commentary. Imagine the emotional toll of continually being the target of mean-spirited bills in Congress to remove birthright citizenship, which would leave a person without a nation. Such inflammatory rhetoric may serve political ends, but it can cause a lot of collateral damage in its wake. So-called anchor babies must bear the pain of being called out as the Other in media and public discourse, and even by the president of the United States. They are made to feel as if they do not belong to the nation of which they feel so profoundly a part.[9]

I find that anchor baby rhetoric is yet another way the children of undocumented immigrants experience the public portrayal of their nonbelonging. Such rhetoric can take an emotional toll on these young adults—and it is especially hard for mothers and young children to process such vitriol. In all of this, however, I offer a positive perspective on such matters; young adults remain resilient even amid such symbolic violence. In part, some of this resilience sprouts from the empowering force of education.

Young adults often pointed to their college education as inspiring a positive sense of self and granting them the tools that enable them to be critical consumers of media and politics. When they think about immigration debates, they can rely on their personal observations, as well as the newfound access to data and research they consumed in their college classes and university events. Importantly, to some, their education was also a reminder that they should be committed to helping their communities, even as they have the privilege of US citizenship or may one day access economic mobility. Indeed, young adults generally felt that some Americans possess a convenient and politically dangerous amnesia about their immigrant heritage that helps them support anti-immigrant policies. They knew that Latinos could hold similar beliefs too, but that their ties to immigrant family members and the racialization of immigration could make their anti-immigrant beliefs harder to reconcile. For the most part, members of mixed-status families could turn to their education as a commitment to honor who they are and where they come from. The college context became a space where young adults could unpack what it means to be part of a mixed-status family. Some, for example, chose to write about or present on undocumented immigration/immigrants for their final papers or class projects.

Still, the college classroom was not exclusively transformative for college-going members of mixed-status families. Students also could find themselves in classes where they have to endure microaggressions from classmates and instructors. In some of these classes, they learn that their classmates brazenly call for the elimination of birthright citizenship for children born to undocumented immigrant parents. This is usually when they discover their classmates would fully support the mass deportation of people like their parents and other loved ones. Nevertheless, by the time Mexican Americans enter the college classroom, they are already familiar with this rhetoric. Despite these more hostile or disappointing experiences, higher education generally instills pride in young adults.

Certainly, education for all who can or want to access it serves as a powerful shield from political vitriol. These findings also provide optimism. Much of the psychological research, for example, captures how children in immigrant families may internalize harmful anti-immigrant rhetoric and display troubling psychological symptoms.[10] Young adults, I believe, transition to adulthood with more tools to make sense of both damaging anti-immigrant rhetoric and the legal uncertainty their families face. Yet, these same young adults also seek to bring dignity for their families and security via economic mobility. Examining these shifts to illegality also serves as a reminder that not everything we can learn about mixed-status families is all doom and gloom. By examining these young adults' experiences and creating space for mixed-status families to talk back, this book aims to highlight their agency, voices, and counterstories. In doing so, we can move away from scholarship that highlights the idea that bureaucratic and legal obstacles constantly bombard citizen children in mixed-status families because of their parentage. Yes, children have these challenges, but they also come of age to become resilient forces in their families and communities.

From a Presidential Campaign to a Presidential Administration

Not long after I finished collecting data for this book, Donald Trump became the forty-fifth president of the United States. Even before Trump was sworn in and able to implement his plans for the country, the election sent a resounding message about the value of a large swath of the American community, most notably people of color, women, and immigrants. Trump's rhetoric specifically targeted Mexicans and their families—and this sad fact was not forgotten by the targets of this vicious vitriol. Yet, for every bit of harmful rhetoric, Mexicans and Mexican Americans responded creatively to claim their worth and dignity. I am reminded of lifelike Trump piñatas I would see at swap meets, parties, and public events across Los Angeles; these piñatas illustrate how Latinos can creatively develop resistance efforts and engage in a rather unorthodox but likely effective strategy to release pent-up frustration.

Although the presidential campaign stirred up creative responses and resistance, I could not help but think that Trump's rhetoric could cause real damage to the people I was interviewing. Throughout this book, there is certainly a looming specter of a Trump presidency, as well as an urgent sense that Trump was responsible for a growing anti-Mexican sentiment. As much as I loathed bringing his rhetoric and policies into this story, it was necessary context for understanding the lives of members of mixed-status families; in addition, participants themselves directly referenced Trump or the things he said. Mexicans and Mexican Americans would tell me scattered stories of anti-Mexican pejoratives they had heard in social settings and at workplaces—spaces where they once felt safe.

Sergio, a young undocumented man, and his partner recalls hearing Trump-inspired violent threats at a college football game. By his account, he did not feel like he experienced much racism throughout his early years as a child and teenager. Yet, Sergio shares that he feels vulnerable to racism in the Trump era of politics. When I ask him if he experienced discrimination, Sergio narrates an experience at a local sports event:

> You know what? Not until recently. This is all thanks to Mr. Donald Trump. We went tailgating for a USC game. It was at USC. We are in line to buy snacks and drinks and there's these students behind us, two USC students. They were saying, "I hate Mexicans. If I had a Mexican in front of me, I would stab him right now." One of them was defending Mexicans and saying, "You shouldn't talk like that. I know plenty of Mexicans and they are good people and hardworking." I turned around. I said, "Dude, I am Mexican. Do you have an issue with Mexicans?" I think that's the only time I felt really discriminated. Yeah, they were talking about Donald Trump and how they believed he was in the right to kick everyone out.

Sergio recalls that the men talking about violence toward Mexicans were under the influence of alcohol and were probably unaware that he was standing near them. Even though he felt comfortable enough to confront the intoxicated man, Sergio admits that the incident was jarring. Unfortunately, this is just one incident among a rather long list of interactions in which Trump's rhetoric made Mexicans and Mexican Americans feel unsafe or othered.

Shortly after the 2016 election, somewhat similar stories surfaced across the country—from schoolchildren chanting "build the wall" to their Latino peers to Trump-inspired taunts hurled at Latino high school basketball players.[11] Such cases seem to reflect a broader increase in hate crimes that arguably are partially attributed to racial discourse and hate speech dispersed during and shortly after the election.[12] In the years since collecting data for this book, I have often been overwhelmed and disappointed with the threats and abuses directed at many marginalized communities. The human rights abuses directed at newly arrived Central American refugees, including family separation policies and the caging of refugee children, are illustrative of everything that is wrong with current immigration policies. The rampant state-sanctioned killings of unarmed Black men and women that have been filmed by onlookers on the street is also a shameful reminder of so much that is twisted, cruel, and unrelenting in a White supremacist society.

Trump's campaign and presidency were also distinctly anti-Mexican. When Sergio shares that he overheard a college student declare, "I hate Mexicans. If I had a Mexican in front of me, I would stab him right now," this statement was said while the student was praising Trump's rhetoric concerning Mexican people. The quote is also clearly violent and marks millions of Mexican-origin people as vulnerable to such extreme aggression, and such comments mirror the violence that is actually inflicted on Mexican and Latino communities. The El Paso mass shooting of 2019, for example, was explicitly an attack on Mexicans, as the shooter expressed his goal to shoot "as many Mexicans as possible."[13] It also stands as one of the deadliest attacks on Latinos in recent history.[14] The White supremacist shooter drove several hours to a Latino and predominantly Mexican-origin community to attack this specific population.[15] Some journalists pointed out that the shooter mimicked Trump's rhetoric in his social media accounts about how "Hispanic" immigrants are an invasion.[16] Even as Latinos resist this harmful rhetoric, it is clear that anti-immigrant and anti-Latino discourse can have real, sometimes fatal consequences.

Still, even while Trump can be the boogeyman to point to regarding the issues I address here, I would be remiss to ignore that long before a reality television star was in the White House, other elected officials and pundits created fertile ground for anti-immigrant and racist discourse and policies. Part of what immigrant families had been dealing with long before Trump was Barack Obama's punitive stance on immigration enforcement—the resulting record-breaking deportation rates under his administration reflect his policy stance and a broad number of elected officials who were unwilling to compromise on immigration reform.

There has been resistance at the policy level, too. For example, when the Trump administration outlined an aggressive immigration plan that would focus on deporting a significant number of undocumented immigrants, California policy makers fought back. California lawmakers successfully passed California Senate Bill 54, more popularly referred to as the "sanctuary state" bill, into law. This bill does the following:

> Expand[s] so-called sanctuary city policies, prohibiting state and local
> law enforcement agencies, including school police and security depart-
> ments, from using resources to investigate, interrogate, detain, detect or
> arrest people for immigration enforcement purposes.[17]

The policy went into effect in January 2018 and can protect a reported
2.3 million undocumented immigrants living in the state of California.[18]

Even with this resistance effort against the priorities of the Trump administration, undocumented immigrants would be pushed to a certain
level of legal vulnerability. At the end of 2016, following the election,
Trump announced plans to deport all eleven million undocumented immigrants, beginning with two to three million immigrants with criminal
records.[19] In September 2017, it appeared that such a plan was going to
be a reality when reports surfaced that the Department of Homeland
Security would conduct mass raids to identify and detain eight thousand
undocumented immigrants. Operation Mega was canceled, reportedly
because resources had to be channeled to hurricane relief in Texas and
Florida.[20] President Trump further expanded detention and deportation
priorities to include noncriminals, although, during the 2017 fiscal year,
approximately 28 percent of deported immigrants did not possess criminal convictions.[21] Then, in June 2019, Trump announced via Twitter that
immigration agents would execute mass immigration raids across the
country, but the operation was later called off, reportedly because the
media had leaked the plan.[22] Two short months later, in August, federal agents arrested 680 immigrants working primarily in poultry plants
across the state of Mississippi.[23] Undeniably, Trump's enforcement actions regarding immigration were punitive.

Undocumented youth, some of whom were protected with DACA,
were soon informed that the Trump administration would rescind the
DACA program beginning in March 2018. When the news was announced in September 2017, it meant that in a matter of months approximately eight hundred thousand DACAmented youth would no
longer be protected from deportation.[24] In making the announcement,
former attorney general Jeff Sessions justified this policy move as one
intended to protect Americans from lawbreaking immigrants who take
jobs that should be reserved for citizens.[25] After some grueling years,
DACA became accessible again in 2020, but then was challenged and

closed to new applicants in 2021.[26] At the same time, there has been a push for the Dream and Promise Act (H.R. 6), which can provide a pathway to citizenship for some immigrants, including DACA-eligible immigrants and those with Temporary Protected Status or Deferred Enforced Departure.[27]

Like all things, the Trump administration came to an end. Aside from a global pandemic, what followed were a series of policy proposals that could legalize undocumented immigrants. The Citizenship for Essential Workers Act could legalize about seven million immigrants who worked as essential workers during the pandemic and undocumented immigrants who lost an essential worker family member due to COVID-19.[28] The Biden administration and congressional Democrats also introduced the US Citizenship Act of 2021, which would legalize many of the immigrants who are featured in this book. Unlike other proposed bills that seek to target specific populations, the US Citizenship Act would be the most inclusive because it can help legalize eleven million undocumented immigrants.[29] Also, in 2021, Mexico implemented a constitutional amendment that grants the descendants of Mexican-origin people Mexican nationality. Mexican nationality includes certain benefits, such as property and voting rights, and the possibility of seeking education and employment in Mexico.[30] Importantly, this constitutional amendment can prevent Mexican-origin people from becoming stateless. For Mexican mixed-status families and undocumented communities, the last few years have entailed much uncertainty, many setbacks, and some room for optimism. It remains to be seen what the policy landscape will look like for mixed-status families in the years ahead.

Moving toward Change: Policy Recommendations

Understandably, much remains at stake for mixed-status families—even for the more privileged among them who live in Los Angeles County's immigrant-accommodating context. Still, while I examined families in an immigrant-friendly context, all mixed-status families—regardless of race/ethnicity or location—have to contend with federal immigration law and, to various extents, the fear of state and community stigma and surveillance. Illegality is still managed when immigrants and their loved ones deal with the constraints attached to undocumented status, including those involving employment, restricted mobility, and blocked access to a wide variety of medical, civic, and economic resources. The most obvious solution that would make a world of difference in the lives of many mixed-status families would undoubtedly be comprehensive immigration reform. Some of the educational and integration challenges faced by youth can be diminished when parents, particularly mothers, become legalized.[31] Further, comprehensive immigration reform would be an appropriate response to a problem that US immigration policies have created in the first place: enduring illegality for millions of people instead of a pathway to become formally integrated into the country. Reform would mean that the harsh consequences of illegality, which scholars have argued are comparable to the outcomes we see with racial and gender inequalities, would partly disappear.[32] However, as Heide Castañeda has argued, the long-term health consequences and trauma of illegality may not be entirely resolved with reform.[33] I agree. And yet, the millions of undocumented people who form part of the United States deserve a new chance at repairing what immigration policies have taken from them all these years. As it turns out, most Americans also support a pathway to citizenship for undocumented immigrants, with 84 percent of Americans and 76 percent of Republicans favoring a citizenship pathway for these immigrants.[34]

Creating a pathway to legal permanent residency and naturalized citizenship is not only humane but also socially responsible. With many parents in this study residing in the country for more than twenty years, it is clear that a humane immigration policy is also overdue. While many families with adult-age children are managing family illegality now, a shift in immigration policy can prevent an entirely new generation of American children from growing up with the ongoing struggle of their parents' state-produced vulnerability. Immigration reform would provide families with real, tangible benefits. Although I would be remiss not to state the obvious: legal status or eventual citizenship should not be the only pathway for families to access a semblance of mobility, economic opportunity, safety, or the tools that allow one to live a dignified life. Legal status and citizenship help, but they do not guarantee these rights. We know from young adults that their citizenship can offer only so much in their lives. Thinking more broadly, in the wake of police killings of Black Americans and the lives and economic stability lost in the times of COVID-19, citizenship does not offer the true human safety, health access, justice, and dignity all people deserve. Thus, I posit that comprehensive immigration reform would yield benefits for some and would be a good starting point, but ultimately it would be limited in its power for true transformative social change for mixed-status families and others.

IRCA, passed over thirty-five years ago, did provide concrete benefits to families. The individuals I interviewed touched on how they had witnessed the benefits of IRCA by seeing how their legalized extended family members were better able to push their families out of poverty, purchase homes, access health insurance, and go on much-cherished international trips to visit the ancestral homeland. These are precisely the opportunities mixed-status families would not take for granted. These opportunities would also do much to provide families with a better quality of life. Adult children of all legal statuses ultimately have the hope that their parents can one day see their home countries again, access affordable health care, and retire with some peace of mind. Undocumented immigrants also have a strong desire to participate in the workforce with legal status because they hope this will mean higher wages, less workplace exploitation, and the security to more safely pursue worker rights.

When DAPA was still a possibility, researchers estimated that newly legalized workers (albeit legalized temporarily) would be able to see a 6 to 10 percent increase in average wages.[35] When parents earn more, children reap the benefits. Given the gains in earnings for legalized workers, researchers predicted that DAPA could have lifted forty thousand of California's children out of poverty.[36] Providing a permanent pathway to legalizing parents should be an important focus for poverty scholars and all who seek to eradicate poverty. These tangible benefits and the sense of safety and pleasure they may provide would make a significant difference for people without legal status and all those who call them family and friends. Legalization is also good for the country because it makes economic sense. When immigrants are formally incorporated, the US economy will benefit from these members of the community who are likely to have more financial security to boost the economy as laborers, taxpayers, and consumers.

These recommendations, in some ways, may become more urgent over time. As parents age into their fifties, sixties, and seventies, the looming questions of retirement and later-in-life health care become harder to ignore. With decades of employment experience to their name, these immigrant workers do not have access to Social Security or any benefits that their tax dollars helped pay for. Their work experience in occupations that tend to be hard on the body also means these workers may feel the wear and tear on their bodies a lot earlier in life. Researchers may already be familiar with the "sandwich generation," or parents who become sandwiched between supporting their children and their aging elderly parents.[37] I believe researchers and policy makers need to consider how the adult children I interviewed here and the many like them can be "sandwiched" in the very near future. And I believe this new sandwich generation will include some adult children who are still relatively young, caring for minor children while their own parents age, and lack government supports for their financial and physical care.

Indeed, both parents and children made these observations and had deep worries about what this would mean for their futures. Daughters, in particular, expressed concern about this situation and knew they would likely be handling more of the caregiving responsibilities when their parents age further. Adult children like Natalia will have to perform financial and physical caregiving when her parents age without the kinds of social programs that are available to seniors with legal authorization. Thus, immigration reform would allow aging immigrants to live out their golden years with some access to social support to alleviate a cumulative social problem. Doing so would clearly help the immigrants in question and their adult children, who may find themselves strapped for time and money while caring for both aging parents and their own families.

In the meantime, in the absence of immigration reform, individual families would be able to benefit from changes to the pivotally important 1996 IIRIRA law. It is precisely this policy that has made sponsoring an undocumented parent so difficult to manage because of the three- or ten-year bar. Eliminating these bars would do much to help families and provide a pathway to welcome new Americans who are often eager to officially become part of a country that has long been their home and is the birthplace of their children. Another alternative to facilitating the legalization of parents would be to expand waivers so that immigrants do not have to demonstrate that their absence would be an extreme hardship only to lawfully present spouses or parents. This current requirement leaves out countless families that do not include citizen or permanent resident spouses or grandparents. Ideally, eliminating the bars or removing any extreme hardship requirement to the waiving of extended family separation would make a tremendous difference for mixed-status families who want to access legalization without exiling loved ones.

Another lesser-known solution to helping undocumented immigrants access legal permanent residency is changing the registry date. Immigrants who entered the United States before January 1, 1970, and have maintained continuous residence may be eligible for a green card.[38] Immigrant parents in this study would not benefit from this law, since they arrived in the United States in the 1980s, the 1990s, and early in the twenty-first century. Changing the registry date to 2010, for instance, would help millions of undocumented immigrants become legal residents and would legalize approximately 81 percent of the greater Los Angeles undocumented population.[39] What's more, the statute itself is uncomplicated, and a bill changing the registry date would also be uncharacteristically easy to accomplish for an immigration law.[40] It also wouldn't be the first time this registry date has been changed—it has been moved three times since first being set for the year 1921.[41] This could create meaningful and inclusive change for many immigrants and families.

Any positive policy shifts should also be accompanied with the proper preparation to support immigrants who may be reluctant to apply for programs because of their previous experiences of exploitation. Immigrants with precarious legal statuses can be easy targets for con artists who present themselves as notaries or lawyers promising much-desired legal papers or work permits. A notary is not trained or equipped to manage immigration cases as a lawyer would. Adding to the confusion, the term notary, or *notario*, in Spanish is a professional title in Latin America that can mean the same thing as lawyer. Holding fraudulent and incompetent notaries and legal professionals accountable is important because they can ruin lives. Part of the reason some families were reluctant to apply for programs like DACA or DAPA or move forward with a pathway to residency is because it seems that just about every immigrant family has someone in their social circle who was swindled by a notary or someone presenting themselves as a legal professional. In the worst cases, immigrants not only are swindled but the actions of their lawyers or notaries result in their deportation or exile. Raúl, for example, attributed the deportation of his parents to their being victims of fraud. Other adult children noted that their parents had lost thousands of dollars to con artists who promised them some sort of legal authorization to be present or labor in the country. Others may have received help from legal professionals who gave bad advice. In observing know-your-rights workshops, I noted that lawyers sometimes reflected on cases they had heard about in which undocumented loved ones were encouraged by their lawyers to leave the country with the promise that they could immediately return with legal authorization. After these clients left the country, however, they found out they would not be able to legally reenter without waiting out an extended bar. Unfortunately, it seemed that these stories about fraud or incompetence were all too common. The unsurprising result of these stories is a community that becomes more insular and less trusting. If there should be a broad amnesty for which undocumented immigrants can apply, these very reasonable fears about engaging with legal professionals and bureaucratic institutions can and will surface. Supporting reputable community organizations that continue to host free and accessible know-your-rights workshops with trusted and diligent lawyers is but one way to address these concerns.

The increasing use of the term "mixed-status" to describe families has benefits that are beyond symbolic. Acknowledging that there are families with members of different immigration statuses rectifies a common misconception that immigration is solely an immigrant issue. Further, by using the term "mixed-status," I believe more appropriate policy solutions and community problem solving can be accomplished. For instance, institutions of higher education can better train staff to advise both undocumented students and students in mixed-status families who may have trouble with the financial aid process. Importantly, if educational staff and gatekeepers at all levels are aware of the challenges faced by mixed-status families, many would be better equipped to support students when they fear or experience family deportation. All forms of resistance and media literacy efforts to create responsible and accurate media about immigration are also immensely important. Understandably, several supports need to be provided to families who have experienced deportation and those who manage a binational separation.

Many of the suggestions I present here are necessary but insufficient for true transformative progress. For one, even if immigrant-friendly comprehensive immigration reform is accomplished, there will still be many families who may not benefit from such a reform, just as there were families who would not have benefited from DAPA if it had become available. Individuals with active deportation orders and/or immigrants with criminal records are not as likely to find themselves eligible for policy relief. Many of the participants I interviewed argued that a pathway to legalization must be earned, and those with criminal records are perceived as not only unworthy but also partially to blame for the stigmatization of all immigrants. How can we honor immigrants who have done right by also creating spaces of human redemption for racialized immigrants who have made mistakes? After all, mistakes committed by undocumented immigrants are often made in a context in which their status and living conditions make committing some infractions all but necessary for survival. These infractions, however, are what eventually make these immigrants the most vulnerable, the most deportable. Their children, then, also live with this heightened sense of deportability. Yet people who work hard and aim to live their lives honestly also want to feel that their struggle will eventually bring them rewards, however small.

Even while undocumented youth have not been central to the story I tell here, we can learn a lot from their politics and organizing. Witnessing some of immigrant youths' smart and inclusive politics tells me that bringing those from the margin to the center works. Immigrant youth movements have not left behind immigrants with criminal records. Undocumented youth, for example, have mobilized for detained immigrants who may have items on their records. Avelica-Gonzalez, for example, has a DUI on his record. Still, activists mobilized for him. The Avelica family story is one of cautious optimism. Avelica-Gonzalez was not deported and, in August 2017, was released from Adelanto Detention Center on bond.[42] An appeals court judge vacated Avelica-Gonzalez's deportation order, but his case has been moved to the lower courts, where his fate may not be determined for several years.[43]

Only time will tell what future political leadership and on-the-ground community resistance will mean for members of mixed-status families. Some things may change; others may stay the same. For families with whom I still have contact, their lives have changed but immigration statuses have remained unaltered or can feel threatened, as was the case with DACA. In the meantime, people keep on living their lives. Some young adults—like the ones in this book—fall in love, complete degrees, change careers, move, return, experience loss, and heal fractured relationships. In the years since this study, some parents have seen their families grow as they become hopeful grandparents and love another generation of US citizens. I think of many of the people in these pages and their loved ones—some of whom I met only in photos. Whether or not they are recognized as citizens, these Americans deserve the opportunity to thrive and be with their families in a country that should finally affirm to them *you belong here*.

ACKNOWLEDGMENTS

I extend my greatest gratitude to all who helped make this project possible. This book is dedicated to the research participants who trusted me with their stories. It is a special honor to impart a bit about their lives here. *Muchas gracias.*

I also extend my appreciation to the funders who helped me pursue this research. This includes support from the UMass Graduate School, the UMass Department of Sociology, the UMass Center for Research on Families, and the Society for the Study of Social Problems. The University of Michigan's National Center for Institutional Diversity also provided funding support for one of the chapters. I am incredibly grateful to the Institute for Citizens & Scholars (previously known as the Woodrow Wilson Foundation), which provided me with a one-year Early Career Enhancement Fellowship to work on the second round of revisions. These supports were invaluable.

Special thanks to Ilene Kalish for believing in this work and to Sonia Tsuruoka, Yasemin Torfilli, Alexia Traganas, Susan Ecklund, and the rest of the NYU Press staff for helping me through the book publishing process. I am thankful to the anonymous reviewers who read a draft of this work and provided helpful feedback.

This book would not have come to fruition were it not for powerful women of color who inspired my interest in sociology. What first drew me to sociology was taking classes in other disciplines taught by Chicana sociologists. In particular, I think of an upper-level Chicano studies class titled "Third World Women and the Chicana" taught by Dr. Mary Pardo at California State University, Northridge (CSUN). I was in the end of my second year at CSUN when I enrolled in this class as an undeclared major thirsty for inspiration and career direction. Mary's class helped me find both of those things. It was in her class that I realized that maybe I, too, could become a college professor. I got a sense of my love for research, feminist texts, and teaching all through her class or the professional opportunities she extended to me later. Thank you, Mary. I am also grateful to Marta Lopez-Garza, Lauren McDonald, Shira Brown, Kris Kouri, Jesse Valdez, Dianne Bartlow, Sheena Malhotra, and Amy Denissen.

While earning my doctoral degree, I had the distinct privilege of working with a wonderful team of amazing feminist mentors who believed in my vision for this book. I am forever grateful and privileged to know my mentor and dear friend Joya Misra. I have learned so much from her during my time at UMass and in the years since. Enobong (Anna) Branch is also an amazing mentor and inspired me from the very beginning when I was taking her graduate course on race and racism. I am thankful to Miliann Kang, who challenged me in the best ways and provided me a space to think through my ideas. Leah Schmalzbauer also provided useful insights and encouragement. At UMass, I also had the privilege of knowing good souls who became my friends. I am thankful to Tim Oechsle, who became my first friend at UMass from day one at orientation. Celeste Vaughan Curington became my kindred sister and blessed me with her humor and brilliance. A very special thanks goes to Mahala Dyer Stewart and Karen Brummond. I am grateful to Alma Castro, Jenny Folsom, and Misun Lim. I thank Juyeon Park, Rodrigo Dominguez Villegas, Sharla Alegria, Chris Smith, Ragini Malhotra, Hebert Rodrigues, Abby Templer-Rodrigues, Carlos Valderrama Renteria, Nathan Meyers, Sonny Nordmarken, Stefanie Robles, Lucius Couloute, Patricia Sanchez-Connally, Patty Leon, Santiago Vidales, Manisha Gupta, Nicole Young, Hind Mari, Beth Berry, and Mamta Dadlani. I am also reminded of the wonderful spirit and support from dear friends throughout the years. I thank Juliane Perez for being another one of my kindred spirits, travel companion, and dearest of friends. I also thank Gabriela Correa, Bodhi Severns, the Perez family, and Zandra Arriola.

I am also thankful to scholars who provided suggestions on earlier iterations of this work, met with me, expressed their encouragement, shared resources, and/or helped me develop as a scholar. These scholars include Mary Romero, Joanna Dreby, April Schueths, Leisy Abrego, Laura Enriquez, Katrina Bloch, Tiffany Taylor, Hae Yeon Choo, Hana Brown, Jennifer Hook, Irene Browne, Marisela Martinez-Cola, Natalie Delia Deckard, Mari Castañeda, Millie Thayer, Naomi Gerstel, Jon

Wynn, Laura Briggs, Krista Harper, Donald Tomaskovic-Devey, Laurel Smith-Doerr, Veronica Montes, and William Lopez.

At the University of Nevada, Las Vegas, Ranita Ray and Georgiann Davis helped me generously with their friendship, as well as resources on how to develop a book proposal, best manage the publishing process, and navigate tenure track life. Thanks also go to Norma Marrun, Constancio Arnaldo, Robert Futrell, Tirth Bhatta, Nirmala Lekhak, Courtney Carter, Brandon Manning, Erika Abad, Anita Tijerina Revilla, Vanessa Núñez, Karen Villa, Steph Landeros, Korey Tillman, and my colleagues and students in the sociology department and across campus.

A number of people were especially generous with me throughout the years. A special shout-out goes to the Hernandez family for providing help, friendship, and temporary housing. A very big nod of appreciation and sincere love go to members of the Orellana family. Special thanks also to the *familia* Jimenez, *familia* Garcia, *familia* Delgado, *familia* Gonzalez, Marlene Cardozo, Jorge Galindo, Aracely Hernandez, Isabel Ocampo, Myisha, Edith Gurrola, Mary Regalado, Lourdes Guerrero, the "Glendale Crew," and many more. I also extend my thanks to a number of people, including community and student leaders, as well as organizations I may not have named here, but that I thank from the bottom of my heart.

I owe a great deal to my family, who were supportive of my educational pursuits, despite it taking so much time away from home. Thank you, Cecilia Rodriguez for being my mother and our family storyteller, and for helping me with my homework all those years. Thank you to Javier Rodriguez, *mi papi* and the person who I always want to make the proudest. Seeing the world from my parents' eyes taught me a lot about the sociological imagination, so in many ways, it's my life with them and their own histories that have shaped my educational pathway and research. I thank my siblings, Javi, Giovanni, Celina, and Carina, because they are among my greatest joys. It has always been a distinct privilege to be their big sister and see how each of them has come into their own as unique, intelligent, adventurous, and kind people. I thank my grandparents Raul and Rosario because when I think of them, what comes to mind is pure, unconditional love. I extend much gratitude also to my *tía* Ana, *tía* Chayo, *tío* Alex, Anthony, Brandon, *tío* Raul, and *nino* Ruben, who also have shown me nothing but love and support. I send appreciation to my *abuelitos, tías, tíos, y primos del lado Rodriguez.* Further, I extend much appreciation and love to Zelideth, Samuel, Carlos, and Ashley. They showed interest in my work from the very beginning, so their questions and check-ins about this project were always welcomed.

I am forever grateful to my husband and partner, who always knew how to keep me grounded but also never clipped my wings when I needed to fly. His sense of humor, along with our sweet little Bento, was everything I needed, especially during the more difficult moments of working on this book. To you, Jose, I dedicate only the most loving musical renditions by Los Panchos because there is just something about a Mexi-Rican collaboration that seems to work so well!

NOTES

INTRODUCTION

1 All names of study participants are pseudonyms. In very few cases, I use a different pseudonym for the same participant when they are quoted multiple times throughout the book. This was done in order to protect their identity.

2 Romero 2011b; N. Cisneros 2013.

3 R. Flores 2015.

4 Diamond 2015.

5 On September 5, 2017, the Trump administration announced plans to rescind the DACA program in March 2018 (Shear and Davis 2017). The DACA program was later restored in 2020, but then blocked again for new applicants in 2021 (USCIS 2021).

6 See Abrego 2006; Abrego and Gonzales 2010; Nicholls 2013; Unzueta Carrasco and Seif 2014; Aranda and Vaquera 2015; Pila 2015; Enriquez 2015, 2020; Gonzales 2011, 2015; Alexis Silver 2018.

7 See Ngai 2003; De Genova 2004.

8 Abrego and Menjívar 2011; Menjívar and Abrego 2012.

9 Baca Zinn 1979; Collins 1991.

10 Santa Ana 2002; Jacobson 2008; Gutierrez 2008; Chavez 2013.

11 S. Cisneros 2015, 277.

12 Bean, Edmonston, and Passel 1990.

13 Nevins 2002.

14 Kossoudji 1992; Massey, Durand, and Malone 2003; Massey, Durand, and Pren 2016.

15 Krogstad, Passel, and Cohn 2019.

16 Hondagneu-Sotelo 1994; Jacobson 2008.

17 Barreto and Segura 2013.

18 Mathema 2017.

19 Waslin 2011.

20 Such enforcement actions are also very lucrative to the many private contractors who profit from having immigrant detainees in their immigrant detention centers (Golash-Boza 2009).

21 US Department of Homeland Security 2013, 2014b; Gonzalez-Barrera and Krogstad 2014.

22 US Department of Homeland Security 2016.

23 Zayas 2015.
24 Golash-Boza and Hondagneu-Sotelo 2013; Das Gupta 2014; Dreby 2015; W. Lopez 2019.
25 J. Johnson 2014.
26 Immigrant Legal Resource Center 2016, 3.
27 For an overview of different assimilation approaches, see Bean, Bachmeier, and Brown 2015, 21–24. For critiques of assimilation paradigms, see Jung 2009; Sáenz and Douglas 2015.
28 Pallares 2014; Chavez 2013.
29 Bloemraad, Korteweg, and Yurdakul 2008, 154.
30 Marshall 1950.
31 Schueths 2009, 2012, 2019; López 2015.
32 Colvin 2008; Kremer, Moccio, and Hammel 2009; Dreby 2015; Zayas 2015.
33 Fix and Zimmerman 2001; Yoshikawa 2011; Luibhéid, Andrade and Stevens 2018; Hamilton, Patler, and Hale 2019.
34 Benhabib 2002; Yuval-Davis 1997.
35 Foner 1988; Glenn 2002; Alexander 2012.
36 Bosniak 2006.
37 Golash-Boza 2016.
38 Interestingly, a small minority of participants—including US citizens and undocumented immigrants—identified as American to challenge US-centric definitions of the term. For example, some participants reasoned that they are American because they live or were born in the Americas or North American continent.
39 Schmalzbauer 2014; Castañeda 2019.
40 Bloemraad 2013; Lash 2017; Flores-González 2017.
41 Glenn 2002.
42 Glenn 2002, 52.
43 Jacobson 2006.
44 Anderson 2006.
45 Jardina 2018.
46 Bloemraad and Trost 2008; Gálvez 2009; Pallares and Flores-González 2010; Pallares 2014; Vega 2015; E. Castañeda 2018.
47 I argue that illegality has been associated with Mexicans, but I am not discounting that illegality is sometimes associated with Latinidad/the larger Latino community or specific Latino groups that are not of Mexican origin.
48 Waters 1990.
49 Telles and Ortiz 2009; Vasquez 2011; Flores-González 2017.
50 Telles and Ortiz 2009; Vasquez 2011.
51 Omi and Winant 1994.
52 Ngai 2003; Romero 2006; Golash-Boza 2012; Alcalde 2016; Garcia 2017.
53 Jiménez 2008.
54 Glenn 2002; Gómez 2007.

55 Gómez 2007.

56 K. Johnson 2007; Romero 2008a; Gabriella Sanchez and Romero 2010; Camacho 2010.

57 Romero 2006; K. Johnson 2007; Rubio-Goldsmith and Romero 2008; Gunkel and Wahl 2012.

58 Romero 2006, 2008c.

59 Siskin 2012; US Department of Homeland Security 2014b.

60 Camacho 2010, 6.

61 Balderrama and Rodriguez 2006.

62 Golash-Boza and Hondagneu-Sotelo 2013.

63 Golash-Boza and Hondagneu-Sotelo 2013.

64 Stumpf 2006; Coutin 2011.

65 D. Hernández 2008.

66 Romero 2001; Rios 2011, 160–161; Aguirre, Rodriguez, and Simmers 2011.

67 Rhodan 2016.

68 Sánchez 1997; Pérez Huber et al. 2008; Lippard 2011.

69 Pérez Huber et al. 2008, 43.

70 This particular burden can impact White women who are partnered with Mexican undocumented men, as Schueths (2014) has demonstrated in her research with mixed-status couples.

71 H. Castañeda 2019, 18.

72 Dreby 2015; Menjívar, Abrego, and Schmalzbauer 2016.

73 Rodriguez 2019.

74 Mathema 2017.

75 Participants refer to themselves in a number of ways, and these labels do not necessarily remain static. Participants called themselves Mexican, Mexican American, Chicano/a, Hispanic, Latino/a, Mexican and Armenian, and Salvadoran Mexican or Mexican Salvadoran. Readers will see that I sometimes reference specific ethnic backgrounds (e.g., Salvadoran, Armenian) in order to honor participants' family ties and ethnic identities. I sometimes use Latino or Latina when specificity is not needed or when speaking about someone who doesn't solely identify as being of Mexican origin or about research that is on the broader Latino experience. I chose not to use Latinx because, to my knowledge, none of the participants had adopted the term at the time of data collection.

76 Luibhéid and Cantú 2005; Das Gupta 2014.

77 Stack 1974; Dill 2011.

78 This part of the data collection was influenced by Dreby's (2015) domestic ethnography.

79 Hochschild 1994.

80 It was during my fieldwork with families that I became aware of the myriad reasons why some families were not eligible for DAPA. Sometimes this was because parents had already been deported and return migrated or had items on their record that could make them ineligible.

81 US Census Bureau 2021a; Nasser 2017.

82 Gonzalez et al. 2020.

83 M. Lopez 2014; Gonzalez et al. 2020.

84 Pew Research Center 2014.

85 Gonzales 2015, 36.

86 Brown and Sanchez 2017.

87 Gonzalez et al. 2020.

88 Portes and Rumbaut 2001, 2006.

89 See Castañeda 2019; Getrich 2019.

90 Tienda and Fuentes 2014.

91 One notable pro-immigrant policy is California Assembly Bill 60. This bill allows undocumented immigrants the option to apply for state driver's licenses. It is important to note that accessing driver's licenses immensely helped immigrant drivers, particularly when being pulled over by police is a significant concern for this population (Schmalzbauer 2014; Enriquez 2015). However, I still found that several undocumented immigrants did not apply for their licenses. For some, being in a governmental database was enough of a deterrent to accessing their license. One young adult noted that her mother refers to her undocumented step-father as a "scaredy-cat" because he refused to apply for a driver's license. For others, their real or assumed ineligibility served as the barrier. In any case, for many immigrants, having driver's licenses available did not mean it was a resource some chose to access.

92 As I will show in this book, the immigrant-friendly context of Los Angeles provided some nuance to the mixed-status family experience. The area sometimes did provide a semblance and perception of safety, but the county was also home to family members who had experienced a family member's deportation. As Angela García (2019) has argued, the immigration politics of place and the subnational laws in effect there will greatly determine the experience of deportability for undocumented immigrants.

93 Abrego and Schmalzbauer 2018; A. García 2019; Valdivia 2019; A. Flores, Escudero, and Burciaga 2019.

94 Office of the Chief of Police of Los Angeles, "Special Order No. 40 Undocumented Aliens," November 27, 1979. However, sheriff departments did participate in 287(g) agreements (Gonzalez et al. 2020).

95 National Immigration Law Center, 2015a.

CHAPTER 1. PARENTS MITIGATING FAMILY ILLEGALITY IN DEPORTATION PLANS

1 Menjívar and Abrego 2012. I appreciate Boehm's (2011, 132) discussion of how immigrant transnational families don't necessarily make individual choices about where family members will live or migrate. Instead, family members are bound by decisions wrapped up in state power and the weighing of various risks.

2 Out of the participants who reported return migrating as a family, one mother shared that she would return migrate with her husband and preadolescent children but would leave a seventeen-year-old daughter in California so that she could attend college.

3 De Genova 2002.

4 Dreby 2012; Zayas 2015.

5 Close to the time of my data collection, a US citizen child of a Mexican parent could be eligible for dual citizenship, but this process required time, money, paperwork, and possibly travel. A popular article citing research and personal experiences of deported/returned families reported that it took one mother four months to arrange dual citizenship for her daughter (Hwang 2017).

6 Medina and Menjívar 2015.

7 Zuñiga and Vivas-Romero 2014; Gándara 2020.

8 Valencia and Black 2002, 83.

9 Valencia and Black 2002.

10 Gándara and Contreras 2009.

11 Dyrness 2012.

12 Villenas and Deyhle 1999.

13 Rios 2011; Ochoa 2013.

14 Vasquez 2011.

15 Telles and Ortiz 2008.

16 Oakes and Guiton 1995.

17 Rios 2011.

18 Yoshikawa 2011:25.

19 Suárez-Orozco and Yoshikawa 2013.

20 Suárez-Orozco et al. 2010.

21 Abrego 2006; Gonzales 2011; 2015.

22 Bean, Bachmeier, and Brown 2015.

23 M. Lopez 2009.

24 Vasquez 2011.

25 Yoshikawa 2011.

26 Ogbu 1990; Suárez-Orozco and Suárez-Orozco 1995.

27 Parents, for example, knew the cultural and pedagogical transition could be a culture shock to children. They worried that their children could struggle with the Spanish language and would fall behind and/or be placed back a grade.

28 I suspect these numbers would be higher if I had been intentional about soliciting this information from participants.

29 Pew Research 2014.

30 Pew Research 2014.

31 US Department of Homeland Security 2006.

32 Foley 2016.

33 Romero 2006; K. Johnson 2007; Rubio-Goldsmith and Romero 2008; Gunkel and Wahl 2012.

34 Sutter 2012; Pallares 2014.
35 Thronson 2006; Colvin 2008. The change in hardship requirements to contest a parent's deportation is arguably against the Convention of the Rights of Children (CRC), a universal document outlining children's most basic of rights (Sutter 2006). Unlike the vast majority of countries, the United States has yet to ratify the CRC (Sutter 2006). Among other rights, the CRC operates under the "best interest of the child" standard and specifies that a child has the right to be cared by his or her parents (Starr and Brilmayer 2003).
36 Menjívar and Abrego 2012.
37 Any parent or guardian can wait for their child in this waiting room, but the overwhelming majority of parents doing so are mothers. In my time there, I witnessed only one father wait in the waiting room for his child.
38 La Rumorosa is a town in Baja California, Mexico, located by the US-Mexico border.
39 Gándara 2020.
40 Gándara 2020.
41 As stated on the US Department of Education website, "There is no single authority in the United States for the recognition of foreign degrees and other qualifications" (US Department of Education, 2008, para. 1). Instead, independent credential evaluation services are often used to evaluate which foreign degrees would be considered valid in the United States.
42 Most public schools in Mexico do not offer special education programs or other similar support services (Santibañéz 2021).
43 Dreby 2010; Abrego 2016, 13.
44 P. Molina 2014.
45 Golash-Boza and Hondagneu-Sotelo 2013.
46 Dreby 2015; Schueths 2019.
47 Social inequality and the cost of higher education are believed to be two reasons why university enrollment in Mexico is lower than in other developed countries (Castiello-Gutiérrez 2020).
48 Ogbu 1990; Suárez-Orozco and Suárez-Orozco 1995.
49 Philbin and Ayón 2016.
50 Montes 2013.
51 Linthicum 2016.
52 Colvin 2008; Kremer, Moccio, and Hammel 2009.
53 Thronson 2006.
54 Medina and Menjívar 2015.
55 Linthicum 2016.
56 P. Molina 2014; Golash-Boza 2015.

CHAPTER 2. NEGOTIATING FAMILY ILLEGALITY AS YOUNG ADULTS
Parts of chapter 2 previously appeared in Rodriguez, Cassaundra. 2019. "Latino/a Citizen Children of Undocumented Parents Negotiating Illegality." *Journal of Marriage and Family* 81:713–728.

1 Gonzales 2011.
2 Dreby (2015) found that undocumented children with same-status or mixed-status siblings perform more housework than US-born children.
3 Fix and Zimmerman 2001.
4 Coll 2010; Abrego and Menjívar 2011; H. Castañeda 2019.
5 Capps, Hagan, and Rodriguez 2004; Brabeck and Xu 2010; Yoshikawa 2011; Abrego and Menjívar 2011; Vargas and Pirog 2016.
6 Vargas and Pirog 2016.
7 Xu and Brabeck 2011.
8 Schmalzbauer 2014; Orellana 2009; Kwon 2015.
9 V. Delgado 2020.
10 Schmalzbauer 2014; Dreby 2015; Getrich 2019; Rodriguez 2019.
11 García Valdivia 2020.
12 Dreby 2015, 112.
13 R. Smith 2006; Louie 2012.
14 R. Smith 2006.
15 Enriquez 2015.
16 Enriquez 2015.
17 Ngai 2004; De Genova 2002.
18 Portes and Rumbaut 2001; Zhou et al. 2008; Telles and Ortiz 2008.
19 Although driving was not a salient citizenship-based responsibility for the young citizens in this study, I did record and observe how driving was a meaningful task and negotiation in other families. For example, among some families headed by mixed-status partners with small children, I noticed that citizen women would more regularly drive to prevent undocumented unlicensed men from doing so.
20 Figueroa 2012.
21 This sense of guilt was also echoed by DACAmented youth who were able to travel outside the United States (unlike their parents) with the Advance Parole program (Ruth and Estrada 2019). However, over time, these youth, like Robert, felt grateful that they could be family ambassadors on these trips.
22 Abrego (2019) also notes how children experienced a "shared vulnerability" (14) when they were in cars with parents. Similarly, this driving experience was also highlighted in Enriquez's (2015) research as an example of how citizen children experience what she calls "multigenerational punishment."
23 Andrews 2018a, 2018b.
24 Enriquez and Millán 2019.
25 Rubio-Hernández and Ayón 2016; Gulbas and Zayas 2017; Barajas-Gonzalez 2018.
26 Rubio-Hernández and Ayón 2016; Barajas-Gonzalez 2018.

27 Abrego 2006, 2008; Abrego and Gonzales 2010; Enriquez 2011; Perez 2011; Gonzales 2011, 2016; Martinez 2014; A. Chang 2016.

28 Vaquera 2016; H. Castañeda 2019, 210–211.

29 Gonzales 2011, 2015.

30 H. Castañeda 2019, 130.

31 Verblow 2013.

32 MALDEF 2017.

33 Chavez 2013.

34 Suárez-Orozco et al. 2011; Galvez 2011; Boehm 2011, 141.

35 Massey and Sánchez 2010.

36 R. Flores 2015; Rodriguez 2016.

37 This section concerns legalizing parents, helping parents access their legal permanent residency, or what can be informally called getting papers for parents. There are legal terms that can describe this process, but for ease of understanding, I will often refer to these processes as the act of legalizing or sponsoring parents. I am not an immigration lawyer, and what follows should be considered my (and my participants') understanding of some immigration policies. Therefore, none of this writing should be considered legal advice.

38 Kendall 2012.

39 Kendall 2012.

40 USCIS 2019.

41 USCIS 2019.

42 Gomberg-Muñoz 2017.

43 H. Castañeda 2019.

44 Sarabia 2012.

45 American Immigration Council 2016, 3.

46 USCIS 2018.

47 This is very similar to Asad's (2020) concept of "system embeddedness."

48 H. Castañeda 2019, 196.

49 USCIS 2011.

50 Gomberg-Muñoz 2017.

51 Other research suggests that parents, too, may also refuse immigration sponsorship help to prevent further clashing with children or to avoid indebtedness to them (García Valdivia 2020).

52 Schmalzbauer and Andrés 2019, 645.

53 For a detailed account of one sort of legalization process for mixed-status families, see Gomberg-Muñoz (2017).

54 Swartz 2009; Swartz et al. 2011.

55 Gonzales 2015.

56 Desmond and Turley 2009.

57 Ovink 2014.

58 Vallejo 2012.

59 Yoshikawa 2011.

60 Passel and Cohn 2009.
61 Estrada 2019.
62 This is not to say that birth order does not matter. For example, these dynamics may play out differently in families where there is a large age gap between older undocumented children and much younger citizen siblings.
63 Abrego 2019.
64 Gonzales 2015, 122–128.
65 Suárez-Orozco and Suárez-Orozco 2001.
66 R. Smith 2006; Louie 2012; Vallejo 2012.
67 Dreby 2015.
68 H. Castañeda 2019; Getrich 2019.
69 Verblow 2013; MALDEF 2017.
70 Rumbaut and Komaie 2010.

CHAPTER 3. TALKING BACK TO "ANCHOR BABY" AND BIRTHRIGHT CITIZENSHIP DISCOURSE

1 I also recognize there is a strand of the anchor baby discourse about American babies born to Chinese maternity tourists. In this chapter, I am referring to debates that relate to families with undocumented parents, not lawfully present tourists.
2 Here, Leonardo used air quotes to challenge notions of educational prestige.
3 Pérez Huber et al. 2008, 48.
4 Montejano 1987; Glenn 2002; Gómez 2007.
5 Brush 2011.
6 Talking back also has some similarities with *testimonios* (see M. García 2014). *Testimonios* are what Das Gupta (2014) has called "forms of life writing that incite social change" (90). However, unlike carefully crafted and explicitly political *testimonios*, I capture interviewees' spontaneous responses.
7 Solórzano and Yosso 2002.
8 R. Delgado 1989; Aguirre 2000; Solórzano and Yosso 2002.
9 Solórzano and Yosso 2002.
10 R. Delgado and Stefancic 1993, 462.
11 See, for example, a number of works that theorize or examine how these debates are racialized, including Chavez 2013, 2017; Oliviero 2013; N. Cisneros 2013; Rodriguez 2016, 2018. See also Romero (2008a) for a review of how immigration and citizenship laws are racialized.
12 A Google search for the term "anchor baby" will reveal a number of dehumanizing images, including political cartoons of pregnant mothers running across the US-Mexico border, brown babies shaped like anchors, and children wearing cartoonish Mexican sombreros or stereotypical Mexican garb. To be sure, there is also resistance to this imagery. A contemporary example includes images that depict Donald Trump or his children as "anchor babies."
13 Zayas 2015, 20.
14 Colvin 2008; Kremer, Moccio, and Hammel 2009; Zayas 2015.

15 Passel and Cohn 2011.
16 Passel and Cohn 2019.
17 Hirsch 2003; Galvez 2011.
18 Massey and Sánchez 2010.
19 Chavez 2013, 74.
20 Galvez 2011; Chavez 2013.
21 N. Molina 2014, 93–95.
22 Lawrence 2000; Briggs 2002; Solinger 2005; Gutiérrez 2008.
23 Roberts 1997; Solinger 2005.
24 Jacobson 2006.
25 Gutiérrez 2008.
26 Cacho 2000.
27 Cacho 2000; Jacobson 2008.
28 Calavita 1996; Cacho 2000; Jacobson 2008; HoSang 2010.
29 Reese 2005.
30 Leiter, McDonald, and Jacobson 2006.
31 Romero 2008b, 2011b; Chavez 2013, 194–195. The term may also date back to the 1980s, when young Vietnamese children in the United States were called anchor children because they were believed to help sponsor relatives still living in Vietnam (Ignatow and Williams 2011).
32 Chavez 2017.
33 Ignatow and Williams 2011.
34 Flores-Yeffal, Vidales, and Plemons 2011; Chavez 2013.
35 Alexandra Silver 2010.
36 US Constitution, Amendment 14. The exception to this statement included the children of foreign diplomats and Native Americans (P. Charles 2012). However, with the passage of the Indian Citizenship Act, Native Americans were explicitly granted birthright citizenship.
37 P. Charles 2012.
38 Haney-López 1996.
39 Gardiner 2018.
40 Kendall 2012.
41 Kopan 2015. At the time, presidential candidate Ted Cruz also stood against birthright citizenship for the children of undocumented immigrants while Hillary Clinton, Marco Rubio, Carly Fiorina, Rick Perry, and Jeb Bush were against changing birthright citizenship (Chavez 2017, 36–37). Jeb Bush later apologized for his use of the term "anchor baby" during a campaign event (Chavez 2017, 37).
42 Lind 2018; LeBlanc 2019.
43 Calavita 1996.
44 For example, Representative Stephen King introduced the Birthright Citizenship Act to Congress by theatrically carrying an over one-foot-high stack of copies of the bill balanced on his shoulder (Chavez 2013). Although the bill itself was only one page long and did not require excessive copies, the rope-tied stack was meant

as a "spectacle" to symbolically represent the supposed burden of undocumented immigrants and their citizen children to the United States (Chavez 2013).

45 Frost 2018.

46 Ngai 2007.

47 Ngai 2007, 2521.

48 Castles and Davidson 2000.

49 Ngai 2007; Kendall 2012. The irony here is that birthright citizenship, along with the Fourteenth Amendment, was implemented for egalitarian purposes. Indeed, the Fourteenth Amendment finally overturned the *Dred Scott* Supreme Court decision and recognized African Americans as US citizens, while the "anti-inheritance rule" in the Constitution suggests that a child is not responsible for the circumstances of their parentage (Rodriguez 2009). Ultimately, the birthright clause was intended to prevent a caste-like system from emerging in the United States, thereby making this clause premised on an equality principle (Rodriguez 2009; Bloemraad 2013).

50 Oliviero 2013.

51 Bloemraad 2013, 57.

52 Public responses to the American-born children of Chinese maternity tourists can vary. Sometimes, these Chinese American children are viewed as potential assets to the United States, and other times, they are positioned as yellow peril threats or opportunistic wealthy elites (Rodriguez 2018).

53 Calavita 2007; Haney-López 1996; Flores-Gonzalez 2017.

54 Solórzano and Yosso 2002, 32.

55 It is not unheard of for governments to create a class of stateless people born within their borders. See Brookshire Childers (2020) for one example of how the Dominican Republic subjugates Dominican-born Haitians living on the island. See also Luibhéid (2013) for an understanding of birthright citizenship debates and anti-immigrant policies in other contexts.

56 I am referring here to the large-scale deportations or "repatriation" of Mexican immigrants and Mexican-origin US citizens that occurred in the 1930s and again in the 1950s (Balderrama and Rodriguez 2006; Blakemore 2018).

57 Rodriguez 2009.

58 Klein 2021.

59 Oliver and Shapiro 1995.

60 Jiménez 2008.

61 This interview was especially emotional, which is why I do not know the specific details concerning how or where Paloma was able to access financial assistance for her family. The amount of financial help she received was $300 per month for a short period.

62 For a detailed and complex analysis of how religiously active Latino immigrants rely on their faith to manage fears of deportability, see Guzman Garcia (2018, 2020).

63 Glenn 2002.

64 Even so, this rhetoric is not without harm. Mexican Americans reported these debates made them angry, frustrated, and disappointed. One person also expressed that she felt chills when talking about the subject.

65 Barajas-Gonzalez, Ayón, and Torres 2018.

66 Chavez 2017, 17.

67 See Serhan and Friedman (2018) for a brief overview.

68 del Bosque 2015.

69 Preston 2016.

70 Chavez 2017, 58.

CHAPTER 4. MORAL BOUNDARIES AND THE RIGHT TO BELONG

1 Barraclough 2011.

2 Loewen 2005.

3 Catanzarite 2000.

4 Gordon and Lenhardt 2008; Gleeson 2010; Andrews 2018a, 2018b.

5 Glenn 2002:188.

6 Amott and Matthaei 1991; Glenn 2002.

7 W. Flores and Benmayor 1997.

8 Rosaldo 1994; Rosaldo and Flores 1997.

9 Ghandnoosh and Rovner 2017.

10 Camacho 2008.

11 Calavita 1992; Ngai 2003; Massey 2007.

12 Glenn 1992.

13 Romero 1992; Branch and Wooten 2012; Wooten and Branch 2012.

14 Maldonado 2009; Harrison and Lloyd 2012.

15 Ngai 2003; Romero 2006, 2008, 2011; Chavez 2013; Rodriguez 2018.

16 Glenn 1986; Hondagneu-Sotelo 2001; Sánchez 2017, 34.

17 Hondagneu-Sotelo 2001.

18 G. Chang 2000.

19 Here I am specifically referencing the slogan of the National Domestic Workers Alliance (NDWA). See www.domesticworkers.org for more details about the organization's mission.

20 For examples, see Saucedo 2006; Lara 2009. There is a sort of paradox that surrounds these claims. On the one hand, immigrants highlight their labor; on the other hand, illegality is constructed as an immigration status to create a necessary but disposable workforce (De Genova 2004).

21 Williamson 2017. Karina, Arturo, and I also spent one spring evening discussing income taxes and filing. Karina files taxes for her family and helps other families do so too. During the course of our conversation, it was clear that she has assisted several undocumented immigrants and mixed-status families file their annual income taxes.

22 Goffman 1963, 11.

23 Goffman 1963, 11.

24 Chavez 2013.

25 Santa Ana 2002.
26 Dowling and Inda 2013.
27 The White House 2014.
28 Liptak and Shear 2016.
29 J. Ross 2016.
30 Nakamura 2017.
31 Abrego 2011.
32 Dreby 2012, 2015.
33 Buenavista 2016.
34 Lamont 2000.
35 Ray 2017.
36 R. Delgado 2016, 684.
37 Menjívar 2016.
38 Coutin 2000; Chauvin and Garcés-Mascareñas 2012; Menjívar and Lakhani 2016.
39 M. Smith 2014.
40 Ghandnoosh and Rovner 2017.
41 J. Ross 2016; Lind 2019.
42 Sampson 2008.
43 Aguirre, Rodriguez, and Simmers 2011.
44 Unzueta Carrasco and Seif 2014.
45 Unzueta Carrasco and Seif 2014.
46 Dingeman-Cerda, Burciaga, and Martinez 2015.
47 Negron-Gonzales 2013; Unzueta Carrasco and Seif 2014; Abrego and Negrón-Gonzales 2020.
48 Rosenblum 2015.
49 California Vehicular Code 40000.11(b).
50 Menjívar and Abrego 2012, 1385.
51 Prieto 2018.
52 Andrews 2018a, 2018b.
53 W. Flores and Benmayor 1997; Stephen 2003.
54 Appelbaum 2017; Elejalde-Ruiz 2017.
55 Bloemraad, Silva, and Voss 2016.
56 Golash-Boza and Hondagneu-Sotelo 2013.
57 Fernandes 2017; McDonough 2017.
58 Dingeman-Cerda, Burciaga, and Martinez 2015, 70.
59 Keller 2019.

CHAPTER 5. NAVIGATING RACIALIZED BELONGING IN SEGREGATED LOS ANGELES

1 Pulido, Barraclough, and Cheng 2012. There have been a few recent exceptions to this pattern, including the two programs called *Vida* (2018–2020) and *Gentefied* (2020–2021), both of which centered on Latino characters in working-class East Los Angeles.
2 Romero 2006; Getrich 2019.

3 Figueroa 2012.
4 C. Charles 2006; Tienda and Fuentes 2014.
5 C. Charles 2006.
6 US Census Bureau 2020b.
7 Bedolla 2000; C. Charles 2006; A. Brown and Lopez 2013.
8 Similar to Sue (2010), I am defining microaggressions as the intentional or unintentional slights and indignities that are extended to people of color.
9 Neckerman and Kirschenman 1991; Massey and Denton 1993; Pulido 2000; Britton and Shin 2013.
10 Logan and Alba 1993; Logan, Alba, and Leung 1996; Cort 2011; Cort, Lin, and Stevenson 2014.
11 Logan and Alba 1993.
12 Massey and Denton 1993; Purnell, Idsardi, and Baugh 1999; Fischer and Massey 2004; Roscigno, Karafin, and Tester 2009.
13 Tienda and Fuentes 2014.
14 Cort 2011.
15 Logan, Stults, and Farley 2004.
16 Rugh and Massey 2014.
17 C. Charles 2006, 150.
18 Iceland 2004.
19 Lobao, Hooks, and Tickamyer 2007.
20 de Certeau et al. 1998.
21 Tickamyer 2000, 806.
22 Glenn 2002.
23 Glenn 2011.
24 Lefebvre 1991, 7.
25 Lewthwaite 2010.
26 George Sánchez 1993.
27 Marcelli and Pastor 2015.
28 US Census Bureau 2021b.
29 Los Angeles Almanac 2022a.
30 Vicente Fernández is a popular longtime Mexican performer known for his *ranchera* music and renditions of Mexican classics.
31 Walderman 1989, 1–2.
32 Connor 2014.
33 US Census Bureau 2020a.
34 A charro is a Mexican cowboy.
35 *Raza* is sometimes incorrectly translated to exclusively mean race, but the term has activist roots and can refer to brown folks or a community of people that are often of Mexican or Latino origin (C. Lopez 2016).
36 *Cumbia* is a Colombian-origin music genre, and *merengue* originates from the Caribbean. Both genres, however, are popular in Central America and among Salvadorans in the United States. *Bandas*, *norteñas*, and *corridos* are distinct Mexican

musical genres. Using musical genres to explain the mix of Mexican and Salvadoran influences in her life is an example of an exchange between two insiders, as I knew without elaboration what Teresa was conveying to me.

37 I appreciate how Ocampo (2020) thoughtfully explains how the "Where are you from?" question is experienced differently based on who is asking this question of a person of color. When this question is addressed to a co-ethnic, the inquiry can be an attempt to form a bond based on familial or ancestral notions of home.

38 Los Angeles Almanac 2022a.

39 Lefebvre 1991, 7.

40 US Census Bureau 2021c; Los Angeles Almanac 2022a.

41 Santa Monica rests on the outskirts of Los Angeles and is populated by mostly White residents (Los Angeles Almanac 2022a). As a beach community, Santa Monica is not unique in this racial representation of residents; White residents of Southern California tend to reside on the outskirts of Los Angeles in coastal, mostly affluent communities (Allen 2002).

42 Vega 2015, 139.

43 Los Angeles Almanac 2022a.

44 Even while participants felt comfortable in Latino spaces, some older first-generation parents disclosed feeling disappointed with what they perceived as a lack of Mexican and Latino solidarity or support. Aside from a cultural idea that Latinos do not support each other, participants turned to national origin, language, and legal status differences as reasons for these divisions.

45 Romero 2006; Flores-González 2017; T. Hernández 2009; Hersch 2011; Ortiz and Telles 2012.

46 None of the participants disclosed identifying as Black, Afro-Latino/x, or Afro-Mexican. However, this does not necessarily mean that Afro-Latinos are not represented in the study. Two participants shared experiences that may suggest they are sometimes racially read as Black or Afro-Latino, but these experiences occurred within the context of family, friend, or coworker interactions.

47 Romero 2001; Rios 2011.

48 Ortiz and Telles 2012.

49 To be clear, I am not suggesting that light-skin privilege does not exist. I am suggesting that the local context of Los Angeles may mean that light-skinned Mexican Americans may still be identified as Mexican Americans and not necessarily read as non-Hispanic White. Aside from skin color, physical features such as hair color and texture, eye color, as well as clothing, names, and accents may also indicate to strangers that a person is Latino or of Mexican origin. It is possible that in other locales that are predominantly White and where Latinos constitute a numerical minority, light skin and non-Indigenous features may more readily mark someone as White-European. See, for example, Gómez Cervantes 2019.

50 Feagin and Cobas 2014.

51 Consider, for example, one nuance pertaining to skin color and racial identification for Mexican Americans; darker-skinned Mexican Americans are more likely

to identify as White on the US Census (Dowling 2014). These choices are shaped by geography, as well as assumptions about how US citizenship implies whiteness (Dowling 2014).

52 Dugdale 2020.
53 Tuan 1998; Tsuda 2014.
54 Jiménez 2008.
55 Zavella 2011, 134; Vega 2015.
56 Feagin and Cobas 2014.
57 Kibria 2002.
58 Kwon 2016.
59 Feagin and Cobas 2008, 2014.
60 A. García 2014.
61 If economic class or immigrant generational status is believed to offset racism in public spaces, the extant sociological research proves otherwise. Middle-class Blacks and Latinos face racism when they navigate public space (Feagin and Sikes 1994; Feagin and Cobas 2008, 2014; Vallejo 2011), as do third-generation Mexican Americans (Vallejo 2011). On the other hand, middle-class *visible markers*, such as driving a newer or well-kept vehicle, were a type of strategy undocumented Latino immigrants used to engage in "legal passing" in restrictive immigration locales (A. García 2019).
62 J. Sanchez et al. 2012.
63 A. García and Schmalzbauer 2017.
64 Rios 2011; Vasquez-Tokos and Norton-Smith 2016.
65 Sue et al. 2007.
66 Hughes et al. 2006.
67 Collins 2004.
68 Dow 2016.
69 Rendón 2019, 206.
70 Miguel and Chhea 2013; Los Angeles Almanac 2022a.
71 Vasquez 2011, 131–133.
72 Flores-González 2017.
73 Vega 2015; Flores-González 2017.
74 Feagin and Cobas 2014.
75 Glenn 2002.
76 Romero 2006; Gardner and Kohli 2009; Romero 2011a.
77 Lee 2015; Peralta 2016; Kenney 2017.
78 Sue et al. 2007; Clark 2007; Vasquez-Tokos and Norton-Smith 2016.
79 Dow 2016.
80 Los Angeles Almanac 2022b.

CONCLUSION
1 R. Sanchez 2017.
2 Castillo 2017.
3 Castillo 2017.

4 R. Sanchez 2017.
5 Gonzales 2015.
6 Ogbu 1990; Suárez-Orozco and Suárez-Orozco 1995.
7 Suárez-Orozco and Suárez-Orozco 1995: 65.
8 Glenn 2002.
9 Chavez 2017, 81.
10 Barajas-Gonzalez, Ayón, and Torres 2018.
11 Wallace and LaMotte 2016; Byron and de la Torre 2017.
12 Petulla, Kupperman, and Schneider 2017; PBS 2017.
13 Anguiano 2019.
14 Garcia-Navarro 2019.
15 I. Sanchez 2019.
16 Anguiano 2019; Wong 2019; Campbell 2019; Baker and Shear 2019.
17 Ulloa 2017b.
18 Ulloa 2017a.
19 Wang 2016.
20 Borunda 2017.
21 Pierce and Selee 2017.
22 Miroff and Sacchetti 2019; McCausland and Ainsley 2019.
23 Jordan 2019.
24 Shear and Davis 2017.
25 Shear and Davis 2017.
26 Dickerson and Shear 2020; USCIS 2021.
27 National Immigration Law Center 2019a.
28 Fwd.us 2021b.
29 Center for Migration Studies.
30 Mendoza 2021.
31 Bean, Bachmeier, and Brown 2015.
32 Dreby 2015; Menjívar, Abrego, and Schmalzbauer 2016.
33 H. Castañeda 2019.
34 Jones 2016.
35 Executive Office of the President 2014.
36 Pastor, Sanchez, and Carter 2015, 5.
37 Miller 1981; Grundy and Henretta 2006.
38 USCIS 2017.
39 Fwd.us 2021a.
40 de la Hoz 2020.
41 de la Hoz 2020.
42 National Day Laborer Organizing Network 2017.
43 Castillo 2018.

BIBLIOGRAPHY

Abrego, Leisy J. 2006. "'I Can't Go to College Because I Don't Have Papers': Incorpora-tion Patterns of Latino Undocumented Youth." *Latino Studies* 4(3):212–231.

———. 2008. "Legitimacy, Social Identity, and the Mobilization of Law: The Effects of Assembly Bill 540 on Undocumented Students in California." *Law & Social Inquiry* 33(3):709–734.

———. 2016. "Illegality as a Source of Solidarity and Tension in Latino Families." *Jour-nal of Latino-Latin American Studies* 8(1):5–21.

———. 2019. "Relational Legal Consciousness of U.S. Citizenship: Privilege, Respon-sibility, Guilt, and Love in Latino Mixed-Status Families." *Law & Society Review* 53(3):641–670.

Abrego, Leisy J., and Roberto G. Gonzales. 2010. "Blocked Paths, Uncertain Futures: The Postsecondary Education and Labor Market Prospects of Undocumented Latino Youth." *Journal of Education for Students Placed at Risk* 15(1):144–157.

Abrego, Leisy J., and Cecilia Menjívar. 2011. "Immigrant Latina Mothers as Targets of Legal Violence." *International Journal of Sociology of the Family* 37(1):9–26.

Abrego, Leisy J., and Genevieve Negrón-Gonzales. 2020. *We Are Not Dreamers: Undocumented Scholars Theorize Undocumented Life in the United States.* Durham, NC: Duke University Press.

Abrego, Leisy J., and Leah Schmalzbauer. 2018. "Illegality, Motherhood, and Place: Un-documented Latinas Making Meaning and Negotiating Daily Life." *Women's Studies International Forum* 67:10–17.

Acuña, Rodolfo. 2010. *Occupied America: A History of Chicanos.* 7th ed. Upper Saddle River, NJ: Prentice Hall.

Aguirre, Adalberto. 2000. "Academic Storytelling: A Critical Race Theory Story of Af-firmative Action." *Sociological Perspectives* 43(2):319–339.

Aguirre, Adalberto, Edgar Rodriguez, and Jennifer K. Simmers. 2011. "The Cultural Production of Mexican Identity in the United States: An Examination of the Mexi-can Threat Narrative." *Social Identities* 17(5):695–707.

Alcalde, Cristina M. 2016. "Racializing Undocumented Immigrants in the Age of Color-Blindness: Millennials' Views from Kentucky." *Latino Studies* 14(2):234–257.

Alexander, Michelle. 2010. *The New Jim Crow: Mass Incarceration in the Age of Color-blindness.* New York: New Press.

Allen, J. P. 2002. "The Tortilla-Mercedes Divide in Los Angeles." *Political Geography* 21(5):701–709.

American Immigration Council. 2016. *The Three- and Ten-Year Bars: How New Rules Expand Eligibility for Waivers.* Washington, DC: American Immigration Council. www.americanimmigrationcouncil.org.

Amott, Teresa L., and Julie A. Matthaei. 1991. *Race, Gender, and Work: A Multi-cultural Economic History of Women in the United States.* Boston: South End Press.

Anderson, Benedict R. O'G. 2006. *Imagined Communities: Reflections on the Origin and Spread of Nationalism.* London: Verso.

Andrews, Abigail L. 2018a. "Moralizing Regulation: The Implications of Policing 'Good' versus 'Bad' Immigrants." *Ethnic and Racial Studies* 41(14):2485–2503.

——. 2018b. *Undocumented Politics: Place, Gender, and the Pathways of Mexican Migrants.* Oakland: University of California Press.

Anguiano, Dani. 2019. "'It's Worse Than Ever': How Latinos Are Changing Their Lives in Trump's America." *The Guardian*, October 7. www.theguardian.com.

Appelbaum, Binyamin. 2017. "Fewer Immigrants Mean More Jobs? Not So, Economists Say." *New York Times*, August 3. www.nytimes.com.

Aranda, Elizabeth, and Elizabeth Vaquera. 2015. "Racism, the Immigration Enforcement Regime, and the Implications for Racial Inequality in the Lives of Undocumented Young Adults." *Sociology of Race and Ethnicity* 1(1):88–104.

Armenta, Amada. 2017. *Protect, Serve, and Deport: The Rise of Policing as Immigration Enforcement.* Oakland: University of California Press.

Asad, Asad. 2020. "On the Radar: System Embeddedness and Latin American Immigrants' Perceived Risk of Deportation." *Law & Society Review* 54(1):133–167.

Baker, Peter, and Ron Nixon. 2017. "Trump Proposal Would Deport More Immigrants Immediately." *New York Times*, February 19. www.nytimes.com.

Baker, Peter, and Michael D. Shear. 2019. "El Paso Shooting Suspect's Manifesto Echoes Trump's Language." *New York Times*, August 4. www.nytimes.com.

Balderrama, Francisco E., and Raymond Rodriguez. 2006. *Decade of Betrayal: Mexican Repatriation in the 1930s.* Albuquerque: University of New Mexico Press.

Barajas-Gonzalez, Gabriela R., Ayón, Cecilia, and Franco Torres. 2018. "Applying a Community Violence Framework to Understand the Impact of Immigration Enforcement Threat on Latino Children." *Social Policy Report* 31(3):1–24.

Barraclough, Laura R. 2011. *Making the San Fernando Valley.* Athens: University of Georgia Press.

Barreto, Matt, and Gary Segura. 2013. "Poll of Undocumented Immigrants Reveals Strong Family and Social Connections in America." *Latino Decisions*, April 15. www.latinodecisions.com.

Bean Frank D., Barry Edmonston, and Jeffrey S. Passel. 1990. *Undocumented Migration to the United States: IRCA and the Experience of the 1980s.* New York: Urban Institute Press.

Bean, Frank D., Mark A. Leach, Susan K. Brown, James D. Bachmeier, and John R. Hipp. 2011. "The Educational Legacy of Unauthorized Migration: Comparisons across U.S.-Immigrant Groups in How Parents' Status Affects Their Offspring." *International Migration Review* 45(2):348–385.

Bean, Frank D., James D. Bachmeier, and Susan K. Brown. 2015. *Parents without Papers: The Progress and Pitfalls of Mexican-American Integration*. New York: Russell Sage Foundation.

Bedolla, Lisa Garcia. 2000. "They and We: Identity, Gender, and Politics among Latino Youth in Los Angeles." *Social Science Quarterly* 81(1):106–122.

Benhabib, Seyla. 2002. *The Claims of Culture: Equality and Diversity in the Global Era*. Princeton, NJ: Princeton University Press.

Bhabha, Jaqueline. 2004. "The Mere Fortuity of Birth: Are Children Citizens?" *Differences: A Journal of Feminist Cultural Studies* 15(2):91–117.

Blakemore, Erin. 2018. "The Largest Mass Deportation in American History." *History*, March 23. www.history.com.

Bloemraad, Irene. 2013. "Being American / Becoming American: Birthright Citizenship and Immigrants' Membership in the United States." *Studies in Law, Politics and Society* 60:55–84.

Bloemraad, Irene, Anna Korteweg, and Gökçe Yurdakul. 2008. "Citizenship and Immigration: Multiculturalism, Assimilation, and Challenges to the Nation-State." *Annual Review of Sociology* 34:153–179.

Bloemraad, Irene, Fabiana Silva, and Kim Voss. 2016. "Rights, Economics, or Family? Frame Resonance, Political Ideology, and the Immigrant Rights Movement." *Social Forces* 94(4):1647–1674.

Bloemraad, Irene, and Christine Trost. 2008. "It's a Family Affair: Intergenerational Mobilization in the Spring 2006 Protests." *American Behavioral Scientist* 52(4):507–532.

Boehm, Deborah A. 2012. *Intimate Migrations: Gender, Family, and Illegality among Transnational Mexicans*. New York: New York University Press.

Borunda, Daniel. 2017. "ICE's Canceled Operation Mega Raises Immigrant Rights Advocates." *USA Today*, September 11. www.usatoday.com.

Bosniak, Linda. 2006. *The Citizen and the Alien: Dilemmas of Contemporary Membership*. Princeton, NJ: Princeton University Press.

Brabeck, Kalina, and Qingwen Xu. 2010. "The Impact of Detention and Deportation on Latino Immigrant Children and Families: A Quantitative Exploration." *Hispanic Journal of Behavioral Sciences* 32(3):341–361.

Branch, Enobong H., and Melissa E. Wooten. 2012. "Suited for Service: Racialized Rationalizations for the Ideal Domestic Servant from the Nineteenth to the Early Twentieth Century." *Social Science History* 36(2):169–189.

Briggs, Laura. 2002. *Reproducing Empire: Race, Sex, Science, and U.S. Imperialism in Puerto Rico*. Berkeley: University of California Press.

Britton, Marcus L., and Heeju Shin. 2013. "Metropolitan Residential Segregation and Very Preterm Birth among African American and Mexican-Origin Women." *Social Science and Medicine* 98:37–45.

Brown, Susan K., and Alejandra Jazmin Sanchez. 2017. "Parental Legal Status and the Political Engagement of Second-Generation Mexican Americans." *RSF: The Russell Sage Foundation Journal of the Social Sciences* 3(4):136–147.

Brown, Anna, and Mark Hugo Lopez. 2013. *Mapping the Latino Population, by State, County and City*. Washington, DC: Pew Research Center. www.pewhispanic.org.

Brush, Lisa D. 2011. *Poverty, Battered Women, and Work in U.S. Public Policy*. New York: Oxford University Press.

Buenavista, Lachica T. 2016. "Model (Undocumented) Minorities and 'Illegal' Immigrants: Centering Asian Americans and US Carcerality in Undocumented Student Discourse." *Race Ethnicity and Education* 10(28):1–14.

Byron, Ken, and Vanessa de la Torre. 2017. "Canton School Officials Apologize For 'Trump' Chant against Hartford Basketball Team." *Hartford Courant*, March 2. www.courant.com.

Cacho, Lisa Marie. 2000. "'The People of California are Suffering': The Ideology of White Injury in Discourses of Immigration." *Cultural Values* 4(4):389–418.

Calavita, Kitty. 1992. *Inside the State: The Bracero Program, Immigration, and the I.N.S.* New York: Routledge.

———. 1996. "The New Politics of Immigration: 'Balanced-Budget Conservatism' and the Symbolism of Proposition 187." *Social Problems* 43(3):284–305.

———. 2000. "The Paradoxes of Race, Class, Identity, and 'Passing': Enforcing the Chinese Exclusion Acts, 1882–1910" *Law & Social Inquiry* 25(1):1–40.

———. 2007. "Immigration Law, Race, and Identity." *Annual Review of Law and Social Science* 3:1–20.

Camacho, Alicia Schmidt. 2008. "Migrant Modernisms: Racialized Development under the Bracero Program." In *Migrant Imaginaries: Latino Cultural Politics in the U.S.-Mexico Borderlands*, edited by A. S. Camacho, 62–111. New York: New York University Press.

———. 2010. "Hailing the Twelve Million." *Social Text* 28(4):1–24.

Campbell, Alexia Fernández. 2019. "Trump Described an Imaginary 'Invasion' at the Border 2 Dozen Times in the Past Year." *Vox*, August 7. www.vox.com.

Capps, Randy, Jacqueline Hagan, and Nestor Rodriguez. 2004. "Border Residents Manage the U.S. Immigration and Welfare Reforms." In *Immigrants, Welfare Reform, and the Poverty of Policy*, edited by P. Kretsedemas and A. Aparicio, 229–250. Westport, CT: Praeger.

Carcomo, Cindy. 2015. "What's the Plan B If You Get Deported? A Generational Divide." *Los Angeles Times*, September 29. www.latimes.com.

Carter, Robert T. 2007. "Racism and Psychological and Emotional Injury: Recognizing and Assessing Race-Based Traumatic Stress." *Counseling Psychologist* 35(1):13–105.

Castañeda, Ernesto. 2018. *A Place to Call Home: Immigrant Exclusion and Urban Belonging in New York, Paris, and Barcelona*. Stanford, CA: Stanford University Press.

Castañeda, Heide. 2019. *Borders of Belonging: Struggle and Solidarity in Mixed-Status Immigrant Families*. Redwood City, CA: Stanford University Press.

Castiello-Gutiérrez, Santiago. 2020. "No Fees to Enroll Them All? The State of College Access in Mexico." *Journal of Comparative and International Higher Education* 12:27–38.

Castillo, Andrea. 2017. "Immigrant Arrested by ICE after Dropping Daughter Off at School, Sending Shockwaves through Neighborhood." *Los Angeles Times*, March 3. www.latimes.com.

———. 2018. "A Dream Displaced: Part 3. How One L.A. Father's Arrest Put an Entire Neighborhood on Edge." *Los Angeles Times*, April 5. www.latimes.com.

Castles, Stephen, and David Alastair. 2000. *Citizenship and Migration: Globalization and the Politics of Belonging*. Basingstoke: Macmillan.

Catanzarite, Lisa. 2000. "Brown-Collar Jobs: Occupational Segregation and Earnings of Recent Immigrant Latinos." *Sociological Perspectives* 43(1):45–75.

Center for Migration Studies. 2021. "The US Citizenship Act of 2021: What's Inside and Who Could Be Eligible for Immigration Relief." www.cmsny.org.

Chang, Aurora. 2016. "Undocumented Intelligence: Laying Low by Achieving High—an 'Illegal Alien's' Co-option of School and Citizenship." *Race, Ethnicity and Education* 19(6):1164–1176.

Chang, Grace. 2000. *Disposable Domestics: Immigrant Women Workers in the Global Economy*. New York: South End Press.

Charles, Camille Z. 2006. *Won't You Be My Neighbor? Race, Class, and Residence in Los Angeles*. New York: Russell Sage Foundation.

Charles, Patrick J. 2012. "Decoding the Fourteenth Amendment's Citizenship Clause: Unlawful Immigrants, Allegiance, Personal Subjection, and the Law." *Washburn Law Journal* 51(2):211–260.

Charmaz, Kathy. 2006. *Constructing Grounded Theory: A Practical Guide through Qualitative Analysis*. London: Sage.

Chauvin, Sébastien, and Blanca Garcés-Mascareñas. 2012. "Beyond Informal Citizenship: The New Moral Economy of Migrant Illegality." *International Political Sociology* 6(3):241–259.

Chavez, Leo R. 2013. *The Latino Threat: Constructing Immigrants, Citizens, and the Nation*. 2nd ed. Stanford, CA: Stanford University Press.

———. 2017. *Anchor Babies and the Challenge of Birthright Citizenship*. Stanford, CA: Stanford University Press.

Cisneros, Natalie. 2013. "'Alien' Sexuality: Race, Maternity, and Citizenship." *Hypatia* 28(2):290–306.

Cisneros, Sandra. 2015. *A House of My Own: Stories from My Life*. New York: Penguin Random House.

Coll, Kathleen M. 2010. *Remaking Citizenship: Latina Immigrants and New American Politics*. Stanford, CA: Stanford University Press.

Collins, Patricia Hill. 2004. *Black Sexual Politics: African Americans, Gender, and the New Racism*. New York: Routledge.

Colvin, Amanda. 2008. "Birthright Citizenship in the United States: Realities of de Facto Deportation and International Comparisons toward Proposing a Solution." *Saint Louis University Law Journal* 53(1):219–246.

Connor, Michan A. 2014. "'These Communities Have the Most to Gain from Valley Cityhood': Color-Blind Rhetoric of Urban Secession in Los Angeles, 1996–2002." *Journal of Urban History* 40(1):48–64.

Cort, David A. 2011. "Reexamining the Ethnic Hierarchy of Locational Attainment: Evidence from Los Angeles." *Social Science Research* 40(6):1521–1533.

Cort, David A., Ken-Hou Lin, and Gabriela Stevenson. 2014. "Residential Hierarchy in Los Angeles: An Examination of Ethnic and Documentation Status Differences." *Social Science Research* 45:170–183.

Coutin, Susan Bibler. 2000. *Legalizing Moves: Salvadoran Immigrants' Struggle for U.S. Residency.* Ann Arbor: University of Michigan Press.

———. 2011. "The Rights of Noncitizens in the United States." *Annual Review of Law and Social Science* 7:289–308.

Das Gupta, Monisha. 2014. "'Don't Deport Our Daddies': Gendering State Deportation Practices and Immigrant Organizing." *Gender & Society* 28(1):1–27.

Deckard, Natalie Delia, and Irene Browne. 2015. "Constructing Citizenship: Framing Unauthorized Immigrants in Market Terms." *Citizenship Studies* 19(6–7):664–681.

de Certeau, Michel, Luce Giard, Pierre Mayol, and Timothy J. Tomasik. 1998. *The Practice of Everyday Life.* Vol. 2. Minneapolis: University of Minnesota Press.

De Genova, Nicholas. 2002. "Migrant 'Illegality' and Deportability in Everyday Life." *Annual Review of Anthropology* 31(1):419–447.

———. 2004. "The Legal Production of Mexican/Migrant 'Illegality.'" *Latino Studies* 2(2):160–185.

de la Hoz, Felipe. 2020. "This Simple Change Could Legalize Millions of Immigrants." *The Nation*, September 1. www.thenation.com.

del Bosque, Melissa. 2015. "Children of Immigrants Denied Citizenship." *Texas Observer*, July 13. www.texasobserver.org.

Delgado, Richard. 1989. "Storytelling for Oppositionists and Others: A Plea for Narrative." *Michigan Law Review* 87(8):2411–2441.

Delgado, Richard, and Jean Stefancic. 1993. "Critical Race Theory: An Annotated Bibliography." *Virginia Law Review* 79(2):461–516.

Delgado, Vanessa. 2020. "'They Think I'm a Lawyer': Undocumented College Students as Legal Brokers for Their Undocumented Parents." *Law & Policy* 42(3):261–283.

Desmond, Matthew, and Ruth N. López Turley. 2009. "The Role of Familism in Explaining the Hispanic-White College Application Gap." *Social Problems* 56(2):311–334.

Diamond, Jeremy. 2015. "Donald Trump Jumps In: Donald's Latest White House Run Is Officially On." *CNN*, June 17. www.cnn.com.

Dickerson, Caitlin, and Michael D. Shear. 2020. "Judge Orders Government to Fully Reinstate DACA Program." *New York Times*, December 4. www.nytimes.com.

Dill, Bonnie Thornton. 2011. "Fictive Kin, Paper Sons, and *Compadrazgo.*" In *The Social Construction of Difference and Inequality: Race, Class, Gender, and Sexuality*, edited by T. E. Ore, 240–257. Dubuque, IA: McGraw-Hill.

Dingeman-Cerda, Katie, Edelina Muñoz Burciaga, and Lisa M. Martinez. 2015. "Neither Sinners nor Saints: Complicating the Discourse of Noncitizen Deservingness." *Association of Mexican-American Educators* 9(3):62–73.

Dow, Dawn M. 2016. "The Deadly Challenges of Raising African American Boys." *Gender & Society* 30(2):161–188.

Dowling, Julie A. 2014. *Mexican Americans and the Question of Race*. Austin: University of Texas Press.

Dowling, Julie A., and Jonathan Xavier Inda. 2013. *Governing Immigration through Crime: A Reader*. Stanford, CA: Stanford University Press.

Dreby, Joanna. 2010. *Divided by Borders: Mexican Migrants and Their Children*. Berkeley: University of California Press.

———. 2012. "The Burden of Deportation on Children in Mexican Immigrant Families." *Journal of Marriage and Family* 74(4):829–845.

———. 2015. *Everyday Illegal: When Policies Undermine Immigrant Families*. Berkeley: University of California Press.

Dugdale, Emily E. 2020. "As Palmdale Grapples with a Hanging Death, Locals Recall the Area's Racist History." NPR, June 30. www.npr.org.

Dyrness, Andrea. 2011. *Mothers United: An Immigrant Struggle for Socially Just Education*. Minneapolis: University of Minnesota Press.

Elejalde-Ruiz, Alexia. 2017. "Economists, in Letter to Trump, Say Immigration Can Boost Growth, Jobs, Wages." *Chicago Tribune*, April 12. www.chicagotribune.com.

Enloe, Cynthia. 2004. *The Curious Feminist: Searching for Women in a New Age of Empire*. Berkeley: University of California Press.

Enriquez, Laura E. 2011. "'Because We Feel the Pressure and We Also Feel the Support': Examining the Educational Success of Undocumented Immigrant Latina/o Students." *Harvard Educational Review* 81(3):476–500.

———. 2015. "Multigenerational Punishment: Shared Experiences of Undocumented Immigration Status within Mixed-Status Families." *Journal of Marriage and Family* 77(4):939–953.

———. 2020. *Of Love and Papers: How Immigration Policy Affects Romance and Family*. Oakland: University of California Press.

Enriquez, Laura E., and Daniel Millán. 2019. "Situational Triggers and Protective Locations: Conceptualising the Salience of Deportability in Everyday Life." *Journal of Ethnic and Migration Studies*. doi:10.1080/1369183X.2019.1694877.

Estrada, Emir. 2019. *Kids at Work: Latinx Families Selling on the Streets of Los Angeles*. New York: New York University Press.

Executive Office of the President, Council of Economic Advisors. 2014. *The Economic Effects of Administrative Action on Immigration*. Washington, DC. www.whitehouse.gov.

Feagin, Joe R., and José A. Cobas. 2008. "Latinos/as and White Racial Frame: The Procrustean Bed of Assimilation." *Sociological Inquiry* 78(1):39–53.

———. 2014. *Latinos Facing Racism: Discrimination, Resistance, and Endurance*. Boulder, CO: Paradigm Publishers.

Feagin, Joe R., and Melvin P. Sikes. 1994. *Living with Racism: The Black Middle-Class Experience*. Boston: Beacon Press.

Fernandes, Sujatha. 2017. "We Need to Fight for All Undocumented Migrants, Not Just Dreamers." *The Nation*, September 8. www.thenation.com.

Figueroa, Ariana Mangual. 2012. "'I Have Papers So I Can Go Anywhere!': Everyday Talk about Citizenship in a Mixed-Status Mexican Family." *Journal of Language, Identity and Education* 11:291–311.

Fischer, Mary J., and Douglas S. Massey. 2004. "The Ecology of Racial Discrimination." *City and Community* 3(3):221–241.

Fix, Michael, Margie McHugh, Aaron Terrazas, and Laureen Laglagaron. 2008. *Los Angeles on the Leading Edge: Immigrant Integration Indicators and Their Policy Implications*. Washington, DC: Migration Policy Institute.

Fix, Michael, and Wendy Zimmerman. 2001. "All under One Roof: Mixed-Status Families in an Era of Reform." *International Migration Review* 35(2):397–419.

Flores, Andrea, Kevin Escudero, and Edelina Burciaga. 2019. "Legal-Spatial Consciousness: A Legal Geography Framework for Examining Migrant Illegality." *Law & Policy* 41(1):12–33.

Flores, Reena. 2015. "Donald Trump: 'Anchor Babies' Aren't American Citizens." CBS News, August 19. www.cbsnews.com.

Flores, William, and Rina Benmayor. 1997. *Latino Cultural Citizenship: Claiming Identity, Space, and Rights*. Boston: Beacon Press.

Flores-Yeffal, Nadia Y., Guadalupe Vidales, and April Plemons. 2011. "The Latino Cyber-Moral Panic Process in the United States." *Information, Communication & Society* 14(4):568–589.

Foley, Elise. 2016. "Obama Administration Defends Deportation Raids on Families." *Huffington Post*, January 4. www.huffingtonpost.com.

Foner, Eric. 1988. *Reconstruction: America's Unfinished Revolution, 1863–1877*. New York: Harper and Row.

Frost, Natasha. 2018. "The Trump Family's Immigrant Story." *History Stories*, July 13. www.history.com.

Fry, Richard, and Jeffrey S. Passel. 2009. *Latino Children: A Majority Are U.S.-Born Offspring of Immigrants*. Pew Research Center Report. www.pewhispanic.org.

Fuligni, Andrew J., Vivian Tseng, and May Lam. 1999. "Attitudes toward Family Obligations among American Adolescents with Asian, Latin American, and European Backgrounds." *Child Development* 70(4):1030–1044.

Fwd.us. 2021a. "Immigration Registry: A Potential Pathway to Citizenship for Many Immigrants." April 15. www.fwd.us.

———. 2021b. "Statement on the Citizenship for Essential Workers Act." March 18. www.fwd.us.

Gálvez, Alyshia. 2009. *Guadalupe in New York: Devotion and the Struggle for Citizenship Rights among Mexican Immigrants*. New York: New York University Press.

———. 2011. *Patient Citizens, Immigrant Mothers: Mexican Women, Public Prenatal Care, and the Birth Weight Paradox*. Piscataway, NJ: Rutgers University Press.

Gándara, Patricia. 2020. "The Students We Share: Falling through the Cracks on Both Sides of the US-Mexico Border." *Ethnic and Racial Studies* 43(1):38–59.

Gándara, Patricia, and Frances Contreras. 2009. *The Latino Educational Crisis: The Consequences of Failed Policies*. Cambridge, MA: Harvard University Press.

García, Angela S. 2014. "Hidden in Plain Sight: How Unauthorised Migrants Strategically Assimilate in Restrictive Localities in California." *Journal of Ethnic and Migration Studies* 40(12):1895–1914.

———. 2019. *Legal Passing: Navigating Undocumented Life and Local Immigration Law*. Oakland: University of California Press.

García, Angela S., and Leah Schmalzbauer. 2017. "Placing Assimilation Theory: Mexican Immigrants in Urban and Rural America." *Annals of the American Academy of Political and Social Science* 672(1):64–82.

García, Mario T. 2014. *The Latino Generation: Voices of the New America*. Chapel Hill: University of North Carolina Press.

García, San Juanita. 2017. "Racializing 'Illegality': An Intersectional Approach to Understanding How Mexican-Origin Women Navigate an Anti-immigrant Climate." *Sociology of Race and Ethnicity* 3(4):474–490.

Garcia-Navarro, Lulu, 2019. "The Media Erased Latinos from the Story." *The Atlantic*, August 9. www.theatlantic.com.

García Valdivia, Isabel. 2020. "Legal Power in Action: How Latinx Adult Children Mitigate the Effects of Parents' Legal Status through Brokering." *Social Problems*. doi:10.1093/socpro/spaa027.

Gardiner, Dustin. 2018. "Before Trump, Arizona State Lawmakers Tried to End Birthright Citizenship." *AZ Central*, October 31. www.azcentral.com.

Gardner, Trevor, II, and Aarti Kohli. 2009. "The C.A.P. Effect: Racial Profiling in the ICE Criminal Alien Program." Berkeley, CA: Chief Justice Earl Warren Institute on Race, Ethnicity and Diversity, Berkeley Law Center for Research and Administration. www.law.berkeley.edu.

Getrich, Christina M. 2013. "'Too Bad I'm Not an Obvious Citizen': The Effects of Racialized US Immigration Enforcement Practices on Second-Generation Mexican Youth." *Latino Studies* 11(4):462–482.

———. 2019. *Border Brokers: Children of Mexican Immigrants Navigating U.S. Society, Laws, and Politics*. Tucson: University of Arizona Press.

Ghandnoosh, Nazgol, and Josh J. Rovner. 2017. *Immigration and Public Safety*. Washington, DC: Sentencing Project. www.sentencingproject.org.

Glaser, Barney G., and Anselm L. Strauss. 1967. *The Discovery of Grounded Theory: Strategies for Qualitative Research*. Chicago: Aldine.

Glenn, Evelyn Nakano. 1986. *Issei, Nisei, War Bride: Three Generations of Japanese American Women in Domestic Service*. Philadelphia: Temple University Press.

———. 1992. "From Servitude to Service Work: Historical Continuities in the Racial Division of Paid Reproductive Labor." *Signs* 18(1):1–43.

———. 2002. *Unequal Freedom: How Race and Gender Shaped American Citizenship and Labor*. Cambridge, MA: Harvard University Press.

———. 2011. "Constructing Citizenship: Exclusion, Subordination, and Resistance." *American Sociological Review* 76(1):1–24.

Goffman, Erving. 1963. *Stigma: Notes on the Management of Spoiled Identity.* Englewood Cliffs, NJ: Prentice-Hall.

Golash-Boza, Tanya. 2009. "A Confluence of Interests in Immigration Enforcement: How Politicians, the Media, and Corporations Profit from Immigration Policies Destined to Fail." *Sociology Compass* 3:293–294.

———. 2012. *Immigration Nation: Raids, Detentions, and Deportations in Post-9/11 America.* Boulder, CO: Paradigm Publishers.

———. 2015. *Deported: Immigrant Policing, Disposable Labor, and Global Capitalism.* New York: New York University Press.

———. 2016a. "Feeling Like a Citizen, Living as a Denizen: Deportees' Sense of Belonging." *American Behavioral Scientist* 60(13):1575–1589.

———. 2016b. "The Parallels between Mass Incarceration and Mass Deportation: An Intersectional Analysis of State Repression." *Journal of World-Systems Research* 22(2):484–509.

———. 2019. "Punishment beyond the Deportee: The Collateral Consequences of Deportation." *American Behavioral Scientist.* doi:10.1177/0002764219835259.

Golash-Boza, Tanya, and Pierrette Hondagneu-Sotelo. 2013. "Latino Immigrant Men and the Deportation Crisis: A Gendered Racial Removal Program." *Latino Studies* 11(3):271–292.

Gomberg-Muñoz, Ruth. 2017. *Becoming Legal: Immigration Law and Mixed-Status Families.* New York: Oxford University Press.

Gómez, Laura E. 2007. *Manifest Destinies: The Making of the Mexican American Race.* New York: New York University Press.

Gómez Cervantes, Andrea. 2019. "'Looking Mexican': Indigenous and Non-Indigenous Latina/o Immigrants and the Racialization of Illegality in the Midwest." *Social Problems.* doi:10.1093/socpro/spz048.

Gonzalez, Dahlia, Sabrina Kim, Cynthia Moreno, and Edward-Michael Muña. 2020. "State of Immigrants in Los Angeles." California Community Foundation and USC Center for the Study of Immigrant Integration (CSII). www.dornsife.usc.edu.

Gonzalez-Barrera, Ana and Jens Manuel Krogstad. 2014. "U.S. Deportations of Immigrants Reach Record High in 2013." Washington, DC: Pew Research Center. www.pewresearch.org.

Gonzales, Roberto G. 2011. "Learning to Be Illegal: Undocumented Youth and Shifting Legal Contexts in the Transition to Adulthood." *American Sociological Review* 76(4):602–619.

———. 2015. *Lives in Limbo: Undocumented and Coming of Age in America.* Berkeley: University of California Press.

Gonzales, Roberto G., Veronica Terriquez, and Stephen P. Ruszczyk. 2014. "Becoming DACAmented: Assessing the Short-Term Benefits of Deferred Action for Childhood Arrivals (DACA)." *American Behavioral Scientist* 58(14):1852–1872.

Gonzalez, Dalia, Sabrina Kim, Cynthia Moreno, and Edward-Michael Muña. 2020. *State of Immigrants in Los Angeles.* Los Angeles: California Community Foundation and USC Center for the Study of Immigrant Integration (CSII).

Gordon, Jennifer, and R. A Lenhardt. 2008. "Rethinking Work and Citizenship." *UCLA Law Review* 55(5):1161–1238.

Grundy, Emily, and John C. Henretta. 2006. "Between Elderly Parents and Adult Children: A New Look at the Intergenerational Care Provided by the 'Sandwich Generation.'" *Ageing & Society* 26(5):707–722.

Gulbas, Lauren, and Luis Zayas. 2017. "Exploring the Effects of U.S. Immigration Enforcement on the Well-Being of Citizen Children in Mexican Immigrant Families." *Russell Sage Foundation Journal of the Social Sciences* 3(4):53–69.

Gunkel, Steven E., and Ana-María González Wahl. 2012. "Unauthorized Migrants and the (Il)Logic of 'Crime Control': A Human Rights Perspective on US Federal and Local State Immigration Policies." *Sociology Compass* 6(1):26–45.

Gutiérrez, Elena R. 2008. *Fertile Matters: The Politics of Mexican-Origin Women's Reproduction.* Austin: University of Texas Press.

Gutmann, Matthew. C. 1996. *The Meanings of Macho: Being a Man in Mexico City.* Berkeley: University of California Press.

Guzman Garcia, Melissa. 2018. "Spiritual Citizenship: Immigrant Religious Participation and the Management of Deportability." *International Migration Review* 52(2):404–429.

———. 2020. "Mobile Sanctuary: Latina/o Evangelicals Redefining Sanctuary and Contesting Immobility in Fresno, CA." *Journal of Ethnic and Migration Studies.* doi: 10.1080/1369183X.2020.1761780.

Hamilton, Erin R., Caitlin C. Patler, and Jo Mhairi Hale. 2019. "Growing Up without Status: The Integration of Children in Mixed-Status Families." *Sociology Compass* 13(6):1–14.

Haney-López, Ian. 1996. *White by Law: The Legal Construction of Race.* New York: New York University Press.

Harrison, Jill L., and Sarah E. Lloyd. 2012. "Illegality at Work: Deportability and the Productive New Era of Immigration Enforcement." *Antipode* 44(2):365–385.

Hernández, David. 2008. "Pursuant to Deportation: Latinos and Immigrant Detention." *Latino Studies* 6(1–2):35–63.

Hernández, Tanya K. 2009. "Latinos at Work: When Color Discrimination Involves More Than Color." In *Shades of Difference: Why Skin Color Matters,* edited by Evelyn Nakano Glenn, 236–244. Palo Alto, CA: Stanford University Press.

Hersch, Joni. 2011. "The Persistence of Skin Color Discrimination for Immigrants." *Social Science Research* 40(5):1337–1349.

Hirsch, Jennifer S. 2003. *A Courtship after Marriage: Sexuality and Love in Mexican Transnational Families.* Berkeley: University of California Press.

Hochschild, Arlie. 1994. "The Commercial Spirit of Intimate Life and the Abduction of Feminism: Signs from Women's Advice Books." *Theory, Culture & Society* 11:1–24.

Hondagneu-Sotelo, Pierrette. 1994. *Gendered Transitions: Mexican Experiences of Immigration*. Berkeley: University of California Press.

Hondagneu-Sotelo, Pierrette, and Ernestine Avila. 1997. "'I'm Here, but I'm There': The Meanings of Latina Transnational Motherhood." *Gender & Society* 11(5):548–571.

HoSang, Daniel Martinez. 2010. *Racial Propositions: Ballot Initiatives and the Making of Postwar California*. Berkeley: University of California Press.

Hughes, Diane, James Rodriguez, Emilie P. Smith, Deborah J. Johnson, Howard C. Stevenson, and Paul Spicer. 2006. "Parents' Ethnic-Racial Socialization Practices." *Developmental Psychology* 42(5):747–770.

Hwang, Kristen. 2017. "As American Kids Pour across the Border, Mexican Schools Struggle to Keep Up." *Desert Sun*, September 5. www.desertsun.com.

ICE. 2017. "Fiscal Year 2016 ICE Enforcement and Removal Operations Report." www.ice.gov.

Iceland, John. 2004. "Beyond Black and White: Metropolitan Residential Segregation in Multi-ethnic America." *Social Science Review* 33:248–271.

Ignatow, Gabe, and Alexander T. Williams. 2011. "New Media and the 'Anchor Baby' Boom." *Journal of Computer Mediated Communication* 17(1):60–76.

Immigrant Legal Resource Center. 2016. *Life under PEP-COMM*. San Francisco: Immigrant Legal Resource Center. www.ilrc.org.

Jacobson, Robin. 2006. "Characterizing Consent: Race, Citizenship, and the New Restrictionists." *Political Research Quarterly* 59(4):645–654.

———. 2008. *The New Nativism: Proposition 187 and the Debate over Immigration*. Minneapolis: University of Minnesota Press.

Jardina, Ashley. 2018. "What Americans Really Think about Birthright Citizenship." *Washington Post*, November 2. www.washingtonpost.com.

Jiménez, Tomás. R. 2008. "Mexican Immigrant Replenishment and the Continuing Significance of Ethnicity and Race." *American Journal of Sociology* 113(6):1527–1567.

Johnson, Jeh Charles. 2014. *Secure Communities*. Washington, DC: US Department of Homeland Security. www.dhs.gov.

Johnson, Kevin. 2007. *Opening the Floodgates: Why America Needs to Rethink Its Borders and Immigration Laws*. New York: New York University Press.

Jones, Jeffrey M. 2016. "More Republicans Favor Path to Citizenship Than Wall." www.gallup.com.

Jordan, Miriam. 2019. "ICE Arrests Hundreds in Mississippi Raids Targeting Immigrant Workers." *New York Times*, August 7. www.nytimes.com.

Jung, Moon-Kie. 2009. "The Racial Unconscious of Assimilation Theory." *Du Bois Review: Social Science Research on Race* 6(2):375–395.

Kalin, Betsy. 2015. *East LA Interchange*. DVD. Los Angeles: Bluewater Media.

Keller, Bill. 2019. "What Do Abolitionists Really Want?" *The Marshall Project*. www.themarshallproject.org.

Kendall, Emily C. 2012. "Amending the Constitution to Save a Sinking Ship? The Issues Surrounding the Proposed Amendment of the Citizenship Clause and 'Anchor Babies.'" *Berkeley La Raza Law Journal* 22:349–381.

Kenney, Andrew. 2017. "Lawsuit: American Citizen Wrongfully Detained by ICE in Colorado Two Years Ago." *Denverite*, March 8. www.denverite.com.

Kibria, Nazli. 2002. *Becoming Asian American: Second-Generation Chinese and Korean American Identities*. Baltimore: Johns Hopkins University Press.

Kim, Nadia. 2007. "A Return to More Blatant Class and Race Bias in U.S Immigration Policy?" *Du Bois Review: Social Science Research on Race* (4)2: 469–477.

Klein, Christopher. 2021. "Born in the USA: The Chinese Immigrant Son Who Fought for Birthright Citizenship." *History Stories*, March 18. www.history.com.

Kopan, Tal. 2015a. "Birthright Citizenship: Can Donald Trump Change the Constitution?" CNN, August 18. www.cnn.com.

———. 2015b. "Controversial Term 'Anchor Baby' Drops into the 2016 Race." CNN, August 21. www.cnn.com.

Kossoudji, Sherrie A. 1992. "Playing Cat and Mouse at the U.S.-Mexican Border." *Demography* 29(2):159–180.

Kremer, James, Kathleen Moccio, and Joseph Hammel. 2009. *Severing a Lifeline: The Neglect of Citizen Children in America's Immigration Enforcement Policy*. Minneapolis: Urban Institute.

Krogstad, Jens Manuel, Jeffrey S. Passel, and D'Vera Cohn. 2019. *5 Facts about Illegal Immigration in the U.S.* Washington, DC: Pew Research Center. www.pewresearch. org.

Kwon, Hyeyoung. 2015. "Intersectionality in Interaction: Immigrant Youth Doing American from an Outsider-Within Position." *Social Problems* 62(4):623–641.

Lamont, Michèle. 2000. *The Dignity of Working Men: Morality and the Boundaries of Race, Class, and Immigration*. Cambridge, MA: Harvard University Press.

Lara, Dulcinea, Dana Greene, and Cynthia Bejarano. 2009. "A Critical Analysis of Immigrant Advocacy Tropes: How Popular Discourse Weakens Solidarity and Prevents Broad, Sustainable Justice." *Social Justice* 36(2):21–37.

Lash, Cristina L. 2017. "Defining 'American' in the Context of Immigration: A Case Study of Helping Hands Elementary." *Ethnic and Racial Studies* 40(6):871–890.

Lawrence, Jane. 2000. "The Indian Health Service and the Sterilization of Native American Women." *American Indian Quarterly* 24(3):400–419.

Lawston, Jodie M., and Martha Escobar. 2009. "Policing, Detention, Deportation, and Resistance: Situating Immigrant Justice and Carcerality in the 21st Century." *Social Justice* 36(2):1–6.

LeBlanc, Paul. 2019. "Trump Again Says He's Looking 'Seriously' at Birthright Citizenship Despite 14th Amendment." CNN, August 22. www.cnn.com.

Lee, Esther Yu Hsi. 2015. "What One Man Did When He Was Accidentally Deported to Mexico." *Think Progress*, July 4. https://thinkprogress.org.

Lefebvre, Henri. 1991. "A Critique of Space." In *The Production of Space*. Oxford: Blackwell.

Leiter, Valerie, Jennifer Lutzy McDonald, and Heather T. Jacobson. 2006. "Challenges to Children's Independent Citizenship Immigration, Family and the State." *Childhood* 13(1):11–27.

Lewthwaite, Stephanie. 2010. "Race, Place, and Ethnicity in the Progressive Era." In *A Companion to Los Angeles*, edited by W. Deverell and G. Hise, 40–55. Chichester, West Sussex, UK: Wiley-Blackwell.

Lind, Dara. 2018. "Birthright Citizenship, Explained." *Vox*, October 30. www.vox.com.

———. 2019. "Trump Has a Long History of Fearmongering about Immigrant Murder." *Vox*, February 5. www.vox.com.

Linthicum, Kate. 2016. "Nearly Half a Million U.S. Citizens Are Enrolled in Mexican Schools. Many of Them Are Struggling." *Los Angeles Times*, September 14. www.latimes.com.

Lippard, Cameron D. 2011. "Racist Nativism in the 21st Century." *Sociology Compass* 5(7):591–606.

Liptak, Adam, and Michael D. Shear. 2016. "Supreme Court Tie Blocks Obama Immigration Plan." *New York Times*, June 23. www.nytimes.com.

Lobao, Linda. 1996. "A Sociology of the Periphery versus a Peripheral Sociology: Rural Sociology and the Dimension of Space." *Rural Sociology* 61(1):77–102.

Lobao, Linda M., Gregory Hooks, and Ann R. Tickamyer. 2007. *The Sociology of Spatial Inequality*. Albany: State University of New York Press.

Loewen, James W. 2005. *Sundown Towns: A Hidden Dimension of American Racism*. New York: New Press.

Logan, John R., and Richard D. Alba. 1993. "Locational Returns to Human Capital: Minority Access to Suburban Community Resources." *Demography* 30(2):243–268.

Logan, John R., Richard Alba, and Shu-yin Leung. 1996. "Minority Access to White Suburbs: A Multiregional Comparison." *Social Forces* 74(3):851–881.

Logan, John R., Brian J. Stults, and Reynolds Farley. 2004. "Segregation of Minorities in the Metropolis: Two Decades of Change." *Demography* 41(1):1–22.

Lopez, Cristina G. 2016. "No, Conservative Media, That's Not What 'La Raza' Means in Spanish." *Media Matters for America*. https://mediamatters.org.

López, Jane L. 2015. "'Impossible Families': Mixed-Citizenship Status Couples and the Law." *Law & Policy* 37(1–2):93–118.

Lopez, Mark H. 2009. *Latinos and Education: Explaining the Attainment Gap*. Washington, DC: Pew Research Center. www.pewhispanic.org.

———. 2014. *In 2014, Latinos Will Surpass Whites as Largest Racial/Ethnic Group in California*. Washington, DC: Pew Research Center. www.pewresearch.org.

Lopez, William D. 2019. *Separated: Family and Community in the Aftermath of an Immigration Raid*. Baltimore: Johns Hopkins University Press.

Los Angeles Almanac. 2022a. "City of Los Angeles Neighborhoods Population & Race, 2010." www.laalmanac.com.

———. 2022b. "Hispanics/Latinos in Los Angeles County by the Numbers." www.laalmanac.com.

Louie, Vivian S. 2012. *Keeping the Immigrant Bargain: The Costs and Rewards of Success in America*. New York: Russell Sage Foundation.

Luibhéid, Eithne. 2013. *Pregnant on Arrival: Making the Illegal Immigrant*. Minneapolis: University of Minnesota Press.

Luibhéid, Eithne, Rosi Andrade, and Sally Stevens. 2018. "Intimate Attachments and Migrant Deportability: Lessons from Undocumented Mothers Seeking Benefits for Citizen Children." *Ethnic and Racial Studies* 41(1):17–35.

Luibhéid, Eithne, and Lionel Cantú. 2005. *Queer Migrations: Sexuality, U.S. Citizenship, and Border Crossings.* Minneapolis: University of Minnesota Press.

MALDEF. 2017. "A History of Efforts to Challenge DACA in Federal Courts." www. maldef.org.

Maldonado, Maria Marta. 2009. "'It Is Their Nature to Do Menial Labour': The Racialization of Latino/a Workers' by Agricultural Employers." *Ethnic and Racial Studies* 32(6):1017–1036.

Mapping Los Angeles. 2000. "Central L.A." *Los Angeles Times.* http://maps.latimes. com.

Marcelli, Enrico A., and Manuel Pastor. 2015. "Unauthorized and Uninsured: Boyle Heights and Los Angeles County." https://dornsife.usc.edu.

Marchevsky, Alejandra, and Jeanne Theoharis. 2000. "Welfare Reform, Globalization, and the Racialization of Entitlement." *American Studies* 41(2/3):235–265.

Marshall, T. H. 1950. *Citizenship and Social Class; Essays.* Garden City, NY: Doubleday.

Martinez, Lisa M. 2014. "Dreams Deferred: The Impact of Legal Reforms on Undocumented Latino Youth." *American Behavioral Scientist* 57(14):1873–1890.

———. 2015. "The Immigrant Rights Movement: Then and Now." Mobilizing New Ideas, December 3. https://mobilizingideas.wordpress.com.

Massey, Douglas S. 2007. *Categorically Unequal: The American Stratification System.* New York: Russell Sage Foundation.

Massey Douglas S., and Nancy A. Denton. 1993. *American Apartheid: Segregation and the Making of the Underclass.* Cambridge, MA: Harvard University Press.

Massey Douglas S., Jorge Durand, and Nolan J. Malone. 2003. *Beyond Smoke and Mirrors: Mexican Immigration in an Era of Economic Integration.* New York: Russell Sage Foundation.

Massey, Douglas S., Jorge Durand, and Karen A. Pren. 2016. "Why Border Enforcement Backfired." *American Journal of Sociology* 121(5):1557–1600.

Massey, Douglas S., and Magaly Sánchez. 2010. *Brokered Boundaries: Creating Immigrant Identity in Anti-Immigrant Times.* New York: Russell Sage Foundation.

Mathema, Silva. 2017. "Keeping Families Together: Why All Americans Should Care about What Happens to Unauthorized Immigrants." *Center for American Progress.* https://cdn.americanprogress.org.

McCausland, Phil and Julia Ainsley. 2019. "President Trump announces delay of mass immigration raids that were to start Sunday." NBC News, June 22. www.nbcnews. com.

McDonough, Katie. 2017. "DREAMers Played the 'Good Immigrant' Game. It Didn't Protect Them." *Splinter*, September 9. www.splinternews.com.

Medina, Dulce, and Cecilia Menjívar. 2015. "The Context of Return Migration: Challenges of Mixed-Status Families in Mexico's Schools." *Ethnic and Racial Studies* 38(12):2123–2139.

Mendoza, Alexandra. 2021. "Constitutional Amendment Guarantees Nationality to Descendants of Mexicans Born Abroad." *San Diego Union-Tribune*, July 15. www.sandiegouniontribune.com.

Menjívar, Cecilia. 2016. "Immigrant Criminalization in Law and the Media." *American Behavioral Scientist* 60(5–6):597–616.

Menjívar, Cecilia, and Leisy J. Abrego. 2012. "Legal Violence: Immigration Law and the Lives of Central American Immigrants." *American Journal of Sociology* 117(5):1380–1421.

Menjívar, Cecilia, Leisy J. Abrego, and Leah Schmalzbauer. 2016. *Immigrant Families.* Oxford: Polity.

Menjívar, Cecilia, and Sarah M. Lakhani. 2016. "Transformative Effects of Immigration Law: Migrants' Personal and Social Metamorphoses through Regularization." *American Journal of Sociology* 121(6):1818–1855.

Mexican American Legal Defense and Educational Fund. 2009. *AB 540—Access to College for ALL!* Los Angeles: Mexican American Legal Defense and Educational Fund. www.maldef.org.

———. 2017. *U.S.-Born Student Sues Washington, D.C. after Denial of Financial Aid Based on Her Parent's Immigration Status.* Los Angeles: Mexican American Legal Defense and Educational Fund. www.maldef.org.

Miguel, Daisy, and Jenny Chhea. 2013. *The State of Van Nuys.* Los Angeles: UCLA School of Public Affairs. https://vnnc.org.

Miller, Dorothy. 1981. "The 'Sandwich' Generation: Adult Children of the Aging. *Social Work* 26(5):419–423.

Miroff, Nick, and Maria Sacchetti. 2019. "Trump Vows Mass Immigration Arrests, Removals of 'Millions of Illegal Aliens' Starting Next Week." *Washington Post*, June 17. www.washingtonpost.com.

Molina, Natalia. 2014. *How Race Is Made in America: Immigration, Citizenship, and the Historical Power of Racial Scripts.* Berkeley: University of California Press.

Molina, Paola. 2014. *Re-immigration after Deportation: Family, Gender, and the Decision to Make a Second Attempt to Enter the U.S.* El Paso, TX: LFB Scholarly Publishing.

Montejano, David. 1987. *Anglos and Mexicans in the Making of Texas, 1836–1986.* Austin, TX: University of Texas Press.

Montes, Veronica. 2013. "The Role of Emotions in the Construction of Masculinity." *Gender & Society* 27(4):469–490.

Nakamura, David. 2017. "Blame Game: Trump Casts Immigrants as Dangerous Criminals, but the Evidence Shows Otherwise." *Washington Post*, March 24. www.washingtonpost.com.

Nasser, Haya El. 2017. "More Than Half of U.S. Population in 4.6 Percent of Counties." United States Census Bureau. www.census.gov.

National Day Laborer Organizing Network. 2017. "Breaking: Romulo Avelica Released after Six Months of Immigration Detention." http://ndlon.org.

National Immigration Law Center. 2015a. "*Breaking the Ice*: NILC Calls for ICE-Free Los Angeles." Los Angeles: National Immigration Law Center. www.nilc.org.

———. 2015b. "Frequently Asked Questions: The Obama Administration's DAPA and Expanded DACA Programs." Los Angeles: National Immigration Law Center. www.nilc.org.

———. 2019a. "Frequently Asked Questions American Dream and Promise Act of 2019." Los Angeles: National Immigration Law Center. www.nilc.org.

———. 2019b. "Summary of Dream and Promise Act of 2019 (H.R. 6)." Los Angeles: National Immigration Law Center. www.nilc.org.

Neckerman, Kathryn M., and Joleen Kirschenman. 1991. "Hiring Strategies, Racial Bias, and Inner-City Workers." *Social Problems* 38(4):433–447.

Negrón-Gonzales, Genevieve. 2013. "Navigating 'Illegality': Undocumented Youth and Oppositional Consciousness." *Children and Youth Services Review* 35(8):1284–1290.

Nevins, Joseph. 2002. *Operation Gatekeeper: The Rise of the "Illegal Alien" and the Making of the U.S.-Mexico Boundary*. New York: Routledge.

Ngai, Mae. 2003. *Impossible Subjects: Illegal Aliens and the Making of Modern America*. Princeton, NJ: Princeton University Press.

Nicholls, Walter. 2013. *The DREAMers: How the Undocumented Youth Movement Transformed the Immigrant Rights Debate*. Stanford, CA: Stanford University Press.

Oakes, Jeannie, and Gretchen Guiton. 1995. "Matchmaking: The Dynamics of High School Tracking Decisions." *American Educational Research Journal* 32(1):3–33.

Ocampo, Anthony C. 2020. "On Adobo and Anxiety: A Meal at Savannah's Only Filipino Eatery Becomes a Second-Generation Identity Crisis." Southern Foodways Alliance. www.southernfoodways.org

Ochoa, Gilda L. 2013. *Academic Profiling: Latinos, Asian Americans, and the Achievement Gap*. Minneapolis: University of Minnesota Press.

Ogbu, John U. 1990. "Minority Status and Literacy in Comparative Perspective." *Daedalus* 119(2):141–168.

Ojeda, Lizette, Lisa Flores, Rocio Meza, and Alejandro Morales. 2011. "Culturally Competent Qualitative Research with Latino Immigrants." *Hispanic Journal of Behavioral Sciences* 33(2):184–203.

Oliver, Melvin L., and Thomas M. Shapiro. 1995. *Black Wealth/White Wealth: A New Perspective on Racial Inequality*. New York: Routledge.

Oliviero, Katie E. 2013. "The Immigration State of Emergency: Racializing and Gendering National Vulnerability in Twenty-First-Century Citizenship and Deportation Regimes." *Feminist Formations* 25(2):1–29.

Omi, Michael, and Howard Winant. 1994. *Racial Formation in the United States*. New York: Routledge.

Orellana, Marjorie. 2009. *Translating Childhoods: Immigrant Youth, Language, and Culture*. New Brunswick, NJ: Rutgers University Press.

Ortiz, Vilma, and Edward Telles. 2012. "Racial Identity and Racial Treatment of Mexican Americans." *Race and Social Problems* 4(1):41–56.

Ovink, Sarah M. 2014. "'They Always Call Me an Investment': Gendered Familism and Latino/a College Pathways." *Gender & Society* 28(2):265–288.

Pallares, Amalia. 2010. "Representing 'La Familia.'" In ¡*Marcha! Latino Chicago and the Immigrant Rights Movement*, edited by A. Pallares and N. Flores-González, 215–236. Urbana: University of Illinois Press.

———. 2014. *Family Activism: Immigrant Struggles and the Politics of Noncitizenship*. New Brunswick, NJ: Rutgers University Press.

Passel, Jeffrey S., and D'Vera Cohn. 2011. "Unauthorized Immigrant Population: National and State Trends, 2010." Washington, DC: Pew Research Center. www.pewhispanic.org.

———. 2019. "Mexicans Decline to Less Than Half the U.S. Unauthorized Immigrant Population for the First Time." Washington, DC: Pew Research Center. www.pewresearch.org.

Passel, Jeffrey S., and Paul Taylor. 2010. *Unauthorized Immigrants and Their U.S.-Born Children*. Washington, DC: Pew Research Center. www.pewhispanic.org.

Pastor, Manuel, Jared Sanchez, and Vanessa Carter. 2015. *The Kids Aren't Alright—But They Could Be: The Impact of Deferred Action for Parents of Americans and Lawful Permanent Residents (DAPA) on Children*. Los Angeles: Center for the Study of Immigrant Integration.

PBS. 2017. "Post-election Spike in Hate Crimes Persists in 2017." *PBS News Hour*, August 12. www.pbs.org.

Peralta, Eyder. 2016. "You Say You're an American, But What If You Had to Prove It or Be Deported?" NPR, December 22. www.npr.org.

Pérez, William. 2012. *Americans by Heart: Undocumented Latino Students and the Promise of Higher Education*. New York: Teachers College Press.

Pérez Huber, Lindsay, Corina Benavides Lopez, Maria C. Malagona, Veronica Velez, and Daniel G. Solorzanoa. 2008. "Getting Beyond the 'Symptom,' Acknowledging the 'Disease': Theorizing Racist Nativism." *Contemporary Justice Review* 11(1):39–51.

Petulla, Sam, Tammy Kupperman, and Jessica Schneider. 2017. "The Number of Hate Crimes Rose in 2016." CNN, November 13. www.cnn.com.

Pew Research Center. 2007. *National Survey of Latinos: As Illegal Immigration Issue Heats Up, Hispanics Feel a Chill*. Washington, DC: Pew Research Center. www.pewhispanic.org.

———. 2014a. "Demographic Profile of Hispanics in California, 2014." www.pewhispanic.org.

———. 2014b. *Quarter of Latinos Know Someone Deported or Detained for Immigration Reasons in the Last Year*. Washington, DC: Pew Research Center. www.pewhispanic.org.

Philbin, Sandy P., and Cecilia Ayón. 2016. "Luchamos por Nuestros Hijos: Latino Immigrant Parents Strive to Protect Their Children from the Deleterious Effects of Anti-immigration Policies." *Children and Youth Services Review* 63:128–135.

Pierce, Sarah, and Andrew Selee. 2017. "Immigration under Trump: A Review of Policy Shifts in the Year since the Election." Washington, DC: Migration Policy Institute. www.migrationpolicy.org.

Pila, Daniela. 2015. "'I'm Not Good Enough for Anyone': Legal Status and the Dating Lives of Undocumented Young Adults." *Sociological Forum* 31(1):138–158.

Portes, Alejandro, and Rubén G. Rumbaut. 2001. *Legacies: The Story of the Immigrant Second Generation.* Berkeley: University of California Press.

———. 2006. *Immigrant America: A Portrait.* 4th ed. Berkeley: University of California Press.

Preston, Julia. 2015. "Administration Asks Court to Lift Order Halting Immigration Programs." *New York Times*, March 12. www.nytimes.com.

———. 2016. "Lawsuit Forces Texas to Make It Easier for Immigrants to Get Birth Certificates for Children." *New York Times*, July 24. www.nytimes.com.

Prieto, Greg. 2018. *Immigrants under Threat: Risk and Resistance in Deportation Nation.* New York: New York University Press.

Pulido, Laura. 2000. "Rethinking Environmental Racism: White Privilege and Urban Development in Southern California." *Annals of the Association of American Geographers* 90(1):12–40.

Pulido, Laura, Laura R. Barraclough, and Wendy Cheng. 2012. *A People's Guide to Los Angeles.* Berkeley: University of California Press.

Purnell, Thomas, William Idsardi, and John Baugh. 1999. "Perceptual and Phonetic Experiments on American English Dialect Identification." *Journal of Language and Social Psychology* 18:10–30.

Ray, Ranita. 2017. "Identity of Distance: How Economically Marginalized Black and Latina Women Navigate Risk Discourse and Employ Feminist Ideals." *Social Problems* 65(1):1–17.

Reed-Sandoval, Amy. 2020. *Socially Undocumented: Identity and Immigration Justice.* New York: Oxford University Press.

Reese, Ellen. 2005. *Backlash against Welfare Mothers: Past and Present.* Berkeley: University of California Press.

Rendón, María G. 2019. *Stagnant Dreamers: How the Inner City Shapes the Integration of Second-Generation Latinos.* New York: Russell Sage Foundation.

Rhodan, Maya. 2016. "Donald Trump Raises Eyebrows with 'Bad Hombres' Line." *Time*, October 19. http://time.com.

Rios, Victor M. 2011. *Punished: Policing the Lives of Black and Latino boys.* New York: New York University Press.

Roberts, Dorothy. 1997. "Who May Give Birth to Citizens?" In *Immigrants Out!*, edited by J. F. Perea, 205–219. New York: New York University Press.

Rodriguez, Cassaundra. 2016. "Experiencing 'Illegality' as a Family? Immigration Enforcement, Social Policies, and Discourses Targeting Mexican Mixed-Status Families." *Sociology Compass* 10(8):706–717.

———. 2018a. "Chinese Maternity Tourists and Their 'Anchor Babies'? Online Commenters' Disdain and Racialized Conditional Acceptance of Non-citizen Reproduction." In *Marginalized Mothers: Advancements in Gender Research*, edited by Katrina Bloch and Tiffany Taylor, 91–106. West Yorkshire, UK: Emerald Press.

———. 2018b. "Fueling White Injury Ideology: Public Officials' Racial Discourse in Support of Arizona Senate Bill 1070." *Sociology of Race and Ethnicity* 4(1):83–97.

———. 2019. "Latino/a Citizen Children of Undocumented Parents Negotiating Illegality." *Journal of Marriage and Family* 81(3):713–728.

Romero, Mary. 1992. *Maid in the U.S.A.* New York: Routledge.

———. 2001. "State Violence, and the Social and Legal Construction of Latino Criminality: From *El Bandido* to Gang Member." *Denver University Law Review* 78(4):1081–1118.

———. 2006. "Racial Profiling and Immigration Law Enforcement: Rounding Up of Usual Suspects in the Latino Community." *Critical Sociology* 32:447–473.

———. 2008a. "Crossing the Immigration and Race Border: A Critical Race Theory Approach to Immigration Studies." *Contemporary Justice Review* 11(1):23–37.

———. 2008b. "'Go After the Women': Mothers against Illegal Aliens (MAIA) Campaign against Mexican Immigrant Women and Their Children." *Indiana Law Journal* 83(4):1355–1389.

———. 2008c. "The Inclusion of Citizenship Status in Intersectionality: What Immigration Raids Tells Us about Mixed-Status Families, the State and Assimilation." *International Journal of Sociology of the Family* 34(2):131–152.

———. 2011a. "Are Your Papers in Order?: Racial Profiling, Vigilantes, and America's Toughest Sheriff." *Harvard Latino Law Review* 14(1):337–358.

———. 2011b. "Constructing Mexican Immigrant Women as a Threat to American Families." *International Journal of Sociology of the Family* 37(1):49–68.

Rosaldo, Renato. 1994. "Cultural Citizenship and Educational Democracy." *Cultural Anthropology* 9(3):402–411.

Rosaldo, Renato, and William V. Flores. 1997. "Identity, Conflict and Evolving Latino Communities: Cultural Citizenship in San Jose California." In *Latino Cultural Citizenship: Claiming Identity, Space, and Rights*, edited by William V. Flores and Rina Benmayor, 57–96. Boston: Beacon Press.

Roscigno, Vincent J., Diana L. Karafin, and Griff Tester. 2009. "The Complexities and Processes of Racial Housing Discrimination." *Social Problems* 56(1):49–69.

Rosenblum, Marc R. 2015. *Understanding the Potential Impact of Executive Action on Immigration Enforcement.* Washington, DC: Migration Policy Institute. www.migrationpolicy.org.

Ross, Janell. 2016. "From Mexican Rapists to Bad Hombres, the Trump Campaign in Two Moments." *Washington Post*, October 20. www.washingtonpost.com.

Rubio-Goldsmith, Pat, and Mary Romero. 2008. "Aliens, Illegals, and Other Kinds of Mexicanness." In *Globalization in America*, edited by A. J. Hattery, D. G. Embrick, and E. Smith, 127–142. Lanham, MD: Rowman and Littlefield.

Rubio-Hernández, Sandy P., and Cecilia Ayón. 2016. "Pobrecitos los Niños: The Emotional Impact of Anti-immigration Policies on Latino Youth." *Children and Youths Services Review* 60:20–26.

Rugh, Jacob S., and Douglas S. Massey. 2014. "Segregation in Post–Civil Rights America: Stalled Integration or End of the Segregated Century?" *Du Bois Review: Social Science Research on Race* 11(2):205–232.

Ruth, Alissa, and Emir Estrada. 2019. "DACAmented Homecomings: A Brief Return to Mexico and the Reshaping of Bounded Solidarity among Mixed-Status Latinx Families." *Hispanic Journal of Behavioral Sciences* 41(2):145–165.

Sáenz, Rogelio, and Karen Manges Douglas. 2015. "A Call for the Racialization of Immigration Studies: On the Transition of Ethnic Immigrants to Racialized Immigrants." *Sociology of Race and Ethnicity* 1(1):166–180.

Sampson, Robert. 2008. "Rethinking Crime and Immigration." *Contexts: Understanding People in Their Social Worlds* 7(1):28–33.

Sanchez, Gabriella, and Mary Romero. 2010. "Critical Race Theory in the US Sociology of Immigration." *Sociology Compass* 4(9):779–788.

Sánchez, George J. 1993. *Becoming Mexican American: Ethnicity, Culture, and Identity in Chicano Los Angeles, 1900–1945*. New York: Oxford University Press.

———. 1997. "Face the Nation: Race, Immigration, and the Rise of Nativism in Late Twentieth Century America." *International Migration Review* 31(4):1009–1030.

Sanchez, Irene. 2019. "El Paso Horror Spotlights Long History of Anti-Latino Violence in the US." CNN, August 5. www.cnn.com.

Sanchez, Jared, Mirabai Auer, Veronica Terriquez, and Mi Young Kim. 2012. "Koreatown: A Contested Community at a Crossroads." USC Program for Environmental and Regional Equity. https://dornsife.usc.edu.

Sanchez, Ray. 2017. "ICE Arrests Undocumented Father Taking Daughter to California School." CNN, March 3. www.cnn.com.

Santa Ana, Otto. 2002. *Brown Tide Rising: Metaphors of Latinos in Contemporary American Public Discourse*. Austin: University of Texas Press.

Santibañéz, Lucrecia. 2021. "Contrasting Realities: How Differences between the Mexican and U.S. Education Systems Affect Transnational Students." In *The Students We Share: Preparing US and Mexican Teachers for Our Transnational Future*, edited by P. Gándara, and B. Jensen, 17–44. Albany: State University of New York Press.

Sarabia, Heidy. 2012. "Perpetual Illegality: Results of Border Enforcement and Policies for Mexican Undocumented Migrants in the United States." *Analyses of Social Issues and Public Policy* 12:49–67.

Saucedo, Leticia M. 2006. "The Employer Preference for the Subservient Worker and the Making of the Brown Collar Workplace." *Ohio State Law Journal* 67(5):961–1035.

Schmalzbauer, Leah. 2014. *The Last Best Place? Gender, Family, and Migration in the New West*. Stanford, CA: Stanford University Press.

Schmalzbauer, Leah, and Alelí Andrés. 2019. "Stratified Lives: Family, Illegality, and the Rise of a New Educational Elite." *Harvard Educational Review* 89(4):635–660.

Schueths, April M. 2009. "Public Policies, Social Myths, and Private Vulnerabilities: The Lives of Mixed Citizenship Status Families in the United States." PhD diss., University of Nebraska–Lincoln.

———. 2012. "'Where Are My Rights?': Compromised Citizenship in Mixed-Status Marriage: A Research Note." *Journal of Sociology and Social Welfare* 39(4):97–109.

———. 2014. "'It's Almost Like White Supremacy': Interracial Mixed-Status Couples Facing Racist Nativism." *Ethnic and Racial Studies* 37(13):2438–2456.

———. 2019. "Not Really Single: The Deportation to Welfare Pathway for US Citizen Mothers in Mixed-Status Marriage." *Critical Sociology* 45(7–8): 1075–1092.

Schueths, April M., and Jodie M. Lawston. 2015. *Living Together, Living Apart: Mixed Status Families and US Immigration Policy*. Seattle: University of Washington Press.

Serhan, Yasmeen, and Uri Friedman. 2018. "America Isn't the 'Only Country' with Birthright Citizenship." *The Atlantic*, October 31. www.theatlantic.com.

Shear, Michael D. 2014. "Obama, Daring Congress, Acts to Overhaul Immigration." *New York Times*, November 21. www.nytimes.com.

Shear, Michael D., and Julie Hirschfeld Davis. 2017. "Trump Moves to End DACA and Calls on Congress to Act." *New York Times*, September 5. www.nytimes.com.

Silver, Alexis M. 2018. *Shifting Boundaries: Immigrant Youth Negotiating National, State, and Small-Town Politics*. Stanford, CA: Stanford University Press.

Silver, Alexandra. 2010. "Top 10 Buzzwords: Anchor Babies." *Time*, December 9. www.time.com.

Siskin, Alison. 2012. *Immigration-Related Detention: Current Legislative Issues*. Congressional Research Service. January 12.

Smith, Michelle. 2014. "Affect and Respectability Politics." *Theory & Event* 17(3):1.

Smith, Robert. 2006. *Mexican New York: Transnational Lives of New Immigrants*. Berkeley: University of California Press.

Solinger, Rickie. 2005. *Pregnancy and Power: A Short History of Reproductive Politics in America*. New York: New York University Press.

Solórzano, Daniel G., and Tara Yosso. 2002. "Critical Race Methodology: Counter-storytelling as an Analytical Framework for Education Research." *Qualitative Inquiry* 8(1):23–44.

Stack, Carol. 1974. *All Our Kin: Strategies for Survival in a Black Community*. New York: Harper and Row.

Starr, Sonja, and Lea Brilmayer. 2003. "Family Separation as a Violation of International Law." *Berkeley Journal of International Law* 21(2):213–287.

Stephen, Lynn. 2003. "Cultural Citizenship and Labor Rights for Oregon Farmworkers: The Case of Pineros y Campesinos Unidos Del Nordoeste (PCUN)." *Human Organization* 62(1):27–38.

Stumpf, Juliet. 2006. "The Crimmigration Crisis: Immigration, Crime, and Sovereign Power." *American University Law Review* 56(2):368–418.

Suárez-Orozco, Carola, Francisco X. Gaytán, Hee Jin Bang, Juliana Pakes, Erin O'Connor, and Jean García Coll Rhodes. 2010. "Academic Trajectories of Newcomer Youth." *Developmental Psychology* 43(3):602–618.

Suárez-Orozco, Carola, and Marcelo Suárez-Orozco. 1995. *Transformations: Immigration, Family Life, and Achievement Motivation among Latino Adolescents*. Stanford, CA: Stanford University Press.

————. 2001. *Children of Immigration*. Cambridge, MA: Harvard University Press.

Suárez-Orozco, Carola, and Hirokazu Yoshikawa. 2013. "Undocumented Status: Implications for Child Development, Policy, and Ethical Research." In *Frameworks and Ethics for Research with Immigrants: New Directions for Child and Adolescent Development*, edited by M. G. Hernández, J. Nguyen, C. L. Saetermoe, and C. Suárez-Orozco, 61–78. San Francisco: Wiley.

Suárez-Orozco, Carola, Hirokazu Yoshikawa, Robert T. Teranishi, and Marcelo Suárez-Orozco. 2011. "Growing Up in the Shadows: The Developmental Implications of Unauthorized Status." *Harvard Educational Review* 81(3):438–473.

Sue, Derald W. 2010. *Microaggressions in Everyday Life: Race, Gender, and Sexual Orientation*. Hoboken, NJ: Wiley.

Sue, Derald W., Christina M. Capodilupo, Gina C. Torino, Jennifer M. Bucceri, Aisha M. B. Holder, Kevin L. Nadal, and Marta Esquilin. 2007. "Racial Microaggressions in Everyday Life: Implications for Clinical Practice." *American Psychologist* 62(4):271–286.

Sutter, Molly H. 2006. "Mixed-Status Families and Broken Homes: The Clash between the U.S. Hardship Standard in Cancellation of Removal Proceedings and International Law." *Transnational Law & Contemporary Problems* 15(2):783–813.

Swartz, Teresa Toguchi. 2009. "Intergenerational Family Relations in Adulthood." *Annual Review of Sociology* 35:191–212.

Swartz, Teresa. T., Minzee Kim, Mayumi Uno, Jeylan Mortimer, and Kirsten Bengtson O'Brien. 2011. "Safety Nets and Scaffolds: Parental Support in the Transition to Adulthood." *Journal of Marriage and Family* 73(2):414–429.

Taylor, Paul, Mark Hugo-Lopez, Jeffrey S. Passel, and Seth Motel. 2011. *Unauthorized Immigrants: Length of Residency, Patterns of Parenthood*. Washington, DC: Pew Research Center. www.pewhispanic.org.

Telles, Edward, and Vilma Ortiz. 2009. *Generations of Exclusion: Mexican Americans, Assimilation, and Race*. New York: Russell Sage Foundation.

Thronson, David B. 2006. "You Can't Get Here from Here: Toward a More Child-Centered Immigration Law." *Virginia Journal of Social Policy & the Law* 14(1):58–86.

————. 2008. "Creating Crisis: Immigration Raids and the Destabilization of Immigrant Families." *Wake Forest Law Review* 43(2):391–418.

Tickamyer, Ann R. 2000. "Space Matters! Spatial Inequality in Future Sociology." *Contemporary Sociology* 29(6):805–813.

Tienda, Marta, and Norma Fuentes. 2014. "Hispanics in Metropolitan America: New Realities and Old Debates." *Annual Review of Sociology* 40(1):499–520.

Tuan, Mia. 1998. *Forever Foreigners or Honorary Whites? The Asian Ethnic Experience Today*. New Brunswick, NJ: Rutgers University Press.

Ulloa, Jazmine. 2017a. "California Becomes 'Sanctuary State' in Rebuke of Trump Immigration Policy." *Los Angeles Times*, October 5. www.latimes.com.

————. 2018a. "What You Need to Know about California's 'Sanctuary State' Bill and How It Would Work." *Los Angeles Times*, April 13. www.latimes.com.

Unzueta Carrasco, Tania A., and Hinda Seif. 2014. "Disrupting the Dream: Undocumented Youth Reframe Citizenship and Deportability through Anti-deportation Activism." *Latino Studies* 12(2):279–299.

US Census Bureau. 2020a. "American Community Survey 5-Year Estimates." Census Reporter Profile page for Los Angeles County—LA (North Central/Arleta & Pacoima) & San Fernando Cities PUMA, CA. http://censusreporter.org.

———. 2020b. "Hispanic or Latino Origin by Race American Community Survey 5-Year Estimates, Table B03002." Census Reporter Profile page. https://censusreporter.org.

———. 2021a. "Los Angeles County, California." Quick Facts. www.census.gov.

———. 2021b. "Quick Facts, 2010, South Gate 90280." https://data.census.gov.

———. 2021c. "Thousand Oaks City, California, Race and Hispanic Origin" Quick Facts. Quick Facts. www.census.gov.

US Citizenship and Immigration Services (USCIS). 2011. "Green Card through LIFE Act (245(i) Adjustment)." www.uscis.gov.

———. 2017. "Green Card through Registry." www.uscis.gov.

———. 2018. "Provisional Unlawful Presence Waivers." www.uscis.gov.

———. 2019. "Unlawful Presence and Bars to Admissibility." www.uscis.gov.

———. 2021. "Consideration of Deferred Action for Childhood Arrivals (DACA)." www.uscis.gov.

US Constitution. Amendment 14, § 1, cl. 1.

US Department of Education. 2008. "Recognition of Foreign Qualifications." www.ed.gov.

US Department of Homeland Security. 2006. *Yearbook of Immigration Statistics: 2005.* Washington, DC: US Department of Homeland Security, Office of Immigration Statistics. www.dhs.gov.

———. 2013. *Immigration Enforcement Actions: 2012. Annual Report.* Washington, DC: US Department of Homeland Security, Office of Immigration Statistics. www.dhs.gov

———. 2014a. *FY 2014 ICE Immigration Removals.* Washington, DC: US Department of Homeland Security, Office of Immigration Statistics. www.ice.gov.

———. 2014b. *Immigration Enforcement Actions: 2013. Annual Report.* Washington, DC: US Department of Homeland Security, Office of Immigration Statistics. www.dhs.gov.

———. 2016. *Immigration Enforcement Actions: 2014. Annual Report.* Washington, DC: US Department of Homeland Security, Office of Immigration Statistics. www.dhs.gov

Valdivia, Carolina. 2019. "Expanding Geographies of Deportability: How Immigration Enforcement at the Local Level Affects Undocumented and Mixed-Status Families." *Law & Policy* 41(1):103–119.

Valencia, Richard R., and Mary S. Black. 2002. "'Mexican Americans Don't Value Education!': On the Basis of the Myth, Mythmaking, and Debunking." *Journal of Latinos and Education* 1(2):81–103.

Vallejo, Jody Agius. 2012. *Barrios to Burbs: The Making of the Mexican-American Middle Class*. Stanford, CA: Stanford University Press.

Valvelde, Miriam. 2016. "Did Donald Trump Promise Mass Deportation of 'Latino Families'?" *Politifact*, July 27. www.politifact.com.

Vaquera, Elizabeth. 2016. "The New Challenges Facing Young Undocumented Immigrants." Scholars Strategy Network. www.scholars.org.

Vargas, Edward, and Maureen A. Pirog. 2016. "Mixed-Status Families and WIC Uptake: The Effects of Risk of Deportation on Program Use." *Social Science Quarterly* 97(3):555–572.

Vasquez, Jessica M. 2011. *Mexican Americans across Generations: Immigrant Families, Racial Realities*. New York: New York University Press.

Vasquez-Tokos, Jessica, and Kathryn Norton-Smith. 2017. "Talking Back to Controlling Images: Latinos' Changing Responses to Racism over the Life Course." *Ethnic and Racial Studies* 40(6):912–930.

Vega, Sujey. 2015. *Latino Heartland: Of Borders and Belonging in the Midwest*. New York: New York University Press.

Verblow, Andrew R. 2013. "*Ruiz v. Robinson*: Stemming the U.S. Citizen Casualties in the War of Attrition against Undocumented Immigrants." *University of Miami Inter-American Law Review* 45(1):195–219.

Villenas, Sofia, and Donna Deyhle. 1999. "Critical Race Theory and Ethnographies Challenging the Stereotypes: Latino Families, Schooling, Resilience and Resistance." *Curriculum Inquiry* 29(4):413–445.

Waldman, Tom. 1989. "Latinos in the Valley: New Power Center in the San Fernando Valley." *California Journal*, October 1.

Wallace, Kelly, and Sandee Lamotte. 2016. "The Collateral Damage after Students' 'Build a Wall' Chant Goes Viral." CNN, December 28. www.cnn.com.

Wang, Amy. 2016. "Donald Trump Plans to Immediately Deport 2 Million to 3 Million Undocumented Immigrants." *Washington Post*, November 14. www.washingtonpost.com.

Waslin, Michele. 2011. *The Secure Communities Program: Unanswered Questions and Continuing Concerns*. Washington, DC: Immigration Policy Center Special Report. www.americanimmigrationcouncil.org.

Waters, Mary C. 1990. *Ethnic Options: Choosing Identities in America*. Berkeley: University of California Press.

Wessler, Seth Freed. 2012. "Nearly 205K Deportations of Parents of U.S. Citizens in Just over Two Years." *Colorlines*, December 17. www.colorlines.com.

The White House. 2014. "Remarks by the President in Address to the Nation on Immigration." Office of the Press Secretary. November 20. https://obamawhitehouse.archives.gov.

Williamson, Vanessa. 2017. *Read My Lips: Why Americans Are Proud to Pay Taxes*. Princeton, NJ: Princeton University Press.

Wong, Julia Carrie. 2019. "Trump Referred to Immigrant 'Invasion' in 2,000 Facebook Ads, Analysis Reveals." *The Guardian*, August 5. www.theguardian.com.

Wooten, Melissa E., and Enobong H. Branch. 2012. "Defining Appropriate Labor: Race, Gender, and Idealization of Black Women in Domestic Service." *Race, Gender & Class* 19(3–4):292–308.

Xu, Qingwen, and Kalina Brabeck. 2012. "Service Utilization for Latino Children in Mixed-Status Families." *Social Work Research* 36(3):209–221.

Yoshikawa, Hirokazu. 2011. *Immigrants Raising Citizens: Undocumented Parents and Their Young Children*. New York: Russell Sage Foundation.

Yuval-Davis, Nira. 1997. "Citizenship and Difference." In *Gender and Nation*, edited by N. Yuval-Davis, 66–88. London: Sage.

Zavella, Patricia. 2011. *I'm Neither Here nor There: Mexicans' Quotidian Struggles with Migration and Poverty*. Durham, NC: Duke University Press.

Zayas, Luis H. 2015. *Forgotten Citizens: Deportation, Children, and the Making of American Exiles and Orphans*. Oxford: Oxford University Press.

Zayas, Luis, and Lauren Gulbas. 2017. "Processes of Belonging for Citizen-Children of Undocumented Mexican Immigrants." *Journal of Child and Family Studies* 26(9):2463–2474.

Zhou, Min, Jennifer Lee, Jody Agius Vallejo, Rosaura Tafoya-Estrada, and Yang Sao Xiong. 2008. "Success Attained, Deterred, and Denied: Divergent Pathways to Social Mobility in Los Angeles's New Second Generation." *Annals of the American Academy of Political and Social Science* 620(1):37–61.

Zoppo, Avalon. 2017. "Here's the Full List of Donald Trump's Executive Orders." NBC News, April 23. www.nbcnews.com.

Zuñiga, Victor, and Maria Vivas-Romero. 2014. "Divided Families, Fractured Schooling, in Mexico: Educational Consequences of Children's Exposition to International Migration." Mexico City: Centro de Estudios Mexicanos Y Centroamericanos.

INDEX

Page numbers in italics indicate Tables.

Marshall, T. H., 10, 11

Massey, Douglas, 100

mass shootings, 191

maternity tourists, Chinese, 213n1, 215n52

matricula (Mexican consular identification), 123

media, 65–66, 73, 102, 118–19, 183

Medicaid, 102

membership: citizenship as, 12–13, 122, 158–59, 180; exclusion, 33. *See also* belonging

men: deportation and, 44, 55, 151; driving responsibilities and, 211n19; fathers, 43–47, 55, 63, 74–75, 89–91, 120–21, 210n37; gendered stereotypes of Mexican Americans, 175–76; policing of Latino, 168; study of working-class, 137; White women partnered with Mexican undocumented, 207n70

Menjívar, Cecilia, 3, 144

merengue, 163, 218n36

Mexican Americans: citizenship and, 12, 156–57, 159; financial help within families and, 83, 88–90; gendered stereotypes, 175–76; LA County population, 22, 156; middle-class, 83, 88; with skin color and spatial change, 167–72, 179–80, 219n49, 219n51; talking back, 104–15; at US-Mexico border, 154–55; Whites and, 158, 159, 164, 165–72, 207n70. *See also* racialized belonging, in segregated LA

Mexican-American War, 15, 96

Mexican consular identification (*matricula*), 123

Mexican nationality, 193

Mexicans: Afro-Latino/Afro-Mexican, 168, 219n46; bodies as criminal, 16; criminalization of, 16, 138, 145; enclaves in LA County, 160–63, 169–70, 171, 178, 181; with familism, 82–83; with illegality racialized, 135, 136–37; LA County population, 22; mixed-status families and racialization, 2, 11, 14–17; "repatriation" of, 215n56

Mexico: education in, 41–42, 43, 46–47, 50, 51, 54, 55, 210n42, 210n47; history with US, 96–97, 105; La Rumorosa, 39, 210n38; social inequality and university enrollment in, 210n47; special education programs in, 210n42. *See also* border, US-Mexico

microaggressions, 164; defined, 218n8; racism and, 25, 157, 159, 165–69, 171, 173–74, 176–81, 188

middle-class: Black Americans, 178; Latinos, 137, 180; lifestyle, 30, 89–90, 133, 220n61; Mexican Americans, 83, 88; Whites, 130, 160

migrants: gender and problem, 101; labor, 16, 127, 132, 151

migration: circular, 6, 7; dehumanization and, 39; labor, 73, 100, 128; return, 30, 37, 38, 45, 55, 207n80, 209n2; violence and, 73, 100

Migration Policy Institute Report, 143

Miguel (pseudonym), family illegality and, 45–47

militarization, of US-Mexico border, 6, 100

mixed-status families: adult children in, 17–18; children in, 59–61; with circular migration, 6, 7; citizenship and, 10; DAPA and, 2; dehumanization of, 2; with family illegality, 3–4, 10, 17, 206n47; in LA County, 1–2, 18, 21–23, 27–29, 36–54, 56; policies for, 198; population of undocumented and, 6–9; question of belonging, 9–14; racialization and Mexican, 2, 11, 14–17; research(er) background, 4–6; researching, 2, 17–21; talking back, 97, 104–15. *See also* family illegality, young adults negotiating

mobility, increased, 61–62

ABOUT THE AUTHOR

CASSAUNDRA RODRIGUEZ is Assistant Professor of Sociology at the University of Nevada, Las Vegas, and a former fellow in the Institute for Citizens & Scholars Career Enhancement Fellowship Program. She specializes in the areas of Latinx sociology, immigration, family, race, and gender. Dr. Rodriguez's current project examines youth and young adult participation in mariachi.